The Medjugorje Messages

Updated through April 02, 2017

The Medjugorje Web
772 N Peace Road
DeKalb, IL 60115
(815)748-0410
http://www.medjugorje.org

ISBN: 978-1-938823-06-0

Table of Contents

Preface

My first knowledge of the phenomena at Medjugorje occurred when I was an Air Force Chaplain serving at Ramstein Air Base, Germany from 1981-1984. One day one of my parishioners, a military policeman, excitedly came into the sacristy after the noon Mass. As I took off my vestments, he showed me a story in *The Catholic Digest* which detailed the account of alleged apparitions of Our Lady in a poor mountainous village in Bosnia-Herzegovina by the name of Medjugorje. Being of Croatian ancestry, my parents having been born in Croatia, I was just as excited as my friend and more so. I could think of nothing more intriguing than the alleged apparitions of the Virgin Mary to six Croatian children. Herzegovina is predominantly Catholic, in which the Croatian people not only are proud of their Catholic faith but also live it exemplarily. I made up my mind then and there to go to Medjugorje.

Being a member of the United States Air Force at the time, however, could have been an obstacle for my entering former Yugoslavia, but eventually I was able to sign up with other Americans for a general tour of Yugoslavia, and I did receive a clearance from military authorities to make the trip. We Americans traveled through Slovenia, Croatia, and Serbia. One day, when we were in Croatia, we had a free day, and so I hired a cab to take me to Medjugorje. The cab driver and I left at 7:00 a.m. and returned around midnight. He spoke some English. Little did I know what would await me in Medjugorje. I really did not know what to expect.

In Medjugorje there were no hotels, no restaurants, no shops, no taxi cabs, and very few English speaking residents. During my one day foray, I was filled with awe and believed what I had seen and felt regarding the alleged apparitions, even though everything was not crystal clear. Fortunately I was even able to be present at an apparition that took place exactly at 6:40 p.m. in the library of the parish rectory. Five visionaries were present; Ivanka was absent. I believe she was in Sarajevo at the time.

About seventy curious pilgrims had filled the rectory yard during that afternoon and were waiting hopefully and anxiously for Father Slavko Barbaric to make his appearance at the door and to invite one or two of us into the library just prior to the apparition. Guess who was called? I can remember an Italian priest becoming quite irate over Father Slavko's choice of me. There were some pilgrims from Ireland, too, and I think there may have been one or two from Austria.

In the rectory library I knelt next to Ivan, one of the visionaries, and I said to myself, "I am not worthy to be in this room." We prayed the rosary in different languages before the apparition. When the moment came for the apparition, the five children simultaneously bobbed their heads in perfect movement as they faced the front wall. Their faces were expressively joyful, their eyes glistened, and their lips were moving. I saw nothing, but I knew that they saw Something. (I have capitalized the last word in the previous sentence deliberately). They saw Something, and that Something was Someone.

Hardly able to contain my happiness and wonder, I then proceeded to St. James Church after the apparition to concelebrate Holy Mass. Marija, one of the visionaries, assisted me in vesting. It was the Solemnity of Corpus Christi, and how fortunate I was to offer Mass in that Communist country, where Christ was present Body, Blood, Soul, and Divinity in the Eucharist and was the great consolation of those religiously and politically enslaved and economically oppressed people.

As I think back over my time in Medjugorje, I will never forget the sight of people going to confession. Confessionals were set up well into the tobacco fields, which surrounded the church, and the lines of penitents were long. A number of priests were administering the Sacrament of Penance. Thinking that I would be able to go to confession in Medjugorje, I had already prepared myself to confess in Latin. However, it would have been hours before my turn to receive the Sacrament of Penance, and my cab driver was anxious to get me back to the hotel in Dubrovnik, where all of us American tourists were staying that night and looking forward to a full schedule the next day.

When I eventually returned to my base in Germany after the trip to Yugoslavia, I had to check in with security personnel to be deprogrammed to make sure that I did not compromise the mission or security of the United States military. Actually, the only person I had talked with in Medjugorje was Vicka, one of the visionaries, a young girl at the time, who was living in her very modest parental home. The taxi driver translated my English into Croatian for Vicka and her Croatian into English for me. My Croatian was faulty. My parents spoke a dialect with a smattering of English and Slovenian from having lived in Willard, Wisconsin, at that time the largest Slovenian rural community outside of Slovenia itself, which is Croatia's neighbor to the west. In addition, my younger sister and I as children had no desire to learn the Croatian language.

Vicka was very frightened. After all, the police were watching the children, and how was she to know that I was not a spy in spite of my telling her that I was an American and of Croatian ancestry? My most urgent question was, "What does the Bishop say?" She shrugged her shoulders and replied in Croatian, "I don't know." She was careful, prudent, and reserved, rightfully so. She not only had to be careful about what she said politically, but she had to weigh her comments about Church authorities also.

In 1994 I returned to Medjugorje with a number of pilgrims. Two months later I was asked to return as the chaplain for a very small group. I did. That was in February 1995.

It was bitterly cold in Medjugorje then. We did climb Mt. Krizevac (Cross Mountain), while the wind fiercely wrapped itself around us. On top of Mt. Krizevac I took pictures, several of them of the cross that the Croatians had erected in 1933 to commemorate the nineteen hundred years since the Passion, Death, and Resurrection of Christ. After the twelfth picture, my camera jammed. Tempted to tear out the film and maybe even to dispose of the camera, I finally conquered my precipitous intentions.

Moving along with the itinerary planned, which was very intense, I developed bronchitis. One day I was too sick to do anything and stayed in bed all day. The house where we were staying did not have central heat. It was a frigid existence for all of us. I remember not showering for a week, tearing up the carpet to throw over myself at night, going to bed with double socks and shoes, and trying to make sense out of such incredible penances. I made up my mind never to return to Medjugorje again in the winter.

As I lay in bed with a fever, I nevertheless felt guilty. Then it was time for evening Mass, and so I convinced myself to get out of bed and to head toward St. James Church. Knowing that I would be late, I felt that I had betrayed the Gospa (Croatian for Our Lady). As I neared St. James Church, suddenly there was a flash of light that seemed to have no plausible explanation. I looked at my watch. It was 5:40 p.m., the time during the winter season at which Our Lady would be appearing to the visionaries. I could not believe it. I later learned that a burst of light of unknown causality was known to accompany Our Lady's visits.

Seeing people going to confession in many languages and participating in evening Masses where the entire church was packed, so much so that people had to stand outside and priests had to go outside to give them Communion made me spellbound. Something was going on, and I was humbled but very proud to be a part of the picture just by being there, even though I could not understand such goings-on.

When I returned to the States, I had my film developed, and I sent the doubles to a family in Texas. The mother and her teenage son had been on the pilgrimage. The father, a doctor, had stayed home. Shortly thereafter, the doctor called me and asked, "Monsignor, did you take a good look at that one picture of the cross? It is a miraculous picture. The cloud formations show God the Father, with his long hair and bushy beard, stretching out his hand toward the cross, and a bird perched on one of His fingers. And in the top corners of the picture are angel heads in cloud formation. This is a picture of the Trinity! The cross indicates Christ, the clouds portray the Father, and the bird is a symbol of the Holy

6

Spirit. I've blown the picture up, framed it, and have it on the wall in my office. Protestants and Catholics alike see it and are amazed. I am going to send you one." The doctor did just that, and I had the picture framed. By the way, this was the final picture I took before my camera jammed.

There are many sequels to the above story. To date I have been to Medjugorje seventeen times, and each time has been a new experience. When I am asked as to why I return, I say, "It is the faith experience. There is such peace there. People are so kind. It is a different world. Midway across the ocean as we head back to the States, I want to go back. It is as if I am homesick."

As a Mariologist, I have concentrated on apparitions in my studies and have been to many of Our Lady's valid shrines throughout the Catholic world, almost all of the more important ones. Fortunately, I have had the humble experience also of addressing English-speaking peoples at Medjugorje in Blessed John Paul II Hall around ten times regarding the criteria used by the Catholic Church in assessing the phenomena of apparitions. I have always enjoyed giving those presentations and have expressed my personal belief to those assembled that I believe in the integrity of the Medjugorje phenomena, but I always articulated a caveat in saying that I would accept the final decision of the Church authorities. This one must do, since apparitions are not part of the public (formal) revelation of the Church. Here we speak of divine faith. Apparitions deal with human faith. They can add nothing to the substance of the Church's doctrine, but they may give us deeper insights, often for devotional purposes, of what has already been revealed through the Written Word (Bible) and the Oral Tradition, those doctrines passed early on from one generation to another and kept infallible because of Christ's promise to Peter, the first Pope.

In my travels to Medjugorje with various pilgrimage companies, I had the good fortune to meet Steve and Ana Shawl, owners of the Medjugorje Web, a pilgrimage company in DeKalb, Illinois. Steve and Ana had me travel with their pilgrimage groups to Medjugorje at least five times in the past. Since Ana is a Croatian-American who speaks Croatian fluently, and since both she and her husband consider Medjugorje to be their "second home," their knowledge of Medjugorje is unparalleled in my estimation. It has been a great joy for me to travel with Medjugorje Web, and it did not surprise me when Steve was to embark on a project that filled my heart with sudden surprise and much joy.

Allow me to explain. Each time that I have traveled to Medjugorje, I wondered why someone did not compile all the messages of the Gospa from 1981 to the present. Was Steve reading my mind? About six weeks ago he called and asked me if I would write the Preface to his new book entitled *The Medjugorje Messages 1981-2012*. I gulped! What I had been waiting for was now becoming a reality! Very quickly I accepted the invitation and also volunteered to edit the book for theological accuracy. This has been a labor of love. However, the real labor of love is the volume itself. Steve's insight to render such a book not only fulfills my longing for such a work, but the book itself presents the Gospa's timely message to today's Church and world. The messages of Our Lady need to be disseminated from beginning to end.

The messages of Our Lady at Medjugorje are revolutionary in their scope. The messages are revolutionary because the Gospa is telling us what we must do to turn back the evil present today throughout the world in biblical proportions. These messages are for everyone, but they are especially meaningful for Catholics. After all, these messages have been imparted to six Croatian visionaries in Herzegovina, which is strongly Catholic, as I have already mentioned.

And what is a message? A message is an announcement. An announcement can refer to something from the past, the present, or the future. A message can be dire in its unraveling. It can also portray a hopeful scenario. It can even be apocalyptic. It can be affirmative. It can also be corrective. A message, however, has a very urgent purpose by its very nature. Something important is at stake.

The messages of Our Lady at Medjugorje to the visionaries wherever they might be at the moment, since not all the visionaries live in Medjugorje at all times or actually do live elsewhere, really dwell on five subjects. These five subjects are the "little stones" or "little pebbles" that form the basis of Our Lady's exhortations to her beloved children. The six visionaries mention these subjects in their talks and contacts with pilgrims. Note that I use the words "little stones" or "little pebbles." Initially I did not understand why the five parts of the Gospa's plans were "stones" at all. Now I understand. If one tosses a stone or a little pebble into the water, it has a ripple effect. Each one of Our Lady's five stones will have a ripple effect if it is accepted and practiced in our lives. The good example will then ultimately influence others to do the same. Good is diffusive of itself.

And what are those "little stones?" She asks for the complete rosary, which means all four mysteries, and this is to be a daily devotion. She calls for monthly confession. She calls for participation at Mass as often as possible and reception of the Eucharist. She talks about fasting on bread and water on Wednesdays and Fridays as the best form of penance. Finally, she talks about reading the Word of God, the Bible.

Now when one prays the rosary, he or she should eventually understand the need for confession. After all, the glorious mysteries basically accent Our Lord's Resurrection. And what was Christ's first gift to His Church on Easter Sunday night? It was the Sacrament of Penance. We read John 20:21-23 that Christ gave us this sacrament when he breathed upon the Apostles and said, "Receive the Holy Spirit. Whose sins you shall forgive, they are forgiven. Whose sins you shall retain, they are retained." The power to forgive sins or not to forgive sins (to retain, in the event that one was not contrite) was given to the Apostles, and this was to be passed on in the Church until the end of time. Confession is good for the soul, and it is the best kept secret in the Catholic Church, in my estimation. I have been told by psychiatrists who were working with the same person whom I was counseling that they could not forgive that person's sins and that only I could. They recognized the power of this sacrament as they sent that person back to me. Those psychiatrists, for the most part, were not even Catholic.

Confession is also a good preparation for the Eucharist, which is another gift from our Lord as detailed in the sixth chapter of St. John's Gospel. Although confession is not strictly necessary for a worthy Communion, unless one is in mortal sin, confession is nevertheless a suitable preparation for the great gift of Jesus' Body, Blood, Soul, and Divinity. To renew our sorrow and to have our sins forgiven is always important, however, and we should not minimize that need.

It has been said that baptism is the most important sacrament but that the Eucharist is the greatest. Our Lady thought so, too. In fact, she once said that if the children had the option of either seeing her or going to Mass, they should go to Mass. Mass is the unbloody Sacrifice of the Cross, in which Christ is offered to the Father under the forms of bread and wine. The elements of bread and wine, after the Consecration of the Mass, also provide the spiritual food for those participating at Mass. This is not a symbol or a pretending. It is the Real Presence. It is Christ himself, Body, Blood, Soul, and Divinity. So lofty is the Eucharist that we cannot even begin to fathom God's goodness in providing this, the greatest of the sacraments, as our act of worship as well as our spiritual food under the sacramental species. Apparently, Our Lady understood this. It is we who fail to appreciate the reality of such goodness on the part of the Almighty. Mass is indeed sacrifice and sacrament.

Fasting on bread and water as the best way to fast is not just a pious act. Our Lord fasted. Fasting was a part of Jewish life. Christ was a Jew and was born of a Jewish mother. Our Lady says that we must fast, except the sick, but the modalities, that is, the kinds of fasting may vary according to the dispositions of the individual and/or that person's condition. There are many ways to fast. Fasting on bread and water is the best, though, and the sick can offer up their sufferings.

Finally, Our Lady tells us that we must read the Scriptures. This is nothing new. St. Jerome reminds us that "to be ignorant of the Scriptures is to be ignorant of Christ." The Word of God is just that! How are we to know

God's Son, the Gospa's Son, if we do not read the Scriptures? Moreover, St. Paul has reminded us that all Scripture is inspired by God and is useful for teaching, for refutation, for correction, and for training in righteousness (2 Timothy 3:16).

The messages of Our Lady, therefore, are not novel. We are not to look upon them as a means to achieve some magical effect. They are theologically oriented, biblically based, and relevantly useful in pursuing the Christian life today. Today, especially, we need all the spiritual helps that we can get.

I have been amazed at the accuracy and depth of theology in Our Lady's messages. To give one example only, Our Lady gave a very theologically accurate answer on October 1, 1981 in response to the question: Are all religions the same? She said, "Members of all faiths are equal before God. God rules over each faith just like a sovereign over his kingdom. In the world, all religions are not the same because all people have not complied with the commandments of God. They reject and disparage them."

Note that Our Lady does not say that all religions are the same or even equal. She states that every *person* is equal before God regardless of his or her religion and that God reigns above all of them. She also states that in the world all religions are not the same because the commandments are not universally kept by all people.

This response has been open to much misinterpretation and confusion. Our Lady does not say that it does not matter what one believes. For example, either Jesus is present Body, Blood, Soul, and Divinity in the Eucharist, or He is not. The Principle of Non-Contradiction does not allow for something to be one thing and the opposite at the same time. Even though one is obligated, however, to seek the truth and to follow it, the Catholic Church does embrace and understand those who are in invincible ignorance and have not been enlightened. Accordingly, those who will be lost are those who have been enlightened but deliberately have refused to accept God's truth, to live morally good lives, and to accept those truths through the instrumentality of the Church.

It is important that we recall the words of Pope Pius XII, who explained in his encyclical *Mystici Corporis* the difference between belonging to the Church *in re* (actually) or *in voto* (indirectly). Catholic theology does teach that there is only one Church having a divine foundation, and we believe that the Catholic faith fulfills that requirement. If it is true, and we believe that it is, then all salvation in some way or other must emanate from the Church's apostolic mission and its divine economy of salvation. However, this in no way disparages those who are not members of the Catholic Church or who have not been enlightened, if the conditions for salvation have not been fulfilled in them through no fault of their own. Indeed all people are equal before God, including people of different religions.

Paragraph 171 of the United States Conference of Catholic Bishops' *Compendium* that was adopted as an aid in understanding the basics of the *Catechism of the Catholic Church* provides a clarification regarding the principle of "no salvation outside the Church": This means that all salvation comes from Christ, the Head, through the Church which is his body. Hence they cannot be saved who, knowing the Church as founded by Christ and necessary for salvation, would refuse to enter her or remain in her. At the same time, thanks to Christ and to his Church, those who through no fault of their own do not know the Gospel of Christ and his Church but sincerely seek God and, moved by grace, try to do his will as it is known through the dictates of conscience can attain eternal salvation.

Let us now move to a final topic. There is much speculation today regarding the ten secrets that each visionary has already received or will receive. We must diligently follow the messages imparted by Our Lady from the beginning of the apparitions in 1981, and by digesting those messages, we will have fervently prepared for the revelations that are destined to occur when the ten secrets have been imparted to all the visionaries. The messages of the Gospa have a personal effect, a parochial effect, and a global effect, and are thus meant for all peoples, even though in particular some messages may pertain only to or more so to Catholics because of the theological implications of the content in those messages. This I have already stated.

The book *The Medjugorje Messages* 1981 – 2014 is a godsend in this troubled age. How refreshing to read these messages and to realize that the Gospa is covering us with the mantle of her protection in preparation for even greater events that will come on the scene when the ten secrets have all been imparted. Like a good mother always intent upon the welfare of her children, the Gospa watches over her earthly children with a careful solicitude. Let us not forget, though, that it is God who uses the Gospa to convey his messages. He sends her, thinking perhaps that if the world will not listen to His son, perhaps it will listen to His Son's Mother. The messages, however, spring from Divinity itself.

May those who read *The Medjugorje Messages* 1981 – 2013 be inspired to listen to Our Lady as she tells us, "Do whatever he tells you." (John 2:1-11)

Reverend Monsignor Matthew G. Malnar
Mariologist
May 1, 2012

Introduction

Dear Reader,

I have to say this book was truly a labor of love, and we are excited to bring you the most complete, updated, and comprehensive collection of Our Lady's messages from Medjugorje. While researching, referencing, and formatting these messages, especially the early years, I was re-inspired by their beauty, and I was again reminded of the spiritual treasure that is contained in these messages from Heaven.

It is difficult to put into words how much Medjugorje means to me personally, and how Our Lady, and God's grace, changed my life forever. My experience with Our Lady is one I will never forget for the rest of my life. I hope by sharing it with you, you will understand why Medjugorje is so important not only to me, but also to you and to the entire world.

Let me first say I did nothing to deserve God's grace or Our Lady's visit, and probably quite the opposite. I take comfort in knowing that when Ivan once asked Our Lady why she chose him, she answered: *"Because I do not always choose the best."* I certainly fit into that category! I know that conversion is a lifelong process and struggle, and as Ivan says, "I try to be better each day." That is our lifelong challenge.

I believe the grace I received that day in March 1995 was, in part, a result of people praying for me. The power of prayer is something that we should never underestimate. If you have a loved one that is lost, pray for him or her unceasingly. God hears every one of our prayers. Miracles do happen, and I am a living witness.

I thank God every day for the opportunity to be even a miniscule part of His plan for the salvation of the world through Medjugorje. I pray that I never disappoint Him.

I guess the best place to start is at the beginning. I was born a cradle Catholic, and lived through the Kumbaya Catechism of the 60's/70's in Catholic school. As a young boy I remember growing up in government subsidized housing during the years my father was going to school for his

PHD. Those were difficult years, and I am certain they stuck with me, and influenced my decisions later in life. I was determined to be successful in life, and to be able to have all the material things I didn't have as a child.

From a young age I was always a hard worker. My first job was as a paperboy in the third grade. I worked all through grade school and high school to make money. Like many teenagers, I found myself seduced and immersed in all the pleasures and false promises "The World" had to offer. Looking back, I do believe if we had prayed the rosary in our family throughout my childhood and teenage years, as Our Lady requests, I would have made different choices in my life.

From my Catholic school years I held many grudges and harbored many misconceptions about the Faith, to such an extent, that I vowed never to set foot in a Catholic Church again. At age twenty I went back to school and became an engineer, which ultimately led to my starting my own computer company towards the end of the 80's. The company was extremely successful, and it fed my endless desire for material things. I remember there were a few years I couldn't even spend all the money I made. I knew there was something missing in my life, and in my heart, but I didn't know what it was. I was constantly trying to fill that void with "Big boy toys," but after each purchase I still felt empty and unfulfilled. What I didn't realize at the time was that the void in my heart could only be filled by God's love and His presence in my life.

It was early 1995, and one evening I went out to dinner with my parents. Our dinner conversation seemed focused on recent television shows about near death experiences and angel stories. My father took the opportunity to ask me if I had ever heard of a place called Medjugorje. I answered, "No, I haven't". My father explained that it was a place in former Yugoslavia where six young people claimed to be receiving apparitions and messages from Our Lady. The idea seemed impossible to me. If this was really taking place, why wasn't it all over the news? I mean, Mother of God visits earth, is big news. My father told me he would give me a series of articles written by a man named Wayne Weible, which were all about this place called Medjugorje.

A few days later, as I sat alone in my house, I felt a strong prompting to read the article. As I picked it up and started to read it, I was overcome with a feeling that this was all true. I had never experienced a feeling like that before, and it was profound. Then, in an instant, there was a beautiful bright white light in front of me that filled my entire field of vision. It was a light I had never seen before. It had depth and life. I could see its beauty, color, and brightness, but also felt its purity and holiness. I was literally pushed back in my chair, and I could feel the warmth of the light on my face. The whole experience is very difficult to explain or put into words, but I knew it was Divine. I knew Our Lady was there before me. I felt indescribable love and peace pouring down upon me. I hadn't cried in over twenty years, and tears were streaming down my face. I was sobbing, but out of pure joy. In an instant, I experienced a moment of clarity. All the grudges I had held against the Church and all the misconceptions I had harbored, were gone, and I was infused with a knowledge of the Catholic faith. I could clearly see the Church in its simplicity, beauty, and truth. I immediately felt a deep love in my heart for the beliefs and traditions of our Faith. It was a feeling like I was home again after a long journey. I then heard Our Lady speak to my heart, and she said, "*Will you help spread my messages?*" It took me about one second to respond, but within that one second it was as if time stood still. In that instant, I understood that this was a very serious and important question. I also understood that my answer was literally choosing God or denying Him. And from the absolute depths of my heart, I answered out loud, "YES! Blessed Mother, but I don't know what to do." I understood that the method of helping to spread Her messages would be through the internet, but I knew nothing about the internet. A moment later the bright white light and Our Lady were gone. I was literally shaking with excitement and in awe at what had just happened.

The next days were busy. I booked a trip to Medjugorje, invited Wayne Weible to our parish, went to confession for the first time in twenty five years, and went to Mass for the first time in fifteen years, I re-learned the rosary and started praying it every day. I also started fasting strictly on bread and water on Wednesdays and Fridays. It was a time of great joy, blessing, and excitement for me. I could not wait to get home each day from work to pray the rosary. I remember searching and searching for a rosary from Medjugorje, and I finally found a woman on the east coast that ran a Marian Center. When the rosaries arrived, I couldn't wait to open the package. They were clear light blue heart-shaped beads, with a note in the box that said they were blessed by Our Lady during an apparition in Medjugorje. I immediately started praying with them. I remember always feeling a warm burning sensation in my chest when I prayed the rosary, and my fingers that held the beads would tingle. Within a few days I noticed the links had turned gold. I could see through the beads, and could see that even the wire inside the bead had turned gold. It was a beautiful gift from Our Lady, and one that I cherish to this day.

The day after Our Lady's visit, I was praying in the morning before work and pondered Our Lady's question. I wondered how this would all work out. I knew nothing about the internet and had no idea where to even begin. I owned a computer hardware company, but in early 1995 the internet was mainly confined to universities. Our company certainly didn't have any involvement or knowledge of the internet at that time. I got into the office and settled down to get some work done. The phone rang, and it was an internet service provider. We spoke, and thirty days later our company was an internet service provider.

I immediately began to work on the web site and named it The Medjugorje Web. I knew nothing about html or how the internet or web pages worked. It was truly a gift from God as I sat down and started hand writing the code for the site. It was effortless for me to learn. To this day, I still do all of our web site work with a simple text editor. I remember sometimes spending eighteen to twenty hours a day typing in Our Lady's messages, and adding content about Medjugorje to the web site. It was a very blessed time filled with great joy. Within a few months, The Medjugorje Web was born. It was the very first web site on Medjugorje, and is still the largest Medjugorje web site with over 4000 pages of content, and receives almost a million hits per day.

My life will always be dedicated to helping Our Lady and Jesus in any way I can. The rest of my story is about how I met my wife Ana. But I will save that, and many other stories of the miracles and wonders we have both experienced taking one hundred fifty plus groups to Medjugorje over the past seventeen years, for an upcoming book called: Medjugorje Calling.

MIR!
Steve Shawl
The Medjugorje Web
http://www.medjugorje.org

Quick Overview

Since June 24, 1981 in a small village called Medjugorje, in Bosnia & Herzegovina, six children (now adults) have been receiving apparitions and messages from the Blessed Virgin Mary or "Gospa," as she is affectionately known in Medjugorje. In addition to her public messages, Our Lady is to give each of the six visionaries a total of ten "secrets" or happenings that will occur on earth in the near future. Some of the secrets pertain to the whole world, while others concern the visionaries themselves or the local village. Only one of the secrets has so far been revealed by the visionaries. In the third secret, Our Lady has promised to leave a permanent, supernatural, indestructible, and visible sign on the mountain where she first appeared. Our Lady said: *"This sign will be given for the atheists. You faithful already have signs and you have become the sign for the atheists. You faithful must not wait for the sign before you convert; convert soon. This time is a time of grace for you. You can never thank God enough for His grace. The time is for deepening your faith, and for your conversion. When the sign comes, it will be too late for many."*

When each of the six visionaries has received all ten secrets, Our Lady will stop appearing to them on a daily basis. Currently, Marija, Vicka, and Ivan have received nine secrets, and Our Lady still appears to them every day. If they are in Medjugorje Our Lady appears at 6:40pm during the summer schedule and 5:40pm during the winter schedule (so as not to disturb evening Mass). If they are not in Medjugorje Our Lady appears to them at 6:40pm wherever they are. No one knows when Our Lady will give the tenth secret to Marija, Ivan, and Vicka.

Mirjana, Jakov, and Ivanka have received all ten secrets, and Our Lady appears to them once per year, and will do so for the rest of their lives. For Ivanka, who received her 10th secret on May 7, 1985, it is on the anniversary date of the apparitions, June 25. For Jakov, who received his 10th secret on September 12, 1998, it is on Christmas day. For Mirjana, who received her 10th secret on Christmas 1982, it is on March 18. In addition, Our Lady told Mirjana that she would experience extraordinary apparitions as well.

And so it was. Beginning on August 2, 1987 Our Lady started appearing to Mirjana on the 2nd of each month to pray with her for unbelievers. Mirjana tells us that it is very important that we pray for the unbelievers in the world, who are described as: Those who have not yet experienced God's love. These 2nd of the month apparitions were private for about ten years. Then, in 1997, Our Lady asked that the apparitions be made public. In 2004 Our Lady started giving public messages during most of these apparitions with Mirjana.

Once Our Lady has stopped appearing, there will be three warnings given to the world. These warnings will be in the form of events on earth. They will occur within Mirjana's lifetime, and Mirjana will witness them. Ten days before each of the warnings, she will advise the priest she chose for this task, Fr. Petar Ljubicic, who will then pray and fast with Mirjana for seven days. Then, three days before each warning is to take place, Fr. Petar will announce to the world what, where, and when the warning will take place. Fr. Petar has no choice and must reveal each warning. After the first warning, the other two will follow in a rather short period of time. That interval will be a period of grace and conversion. After the permanent, visible, supernatural, and indestructible sign appears on Apparition Hill, where Our Lady first appeared in Medjugorje, there will be little time for conversion. For that reason, Our Lady invites us to urgent conversion and reconciliation. The permanent sign will lead to many healings and conversions before the secrets become a reality. According to Mirjana, the events predicted by Our Lady are near. By virtue of this experience, Mirjana proclaims to the world: "Hurry, be converted; open your hearts to God."

The ninth and tenth secrets are serious. They concern chastisements for the sins of the world. Punishment is inevitable, because we cannot expect the whole world to be converted. The punishments can be diminished by prayer and penance, but they cannot be eliminated. Mirjana says that one of the evils that threatened the world, which was contained in the seventh secret, has been averted, thanks to prayer and fasting. That is why Our Lady continues to encourage us to pray and fast: *"You have forgotten that with prayer and fasting you can ward off wars, suspend natural laws."*

In addition to this basic message, Mirjana related an apparition she had in 1982, which sheds some light on certain aspects of Church history. She spoke of an apparition in which Satan appeared to her, and asked Mirjana to renounce Our Lady and to follow him. By doing so she would be happy in love and in life. He added that following Our Lady would only lead to suffering. Mirjana rejected him, and immediately Our Lady appeared and Satan disappeared. Our Lady then gave Mirjana the following message:

"Excuse me for this, but you must realize that Satan exists. One day he appeared before the throne of God and asked permission to submit the Church to a period of trial. God gave him permission to try the Church for one century. This century is under the power of the devil; but when the secrets confided to you come to pass, his power will be destroyed. Even now he is beginning to lose his power and has become aggressive. He is destroying marriages, creating divisions among priests and is responsible for obsessions and murder. You must protect yourselves against these things through fasting and prayer, especially community prayer. Carry blessed objects with you. Put them in your house, and restore the use of holy water."

According to Catholic experts who have studied these apparitions, this message given by Our Lady through Mirjana may shed light on an apocalyptic vision Pope Leo XIII had on October 13, 1884. It was after this vision that Pope Leo XIII introduced the prayer to Saint Michael, which priests used to recite after Low Mass up to the time of the Second Vatican Council. These experts agree that the century of trials foreseen by Leo XIII is about to end.

Since the apparitions began in 1981, approximately 40 million people of all faiths, from all over the world, have visited Medjugorje and have left spiritually strengthened and renewed. Many bring back stories of miracles in the form of healings of mind, body and spirit, supernatural visual signs, and deep conversions back to God. You owe it to yourself, and your loved ones, to investigate with an open mind and heart the messages which are given to us by Our Lady of Medjugorje. I invite you to read these messages, and decide for yourself how they will affect your life and that of your family.

The First Seven Days of The Apparitions

The First Day

It was June 24, 1981, and the feast of John the Baptist. Mirjana Dragicevic and Ivanka Ivankovic were walking alone along the base of Podbrdo (now known as Apparition Hill) heading out of the village. It was a hot summer day, and after walking for a while they felt tired and decided to sit down and rest. Ivanka was looking towards the hill, and Mirjana was facing the opposite direction. In one moment Ivanka said, "I think Our Lady is on the hill." Mirjana didn't even look because the thought of Our Lady appearing seemed to her impossible. Mirjana responded, "Yeah, like Our Lady has nothing else to do that she would come to the two of us."

Mirjana stood up and left, intending to go back to the village, but as she was nearing the first house, she felt an intense call within herself to return. There she found Ivanka in the same spot and she said to Mirjana, "Look now please". Mirjana saw a young woman in a long grey dress holding a baby in her arms. Mirjana said in that instant, she felt every possible emotion. Shortly after, Vicka Ivankovic arrived and also saw Our Lady. She became so frightened she took off her shoes and started running as fast as she could back toward the village. On the way she met two boys, Ivan Dragicevic, and Ivan Ivankovic. Vicka asked them to come with her back to the spot where they saw Our Lady. Finally Milka Pavlovic joined them. It was now about 6pm, and all six of the children saw the amazingly beautiful young woman with a small child in her arms. The woman didn't say anything to them but gestured that they should come closer. But they were too frightened to move, although they immediately believed the woman to be Our Lady.

The Second Day

On the second day, June 25, 1981, the children agreed to meet once again at the same place that Our Lady had previously appeared, in the hope of seeing her again. All of a sudden there was a flash of light. The children looked up and saw Our Lady, this time without the small child. She was smiling and joyful and was indescribably beautiful. With her hands she gestured to them to come closer. As they approached, they fell to their knees. Our Lady said: *"Dear children, be not afraid; I am the Queen of Peace."*

They then began to pray the Our Father, Hail Mary and Glory Be. Our Lady prayed together with them except when they prayed the Hail Mary.

After they had prayed for a while, Our Lady began to speak with the children. Ivanka asked her about her mother, who had died two months previously. Our Lady responded, *"She is happy. She is with me."*

And Mirjana asked Our Lady for some sign to be given to show to the people that they were neither lying nor crazy, as some people had said. Our Lady smiled, and in that moment Mirjana felt she had received a sign. After Our Lady had left, Mirjana noticed that her watch had changed time during the apparition.

Our Lady finally left the children with the words:
"God be with you, my angels!"

When the children asked her if they would see her the following day, Our Lady replied by nodding her head.

According to the visionaries, the whole encounter was indescribable. On that day two of the children, who were in the previous group, were missing: Ivan Ivankovic and Milka Pavlovic. They were replaced by Marija Pavlovic and Jakov Colo. Milka Pavlovic and Ivan Ivankovic never saw Our Lady again, even though they returned to the site of the first apparition in the hope of seeing her.

The Third Day

On June 26, 1981, the six children were full of anticipation. It was again around 6pm, and they were making their way to the same place where they had previously seen Our Lady. They were very happy, although their joy was mixed with fear, wondering what would be the outcome of all this. The children said they could feel an inner pull attracting them to meet with Our Lady.

Suddenly, while the children were still on their way, a light flashed three times. It was a sign indicating Our Lady's presence. On that third day Our Lady appeared even higher up on the hill than on the previous days. All at once Our Lady disappeared. But when the children began to pray, she reappeared. She was cheerful and smiling. Once again her beauty was overwhelming.

As Vicka left her home, her grandmother advised her to carry some holy water with her to make sure the apparition was not something from Satan. When the children were with Our Lady, Vicka sprinkled the holy water in the direction of the vision saying, "If you are Our Blessed Mother, please stay, and if you are not, go away from us." Our Lady smiled and remained with the children. Then Mirjana asked her name, and she replied, *"I am the Blessed Virgin Mary."*

On the same day, coming down Podbrdo (Apparition Hill), Our Lady appeared one more time, but only to Marija, and said, *"Peace, peace, peace and only peace."* Behind her, Marija could see a wooden cross, after which Our Lady repeated, in tears, the following words, *"Peace must reign between man and God, and among all people!"* The area where this took place is a little less than half way up to the spot where Our Lady had appeared, and it is now marked with a wooden cross.

The Fourth Day

On June 27, 1981, Our Lady appeared three times to the children. During these apparitions the children asked Our Lady many questions, and Our Lady responded. For priests, she gave this message:
"May the priests firmly believe, and may they take care of the faith of the people!"

Once again, Jakov and Mirjana asked for a sign, because the people had begun to accuse them of lying or taking drugs. Our Lady replied, *"Do not be afraid of anything."*

Before leaving, when asked if she would come again, Our Lady indicated that she would. On the way down Podbrdo, Our Lady appeared one more time to say good bye with the words:

"May God be with you, my angels; go in peace!"

The Fifth Day

On June 28, 1981, from the early hours of the morning, big crowds started gathering. By noon there were about 15,000 people present. On the same day, the parish priest, Fr. Jozo Zovko, questioned the children about what they had seen and heard in the previous days.

At the usual time Our Lady appeared again. The children prayed with Her, and afterwards they asked Our Lady questions. Vicka, for example, asked, "My dear Lady, what do you want from us, and what do you want from our priests?" Our Lady replied, *"The people should pray and firmly believe."*

Regarding priests, she replied that they should believe firmly and help others to do the same.

On that day Our Lady appeared many times. During one of the apparitions the children asked her why she didn't appear in the parish Church for everyone to see. She replied,

"Blessed are those who have not seen and yet believe."

The Sixth Day

On June 29, 1981 the children were taken to Mostar for a medical examination, after which they were proclaimed "healthy." The statement the head doctor gave was: "The children aren't crazy, but the person who brought them here must be."

The crowds on Apparition Hill that day were greater than ever. As soon as the children arrived at the usual place and began to pray, Our Lady appeared. On that occasion the Blessed Mother exhorted them to have faith, saying, *"The people should believe firmly and have no fear."*

On that day, a woman doctor who was following and observing them, asked if she could touch Our Lady. The children guided her hand to the place where Our Lady's shoulder was, and she felt a tingling sensation. Even though the doctor was an atheist, she said, "Here, something strange is happening!"

On that same day a child named Daniel Setka was miraculously healed. His parents had brought him to Medjugorje, praying specifically for a healing. Our Lady had said that he would be healed if the parents prayed, and fasted, and strongly believed. Little Daniel was healed.

The Seventh Day

On June 30, 1981 two young Communist women suggested to the children that they go by car away from Medjugorje so they could walk around in peace. Their real intention was to take them away from the area and keep them there until after the normal apparition time had passed. However, even though the children were far away from Podbrdo, at the usual time of the apparition, it was as if an interior call prompted them to ask to be let out of the car. The women ignored their request. The engine stalled, and the car coasted to the side of the road. The children got out of the car and started to pray. Our Lady drew near to them from the direction of Podbrdo, which was over a kilometer away. The two women saw the light of Our Lady and became believers. To this day they can be found in the Church each evening praying the rosary and attending Holy Mass.

It wasn't long before the children, as well as the crowds of people, were forbidden to go on Apparition Hill. The police came with dogs and blocked anyone from climbing. Anyone who was caught on the hill was arrested and put in prison. Our Lady continued to appear to the children in secret places, in their homes, and in the fields. The children openly spoke with Our Lady, eagerly asking her advice, and listening to her messages and warnings.

In the meantime, Fr. Jozo began the evening program in the Church, where each day everyone could gather and pray the rosary and celebrate Holy Mass. In those early days Our Lady sometimes appeared to the visionaries in the Church. And on one occasion when Our Lady appeared in the Church during the rosary, Fr. Jozo also saw Our Lady. He immediately stopped praying and spontaneously started to sing a popular hymn: Kako si lijepa, Blazena Djevico Marijo (O how beautiful you are Most Blessed Virgin Mary). The whole church could see that something amazing had happened to him. Afterwards he stated that he had seen Our Lady. Fr. Jozo had not only been doubtful, but openly against even rumors of the apparitions. He now became the children's greatest supporter and defender. He testified his support of the apparitions to the point of being imprisoned for eighteen months.

It has now been over thirty one years since Our Lady has been appearing and giving messages and graces, to bring souls back to her Son Jesus. As you begin to read the messages from 1981, you get a deep sense of Our Lady's love and concern for each one of us, as a mother would have for her children. From this realization, we can then begin to understand the depth of God's love for each one of us. God so loves the world that He would send His mother to us, with special graces, to turn the course of the world from disaster to a course leading to Heaven.

Our Lady's Messages - The Five Stones

In Medjugorje, Our Lady has given us five core "tools" to help us with our conversion, increase our spiritual life, bring and keep us close to God, and protect us from Satan. They are not always easy to follow, and it takes time, effort, and perseverance to live them fully. Our Lady taught the visionaries how to pray and to fast slowly over time. So we can say it is better to start slowly and persevere, than to try to do everything at once and give up.

1. Prayer

Prayer is the center of Our Lady's plan and is the most frequent message she gives in Medjugorje. Our Lady asks us to pray three hours each day, and to pray with the heart. To pray with the heart is to pray with love, trust, and abandonment. Praying with the heart is an encounter with God. In one of Ivan's talks he said, "To pray is our personal decision. The quality of our prayer is a grace. So the more we pray, the more grace we will receive, and the better we will pray."

Contained in our three hours of daily prayer can be:

The Rosary
Joyful, Luminous, Sorrowful, and Glorious Mysteries
Our Lady tells us that the rosary is one of the most powerful prayers against Satan. Our Lady asks that we pray all four mysteries of the rosary each day (Joyful, Luminous, Sorrowful, and Glorious). She also recommends that we always have our rosary with us, and tells us that Satan cannot harm us with the rosary in our hand.

The Peace Chaplet
Creed, 7 Our Father's, Hail Mary's, and Glory Be's
The Peace Chaplet has been prayed for generations in Medjugorje. When Our Lady first started teaching the visionaries to pray, she asked them to continue with this prayer, but to add the Creed at the beginning. Our Lady also asked that this chaplet be prayed every evening right after Holy Mass in Medjugorje.

Holy Mass

Sundays, and Daily Mass when possible.

Our Lady tells us to live the Mass. At Mass we receive the Living Body and Blood, Soul and Divinity of Jesus in the Eucharist. The more we attend Holy Mass the more we will feel a need for holiness, and the closer we will become to God.

Devotions and Novenas

Divine Mercy, St. Bridget Prayers, etc.

We have so many beautiful prayers, devotions, and novenas that are part of our Catholic faith. There are many books and online sources that we can use to enrich our prayer life and obtain graces and blessings.

Free Form Prayers

Prayer is a constant conversation with God.

Prayer is a constant conversation with God throughout our day. It is speaking to heaven about what we are struggling with, what our temptations are, what makes us joyful, and what makes us sad. Our Heavenly Father, Our Blessed Mother, and all the Saints and Angels are at our constant beck and call just waiting to hear from us.

Works of Love, and Mercy

Everything that we do in our day can be prayer.

Everything we do in our day can be offered as a work of charity for the Kingdom of God, whether it is volunteering at a homeless shelter or food pantry, spending time with the elderly, teaching religious education, or visiting the sick or imprisoned. Even one's everyday activities like making dinner for one's family, cleaning the house, mowing the lawn, and going to work can also be works of love and mercy. If we do these simple tasks that take up so much of our day with a joyful heart and offer it as a prayer, then it truly makes the three hours of prayer a day easy to achieve.

"I would like the people to pray along with me these days. And to pray as much as possible! And to fast strictly on Wednesdays and Fridays, and every day to pray at least one Rosary: the joyful, sorrowful and glorious mysteries." August 14, 1984

"You know that I love you and am coming here out of love, so I could show you the path of peace and salvation for your souls. I want you to listen to me and not permit Satan to seduce you. Dear children, Satan is strong enough! Therefore, I ask you to dedicate your prayers so that those who are under his influence may be saved. Give witness by your life, sacrifice your lives for the salvation of the world. Therefore, little children, do not be afraid. If you pray, Satan cannot injure you, not even a little, because you are God's children, and He is watching over you. Pray, and let the Rosary always be in your hands as a sign to Satan that you belong to me."
February 25, 1989

2. Fasting

In Medjugorje, Our Lady asks us to fast on Wednesdays and Fridays from midnight to midnight on bread and water. Our Lady tells us that this is the "best" fast. The amount of bread and water you consume or the frequency at which you consume them is not important. What is important is that we make this sacrifice and offer it to God. I have many times heard people ask the visionaries about including butter, jelly, coffee, etc., in their fasting. Their answer is always the same: "We can only tell you what Our Lady has asked of us."

There will be times when it is impossible, for whatever reason, to fast on bread and water. And, of course, if someone is sick or has a medical condition which prevents them from fasting on bread and water, he can give up other things that he likes such as TV, the internet, coffee, alcohol, sweets, cigarettes, etc. and offer that sacrifice to God.

In both the Old Testament and New Testament, there are many examples of fasting. Jesus fasted frequently. According to tradition, fasting is encouraged especially in times of great temptation or severe trials. After casting out an unclean spirit from a boy Jesus said to his disciples *"This kind can only come out through prayer and fasting."* (Mark 9:29).

We need to realize the power of fasting. Our Lady tells us *"You have forgotten that with prayer and fasting you can ward off wars, suspend natural laws."* By combining prayer and fasting we increase the power of our prayers. This is important to remember when praying for a special or urgent intention. By prayer and fasting we allow our whole being to participate in offering this sacrifice to God. We should also fast because we love God and want to be soldiers that offer our bodies in the battle against evil.

3. Confession

Our Lady asks us to go to monthly confession. Pilgrims who come to Medjugorje are always impressed by the number of people waiting in line for confession and the number of priests hearing confessions. Many priests have had extraordinary experiences during confessions in Medjugorje. Many of our pilgrims who have come with us to Medjugorje go to confession for the first time in 20, 30, 40, even 50 years. It is one of the fruits and miracles of Medjugorje.

Many people have a difficult time with confession. Some have had a bad experience at some point in their life. It is important that we overcome any aversions we may have to confession, and trust in Our Lady's request. Confession is a sacrament, and when we receive absolution, we receive special graces. I know that for many people when they begin to go to monthly confession (or more often if needed) their lives change dramatically. The more you go, the more you become aware of your sins. The harder we work on our sins the more graces God will give us to overcome our sins. When we approach confession with a truly contrite heart, God begins to build us up with the virtues that we lack.

"Make your peace with God and among yourselves. For that, it is necessary to believe, to pray, to fast, and to go to confession." June 26, 1981

"Dear children! Open your heart to God's mercy in this Lenten time. The heavenly Father desires to deliver each of you from the slavery of sin. Therefore, little children, make good use of this time and through meeting with God in confession, leave sin and decide for holiness. Do this out of love for Jesus, who redeemed you all with His blood, that you may be happy and in peace. Do not forget, little children: your freedom is your weakness, therefore follow my messages with seriousness. Thank you for having responded to my call." February 25, 2007

4. Scripture (The Bible)

Usually Our Lady comes to the visionaries happy and joyful. On one occasion, while talking about the Bible, she was crying. Our Lady said: *"You have forgotten the Bible."*

The Bible is a book different from any other book on earth. Vatican II says that all the canonical books of the Bible were, "...written under the inspiration of the Holy Spirit, and they have God as their author." (Dogmatic Constitution on Divine Revelation) There is no writing, even from a saint or inspired person that can be compared with the Bible.

"Dear children! Today I call on you to read the Bible every day in your homes, and let it be in a visible place so as always to encourage you to read it and to pray. Thank you for having responded to my call." October 18, 1984

"Dear children! Today on this great day which you have given to me, I desire to bless all of you and to say: these days while I am with you are days of grace. I desire to teach you and help you to walk the way of holiness. There are many people who do not desire to understand my messages and to accept with seriousness what I am saying. But you I therefore call and ask that by your lives and by your daily living you witness my presence. If you pray, God will help you to discover the true reason for my coming. Therefore, little children, pray and read the Sacred Scriptures so that through my coming you discover the message in Sacred Scripture for you. Thank you for having responded to my call." June 25, 1991

5. Holy Mass

Our Lady asks us to attend Sunday Mass, and when possible, Daily Mass. Our Lady has said to the visionaries that if they have to choose between seeing her and going to Mass, they must choose Holy Mass. This statement tells us just how important Holy Mass and the Eucharist are.

Marija tells us that Our Lady wants us to see the Holy Mass as the highest form of prayer and the center of our lives.

Vicka tells us that the Blessed Mother sees the Mass as the most important and the most holy moment in our lives. We have to be prepared and pure to receive Jesus with great respect. The Mass should be the center of our lives.

"Dear children! I am calling you to a more active prayer and attendance at Holy Mass. I wish your Mass to be an experience of God. I wish especially to say to the young people: be open to the Holy Spirit because God wishes to draw you to Himself in these days when Satan is at work. Thank you for having responded to my call."
May 16, 1985

"Dear children! I wish to call you to a living of the Holy Mass. There are many of you who have sensed the beauty of the Holy Mass, but there are also those who come unwillingly. I have chosen you, dear children, but Jesus gives you His graces in the Mass. Therefore, consciously live the Holy Mass and let your coming to it be a joyful one. Come to it with love and make the Mass your own. Thank you for having responded to my call." April 3, 1986

The Visionaries

 ## Vicka Ivankovic-Mijatovic

Vicka is the oldest of the visionaries, and was born on September 3, 1964, in Bijakovici. She comes from a family of eight children. Her prayer mission given to her by Our Lady is to pray for the sick. Our Lady appeared to her for the first time on June 24, 1981. For her the daily apparitions continue. Our Lady has so far confided nine secrets to her. Vicka married on January 26, 2002, and lives with her husband Mario in the small village of Gradac, a few kilometers north of Medjugorje. They have two children, Sophia Maria and Anton.

Vicka: "Before, I prayed from pure habit. Now I've turned completely to prayer. I commit my life completely to God. I feel sorry for those who do not believe in God, because Our Lady wants no one to be lost. We can help each other find the right way to God. It's up to the people to obey the messages and be converted. Great things are happening here; Our Lady is among us. She wishes to attract everyone to her Son. That's the reason she has been coming so long and so often. Here, everyone feels the nearness and the love of God. As role model and example, Gospa began, in January 1983, to tell me her life story, which took over two years."

The information Our Lady dictated to Vicka over these two years is contained in three hand-written notebooks and will be published when Our Lady tells Vicka it is time.

Ivan Dragicevic

Ivan is the oldest of the two boys who see Our Lady, and was born on May 25, 1965 in Bijakovici. His prayer mission given by Our Lady is to pray for priests, families, and the youth of the world. Although Ivan and Mirjana share the same last name, they are not related.

Our Lady has appeared to him every day since June 24, 1981. Our Lady has confided nine secrets to Ivan. He is now married and resides half the year in the parish of Medjugorje, and half the year in Boston, MA. Ivan and his wife Laureen have four children.

Ivan: "The apparitions made a big difference in my life - the difference between heaven and earth. For example, I arrange my day now so that even during the day I find time to pray. Before, my life had no meaning. Now, I'm filled with inner contentment. The first time I saw Our Lady, a change occurred in my soul and in my heart. Before, I often avoided prayer, but now the difference is so great, I really can't describe it. I'm confident and not afraid, because I know who leads me, and therefore, I'm not afraid of death. People in our parish, and all people, should feel that way."

Mirjana Dragicevic-Soldo

Mirjana was born March 18, 1965 in Sarajevo. Her prayer mission from Our Lady is to pray for all unbelievers. She is the second oldest of the visionaries. Very intelligent, Mirjana graduated from the University of Sarajevo, where her family lived. Mirjana was the second person to see the Blessed Mother on June 24, 1981 in Medjugorje. Although her family lived in Sarajevo, she spent the summers with her grandmother, who lived in Bijakovici. That is how she came to be in Medjugorje that summer. She had daily apparitions from June 24, 1981 until December 25, 1982. On this day, Mirjana received her tenth and final secret from Our Lady. Mirjana was the first visionary to receive all ten secrets.

Since that time, Our Lady only appeared to Mirjana once a year on her birthday, March 18, until August 2, 1987, when Our Lady also began appearing to Mirjana on the second of each month to pray with Mirjana for all unbelievers. Mirjana tells us that Our Lady defines 'unbelievers' as those who have not yet experienced God's love. She tells us that if we only once saw the tears in Our Lady's eyes for all unbelievers, we would all begin praying intensely for this intention. Mirjana lives in Medjugorje with her husband Marko Soldo. They have two daughters.

Mirjana: "I didn't know Marian apparitions existed. I never heard about Lourdes or Fatima. The first day Ivanka had the vision of Our Lady, she was full of enthusiasm and wanted me to look, too. I thought: This can't be real! But, Our Lady gave us strength to accept her as a Mother. I've changed a lot. I realize how empty my heart was. Now I truly feel God, the Mother of God, and the Faith. My relationship with Our Lady has become one of a mother and daughter. Jesus is like a friend, or an older brother. Whoever believes in God and opens himself up to God, needn't be afraid. God will be with him in the future, too. If everyone believed in God, there'd be no war."

Ivanka Ivankovic-Elez

Ivanka was the first person to see Our Lady on June 24, 1981, and is the youngest of the four girls. She was born on July 21, 1966, in Bijakovici. Ivanka's prayer mission from Our Lady is to pray for families. Ivanka has one brother and one sister. Her mother Jagoda died in May 1981. When the apparitions first began, Ivanka asked the Blessed Mother about her mother. Our Lady told her that her mother was with her in heaven. God has allowed Ivanka to see and speak with her mother, who is in heaven, five times over the years.

She had daily apparitions from June 24, 1981, until May 7, 1985. On that day Our Lady confided to her the last of her ten secrets. Our Lady told her that for her entire life she will have an apparition every year on June 25, the anniversary of the apparitions. Ivanka is living in the parish of Medjugorje, and is married with three children.

Ivanka: "When the apparitions began, I was only a child. I prayed and went to church when my parents asked me to. Now when I pray, I feel united with God and Our Lady. Before, when I went to Mass, I didn't feel anything special. Now, I know God is alive at the Holy Mass and gives himself completely to us in the Host. Concerning my own future, I leave it completely to God - my path will go in the direction God leads me. I have some advice for young people: I want to tell them to turn to God as soon as possible because He's the only one who can lead them to happiness and truth. We simply must pray more and live the messages of Medjugorje."

39

Jakov Colo

Jakov is the youngest of the visionaries. He was born on March 6, 1971 in Bijakovici, and was only ten years old when the apparitions began. His prayer mission given by Our Lady is to pray for the sick. Jakov's mother Jaca died on September 5, 1983, and it affected Jakov very deeply since he rarely saw his father, who worked in Germany, as many men did in those days. There were simply no jobs available in Medjugorje or the surrounding area.

He has had daily apparitions since June 25, 1981, and on September 12, 1998, Our Lady confided to him his tenth secret. Our Lady now appears to Jakov only once per year, on Christmas Day. Our Lady literally raised Jakov, since his mother died when he was so young. It was very difficult for him to accept that he would no longer see Our Lady every day. He wondered how he would continue, and, he struggled for months until he realized that through prayer he was now like all of us who do not see Our Lady. He tells us that Our Lady is with each one of us always, and we can experience her in our hearts. Jakov lives in the parish of Medjugorje, and is married with three children.

Jakov: "From the time Our Lady first appeared to me, my life has entirely changed. Now, I pray more and go to Mass every evening. I try, more and more, to fulfill the messages that Our Lady gives us. I feel I'm closer to God now. I believe we have to pray that God's plans will be realized. I now want to live as a Christian. I begin the day with prayer, then go to school. When I get home, I help wherever necessary. To me, the Mass means an encounter with the living God. Our Lady always tells us to pray more."

Marija Pavlovic-Lunetti

Marija is the third oldest of the visionaries. She was born on April 1, 1965, in Bijakovici. Her prayer mission given by Our Lady is to pray for all the souls in purgatory. She has three brothers and two sisters. When the apparitions started, she was studying in Mostar, which is about eighteen miles away from Medjugorje.

Our Lady appeared to her for the first time on June 25, 1981. She still has apparitions every day, and is the visionary to whom Our Lady gives the public message to the world on the 25th of each month. Our Lady has confided nine secrets to her so far. Marija is presently living in Italy, is married, and has four children. She visits Medjugorje a number of times each year.

Marija: "Everything has changed in Medjugorje. People started to pray and listen to Our Lady's messages. Before, I didn't pray enough. Now I want to pray more and more. I'm sure God gives much to everyone who's open to prayer. I tell people they should pray more, and Our Lady will give them peace in all that burdens them. It's not I; it's Our Lady who urges us to nurture prayer, to propagate peace, and to fast. She says that everyone who comes to Medjugorje must be converted. They must encourage other people, too, to pray and fast. God wishes us to pray and fast. God wishes to develop the parish and make it grow more and more in faith. If people accept the messages, God will lead them."

The Messages

The messages given by Our Lady in Medjugorje began on June 25, 1981, and continue to this day. The earliest messages from 1981-1983, recorded by the parish in Medjugorje (Information Center MIR Medjugorje, www.medjugorje.hr), were unfortunately confiscated and destroyed by the Communists.

The 1981-1983 messages found on the following pages were obtained from the works of Fr. René Laurentin and Professor René LeJeune. They were originally recorded in French and translated into English by Juan Gonzales Jr., Ph.D. Although these messages have not been validated by the parish in Medjugorje, great care was taken in their recording, translation, and compilation.

We have also included messages compiled by Fr. Laurentin and Prof. LeJeune from 1984-1986, which are in addition to the weekly messages recorded by the parish in Medjugorje during that same period. We also credit their work for the chapter of messages collected by various authors, as well as the messages given to Jelena Vasilj and her prayer group.

Beginning in March 1984, Our Lady desired the parishioners of St. James Church to come together at the church for one evening a week so that She could direct them in their spiritual life. The priests chose Thursday. So from March 1, 1984 through January 8, 1987, Our Lady gave messages to the parish on Thursday evenings. The messages came almost entirely through Marija Pavlovic, except where noted. These messages were obtained from the parish in Medjugorje.

On January 8, 1987, Our Lady said she would begin giving public messages on the 25th of each month. These messages are given entirely through Marija Pavlovic. The 25th of the month messages, and the annual messages given to Ivanka, Mirjana, and Jakov, included in this book, were also obtained from the parish in Medjugorje.

Beginning on August 2, 1987 Our Lady began appearing to Mirjana on the second of every month to pray with her for unbelievers. Our Lady defines unbelievers as those who have not yet experienced God's love. These second of the month apparitions were private for ten years. Then, in 1997 Our Lady asked that the apparitions be made public. In the fall of 2004 Our Lady began to give public messages during most of the apparitions, and at present, messages are being given on every second of the month. When Mirjana was asked if these messages were only meant for unbelievers, she responded that they were for everyone. The second of the month messages from 2004-2009 were translated from Croatian to English by my wife Ana Shawl, and from 2009-present, by Miki Musa, who is one of the senior guides in Medjugorje.

For me personally, reading these early messages gives me the sense of how Our Lady, from the beginning, led the visionaries and the parish, step by step and day by day. It was important that Our Lady built a solid spiritual foundation within the local people, who would later be serving as an example to the almost 40 million people that have visited Medjugorje. We hope that you are as inspired and spiritually enriched as we have been by these messages from Our Lady in Medjugorje.

I want to take this opportunity to offer a special thank you to Monsignor Matthew Malnar for all his help in proofreading, and editing this book. The endeavor spanned many months, and with Monsignor's expertise in Mariology, Psychology, Canon Law, Theology, and as a Scholar, he helped make this book the most accurate to date on Our Lady's messages from Medjugorje.

The Early Messages 1981-1986

Wednesday, June 24, 1981

The visionaries see a distant apparition of a young woman in a long grey dress holding a baby in her arms on the hill of Crnica (now known as Apparition Hill). The first time was in the afternoon, the second time towards 6:00pm.

Thursday, June 25, 1981

The date of the first apparition for the group of six visionaries, who see Our Lady nearby on the hill. Our Lady says: *"Praised be Jesus!"*

Ivanka: "Where is my mother?" (Her mother had died two months previously.) *"She is happy. She is with me."*

The visionaries: "Will you return tomorrow?" The apparition answers with a nod of her head.

Mirjana: "No one will believe us. They will say that we are crazy. Give us a sign!" The apparition responds only with a smile. Mirjana believed she had received a sign. Her watch had changed time during the apparition. *"Goodbye, my angels. Go in the peace of God."*

Friday, June 26, 1981

In the presence of a crowd of 2,000 to 3,000 people, drawn there by the luminary signs coming from the hill of the apparitions, Vicka sprinkles the apparition with holy water and says: "If you are the Gospa, stay with us, if not, go away." The apparition only smiles.

Ivanka: "Why have you come here? What do you desire?"
"I have come because there are many true believers here. I wish to be with you to convert and to reconcile the whole world."

Ivanka: "Did my mother say anything?"
"Obey your grandmother and help her because she is old."

Mirjana: "How is my grandfather?" (He had recently died.) *"He is well."*

The visionaries, on a request from the crowd: "Give us a sign which will prove your presence." *"Blessed are those who have not seen and who believe."*

Mirjana: "Who are you?" *"I am the Most Blessed Virgin Mary."*

"Why are you appearing to us? We are not better than others."
"I do not necessarily choose the best."

"Will you come back?" *"Yes, to the same place as yesterday."*

On returning to the village after the apparition, Marija sees the Virgin again, in tears, near a cross with rainbow colors:
"Peace, Peace, Peace! Be reconciled! Only Peace. Make your peace with God and among yourselves. For that, it is necessary to believe, to pray, to fast, and to go to confession."

Saturday, June 27, 1981
"Praised be Jesus!"

Jakov: "What do you expect of our Franciscans?"
"Have them persevere in the Faith and protect the Faith of others."

Jakov and Mirjana: "Leave us a sign because the people treat us as liars."
"My angels, do not be afraid of injustice. It has always existed."

The visionaries: "How must we pray?"
"Continue to recite seven Our Father's and seven Hail Mary's and Glory Be's, but also add the Creed. Goodbye, my angels. Go in the peace of God."

To Ivan, aside from the others: *"Be in peace and take courage."*
(Ivan said, "What a beautiful smile when she left me.")

Sunday, June 28, 1981
The visionaries: "What do you wish?"
"That people believe and persevere in the Faith."

Vicka: "What do you expect from the priests?"
"That they remain strong in the Faith and that they help you."

"Why don't you appear to everyone in church?"
"Blessed are they who believe without having seen."

"Will you come back?" *"Yes, to the same place."*

"Do you prefer prayer or singing?" *"Both, praying and singing."*

Vicka: "What do you wish from the crowd which has gathered here?" The visionaries said this question received no response except for a glance filled with love and Our Lady's smile. Then Our Lady disappeared. The visionaries prayed so that she might return because she had not said, *"Goodbye, my angels."* During their song, You Are All Beautiful, she reappears.

Vicka: "Dear Gospa, what do you expect of this people?" She repeated the question three times and finally was given this answer:
"That those who do not see believe as those who see."

Vicka: "Will you leave us a sign so that people believe that we are not liars or comedians?" No other response, only a smile. *"Go in the peace of God,"* she said, as she disappeared.

Monday, June 29, 1981
The visionaries: "Dear Gospa, are you happy to see so many people here today?" *"More than happy."* (She smiles, writes Vicka).

"How long will you stay with us?" *"As long as you will want me to, my angels."*

"What do you expect of the people who have come in spite of the brambles and the heat?" *"There is only one God, one faith. Let the people believe firmly and do not fear anything."*

46

"What do you expect of us?"
"That you have a solid faith and that you maintain confidence."

"Will we know how to endure persecutions, which will come to us because of you?"
"You will be able to, my angels. Do not fear. You will be able to endure everything. You must believe and have confidence in me."

Here Vicka writes a question from Dr. Darinka Glamuzina: "May I touch Our Lady?" She gives this response,
"There have always been Doubting Thomases, but she can approach."

Vicka shows her where to stretch out her hand. Darinka tries to touch her. Our Lady disappears, and then reappears in her light.

The parents of a three-year-old child, Daniel Setka, who had suffered from septicemia since the fourth day of his birth, asked the visionaries to intercede for the handicapped child. "Dear Gospa, is little Daniel going to speak some day? Cure him so that they all will believe us. These people love you very much, dear Gospa. Perform a miracle. Dear Gospa, say something." They repeated this petition and conveyed the response,
"Have them believe strongly in his cure. Go in the peace of God."

The Hidden Phase
(Jun 30, 1981 To Dec 31, 1981)

During this period, Our Lady appeared to the visionaries in hidden places, away from the police patrols that were trying to track them down.

Tuesday, June 30, 1981

Apparition at Cerno. Mirjana: "Are you angry that we were not on the hill?"
"That doesn't matter."

"Would you be angry if we would not return any longer to the hill, but we would wait in the church?" *"Always at the same time. Go in the peace of God."*

On that day, Mirjana thought that she understood that the Gospa would return for three more days, until Friday. But it was only her interpretation.

Thursday, July 2, 1981

Jakov: "Dear Gospa, leave us a sign." The Virgin seemed to consent with a nod, *"Goodbye, my dear angels."*

Saturday, July 4, 1981

The visionaries believe the apparitions had ended, but Our Lady appeared to each one of them separately, where he or she was. No message was preserved.

Tuesday, July 21, 1981

(Vicka's diary - 27th apparition, 6:30pm)
"Just like every day, we spoke with the Gospa. She arrived at 6:30pm, and greeted us," *"Praised be Jesus!"*

Then we asked her if she would give us a sign. She said, "*Yes.*" Then we asked her how much longer she would still continue to visit us. The Blessed Virgin responded,
"My sweet angels, even if I were to leave the sign, many people will not believe. Many people will only come here and bow down. But people must be converted and do penance."

Then we questioned her on the subject of the sick. For some, the Gospa said that they would be cured only if their faith was strong, and for others, no. Then She prepared to depart. Upon leaving, She said to us, *"Go in the peace of God."*

Wednesday, July 22, 1981
(Vicka's diary - 28th apparition, 6:30pm)
On arriving she said, *"Praised be Jesus Christ."*

All of us questioned her on the subject of some sick people who had been recommended to us. Then we prayed with the Blessed Virgin. She only said the Our Father and Glory Be, and during the time that we said the Hail Mary, she was silent. The Gospa told us that,
"A good many people have been converted, and among them some had not gone to confession in forty five years, and now, they are going to Confession. Go in the peace of God."

As Our Lady was departing, a cross appeared in the sky.

Thursday, July 23, 1981
(Vicka's diary - 29th apparition, 6:30pm)
Vicka only mentions the greeting from Our Lady, *"Praised be Jesus Christ."*

Friday, July 24, 1981
(Vicka's diary - 30th apparition, 6:30pm)
"Today, also, we went to the place of the apparitions about 6:20pm, and while praying and singing, we waited for the Blessed Virgin. At exactly 6:30pm we saw the light which slowly approached. Then we saw the Blessed Virgin and heard her customary greeting. To our questions, relative to the majority of the sick, the Gospa answered quickly,"
"Without faith nothing is possible. All those who will believe firmly will be cured."

Saturday, July 25, 1981
(Vicka's diary - 31st apparition, 6:30pm)
After the usual questions on the subject of the ill, the Gospa responded,
"God, help us all!"

Monday, July 27, 1981

(Vicka's diary - 33rd apparition, 6:30pm)

Only four of us came because they put pressure on Ivan, Ivanka and Mirjana to go to Sarajevo. At 6:30pm exactly, the Gospa appeared. Vicka asked her about certain sick people, took some objects which had been given to her by some people, and approached Our Lady so that she could bless them. The Gospa made the Sign of the Cross and said,

"In the name of the Father, and of the Son, and of the Holy Spirit."

Then we questioned her on the subject of the sign, and the Gospa answered,

"Await, it will not be for long. If I will leave you a sign, I will still appear to you."

Vicka asked if we would be able to see her again one more time this evening on the hill. The Gospa agreed and said:

"I will come at 11:15pm. Go in the peace of God."

Saying this, She began to disappear and we saw in the heavens the heart and the cross. Our Lady said:

"My angels, I send you my Son, Jesus, Who was tortured for His faith, and yet He endured everything. You also, my angels, will endure everything."

Jesus had long hair, brown eyes, and a beard. We only saw His head. She said that we prayed and sang beautifully:

"It is beautiful to listen to you. Continue in this manner."

In conclusion she said, *"Don't be afraid for Jozo."*
(The pastor of the parish who had been threatened by the police).

Wednesday, July 29, 1981

(Vicka's diary - 35th apparition, 6:30pm)

Today we waited for the Blessed Virgin in Vicka's room. At exactly 6:30pm, the Gospa came and greeted us, *"Praised be Jesus!"*

Jakov was the first to question her on the subject of a person who was ill. The Blessed Virgin said, *"She will be cured. She must believe firmly."*

Vicka asked Our Lady why she had not come the day before. The Blessed Virgin said something, and smiled, but no one heard it. Then Marija and Jakov asked her about certain sick people. We then took some religious articles, and the four of us approached Our Lady so that she would bless them. As Our Lady was blessing the articles, our hands became very cold.

Jakov asked if we could embrace her. The Blessed Virgin said that we should approach and embrace her. Then we asked her to leave us the sign. She said, *"Yes. Go in the peace of God."*

As Our Lady began to disappear, on the ceiling the Cross and the Heart were visible. The cross, the heart, and the sun are also mentioned in Vicka's diary in later apparitions.

In church we saw the Blessed Virgin a second time toward 8:00pm in the choir loft. While we were praying, the Blessed Virgin prayed with us.

Thursday, July 30, 1981
We did not go to the hill.
(Vicka's diary contains no more observations until Aug 25)

Sometime In July 1981
"Carry out well your responsibilities and what the Church asks you to do."

Sunday, August 2, 1981
Marija sees the Virgin in her room.
"All of you together go to the meadow at Gumno. A great battle is about to take place. A battle between my Son and Satan. Human souls are at stake."

The visionaries, accompanied by about 40 local people, went to the prairie of Gumno, about 200 yards from Vicka's house. Our Lady said,
"Everyone here may touch me."
After many people had touched her, a black stain appeared on her dress. Marija cried. Marinko invited the people who were present to go to confession.

Beginning of August 1981

"What do you wish that we do later?" *"I would like for you to become priests and religious, but only if you yourselves would want it. It is up to you to decide."*

Thursday, August 6, 1981

"I am the Queen of Peace."

Friday, August 7, 1981

On Mt. Krizevac, at 2:00am in the morning:
"That one do penance for sins."

Saturday, August 8, 1981

"Do penance! Strengthen your faith through prayer and the sacraments."

Monday, August 17, 1981

"Do not be afraid. I wish that you would be filled with joy and that the joy could be seen on your faces. I will protect Father Jozo."
(Fr. Jozo was the pastor in Medjugorje who was imprisoned.)

Saturday, August 22, 1981

"Father Jozo has nothing to fear. All that will pass."

Sunday, August 23, 1981

"Praised be Jesus! I have been with Ivan until now. Pray, my angels, for this people. My children, I give you strength. I will give you some of it always. When you need me, call me."

Monday, August 24, 1981

In Vicka's diary, August 25, she writes: Yesterday, Monday the 24th at 10:45am, Mirjana and I were at Ivan's house. We heard a commotion, and we went out running. Outside everybody was looking at the cross on Krizevac. At the spot of the cross, Mirjana, Jakov, Ivan and I saw the Blessed Virgin, and the people saw something like her statue, which then began to disappear, and the cross appeared again. Over the entire sky everyone saw, written in gold letters, the word "MIR" (which means peace in Croatian).

Vicka's diary then reports the apparition on August 25. A little after Our Lady prayed for peace, a large inscription appeared on top of Krizevac. The word "MIR" was seen by the pastor and many persons from the village. The visionaries affirmed that the Blessed Virgin promised that there would still be many other signs as forerunners before the great sign in Medjugorje and in other parts of the world.

Tuesday, August 25, 1981
Some persons who were present asked the visionaries to request of the Blessed Virgin permission to touch her. Our Lady said: *"It is not necessary to touch me. Many are those who do not feel anything when they touch me."*

Our Lady also said that among those present, there was a spy (no other clarification was given).

On the matter of the sign:
"You do not have to become impatient, for the day will come."

Wednesday, August 26, 1981
Today, for the first time, we waited for the Blessed Virgin at the home of Zdenka Ivankovic. There were five of us, because Ivanka had not yet returned. The Blessed Virgin appeared and said, *"Praised be Jesus."*

She said that tomorrow the people did not have to come, and thus we would be by ourselves. Then also:
"Do not give advice to anyone. I know what you feel, and that will pass, also."

Thursday, August 27, 1981
Vicka: "Marija and I came to Jakovs house today about 6:00pm. We helped Jakov's mother prepare supper. At 6:00pm the Blessed Virgin came toward us. I was outside when the Blessed Virgin Mary came. She said that they should not have to make one suffer so."

"We asked her with respect to the sign, and she said:"
"Very soon, I promise you."

We recommended certain sick people to Our Lady. She stayed with us for fifteen minutes. Then we left for the home of Marinko Ivankovic in order to wait for the Blessed Virgin there. She came at 6:30pm. She told Ivan: *"Be strong and courageous."*
She left, and the cross, the heart, and the sun appeared.

Friday, August 28, 1981
At the hour of the apparition, the visionaries wait in the room of Fr. Jozo, who is in prison. The Virgin does not appear. It is the second time that this has happened. They go to church and pray. She then appears to them. *"I was with Father Jozo. That is why I did not come. Do not trouble yourselves if I do not come. It suffices then to pray."*

Today Ivan entered the seminary of Visoko: *"You are very tired. Rest, so that you can find strength. Go in the peace of God. Goodbye."* (From Ivan's journal)

Saturday, August 29, 1981
Jakov: "Are you also appearing to Ivan in the seminary?" *"Yes, just like to you."*

"How is Ivan Ivankovic?" (Son of Pero, cousin of Vicka, and one of four men in Bijakovici who bear this name. He had been arrested by the police on Aug 12, while on the hill of the apparitions, and was imprisoned.) *"He is well. He is enduring everything. All that will pass. Father Jozo sends you greetings."*

"What is the news from our village?" *"My angels, you are doing your penance well."*

"Will you help us in our studies?" *"God's help manifests itself everywhere."*

"Go in the peace of God with the blessing of Jesus and mine. Goodbye." (From Ivan's journal.)

Ivanka: "Will you leave us a sign soon?" *"Again, a little patience."*

Sunday, August 30, 1981

Vicka: "At 6:20pm, we began to pray at the home of Marinko Ivankovic." The Virgin arrived and said, *"Praised be Jesus!"*

Vicka: "People say that since they locked up Fr. Jozo in his cell, the doors unlock by themselves. Is that true?" *"It is true, but no one believes it."*

Ivanka: "How is Mirjana? What are her feelings?" *"Mirjana is sad because she is all alone. I will show her to you."* "Suddenly, we saw Mirjana's face. She was crying."

"Dear Gospa, there are some young people who betray our Faith." *"Yes, there are many."* She mentions some names.

Vicka asks the Virgin concerning a woman who wanted to leave her husband because he was making her suffer. *"Let her remain close to him and accept her suffering. Jesus Himself also suffered."*

On the matter of a sick young boy, *"He is suffering from a very grave illness. Let his parents firmly believe, do penance, then the little boy will be cured."*

Jakov asks her about the sign. *"Again, a little patience."*

Ivan, who had been several days without an apparition: "How will I do in this seminary?" *"Be without fear. I am close to you everywhere and at all times."*

Ivan's diary: "Are the people pious in our village?" *"Your village has become the most fervent parish in Herzegovina. A large number of people distinguish themselves through their piety and their faith."*

End of August 1981

"Which is the best fasting?" *"A fast on bread and water."*

"I am the Queen of Peace."

Tuesday, September 1, 1981

"Will there be a Mass on Mt. Krizevac?" *"Yes, my angels."*

Jakov: "Are the police setting up a trap around the church?"
"There's nothing at all. Have the people pray and remain in church as long as possible. Go in the peace of God."
The cross, the heart, and the sun appeared.

Ivan's diary: "I prayed with her so that Jesus might help me in my vocation. Then we recited the rosary. The Gospa smiled with kindness."
"Do not be afraid. I am close to you and I watch over you."

Wednesday, September 2, 1981

Concerning a young man who hanged himself, Vicka asked, "Why did he do that?" *"Satan took hold of him. This young man should not have done that. The Devil tries to reign over the people. He takes everything into his hands, but the force of God is more powerful, and God will conquer."*

Ivan's diary: "How will things go for Anton, Dario, Miljenko, my friends in the seminary, and for me?"
"You are, and you will always be my children. You have followed the path of Jesus. No one will stop you from propagating faith in Jesus. One must believe strongly."

Thursday, September 3, 1981

Jakov: "When will the sign which was announced come?"
"Again, a little patience."

Friday, September 4, 1981

Ivanka and Marija: "Since we will be far away at school during the week, except on Saturdays and Sundays, what must we do?"
"It is enough for you to pray. Come here Saturdays and Sundays. I will appear to all of you."

To Ivan in the seminary: *"The sign will be given at the end of the apparitions."*
Ivan: "When will that be?" *"You are impatient, my angel. Go in the peace of God."*

Saturday, September 5, 1981

Ivan's diary: "I was praying in the chapel. The Gospa came when I was reciting the Our Father."

"Praised be Jesus and Mary."
(Our Lady was using a salutation of pious people in Croatia, probably with the desire to revive it.)

"Go in the peace of God, my angel. May the blessing of God accompany you. Amen. Goodbye."

Sunday, September 6, 1981

Ivan's diary: "I was praying in the chapel. Suddenly there was a great light."
"Pray especially on Sunday, so that the great sign, the gift of God may come. Pray with fervor and a constancy so that God may have mercy on His great children. Go in peace, my angel. May the blessing of God accompany you. Amen. Goodbye."

Monday, September 7, 1981

Ivan's diary: *"Be converted, all of you who are still there. The sign will come when you will be converted."*

Tuesday, September 8, 1981

Ivan's diary: *"I ask you only to pray with fervor. Prayer must become a part of your daily life, to permit the true Faith to take root."*

Jakov wishes the Blessed Virgin a happy birthday. She answers:
"It is for me a beautiful day. With respect to you, persevere in the Faith and in prayer. Do not be afraid. Remain in joy. It is my desire. Let joy appear on your faces. I will continue to protect Father Jozo."

Thursday, September 10, 1981

Ivan's diary: "We prayed a lot. Prayers filled with joy and love, prayers of the heart." Then She says, *"Go in the peace of God, my angel. Amen. Goodbye."*

Sunday, September 13, 1981

Ivan's diary: "The students in the seminary prayed the rosary after they had gone to confession. The Virgin came near the image of Jesus and said:" *"There is your Father, my angel. Go in the peace of God, my angels."*

Christ is our Brother, but in a sense, also our Father: In an apparition to Gemma Galgani, Jesus said, *"I am your Father. Your Mother, here she is."* And He pointed out to Gemma the Blessed Virgin.

Monday, September 14, 1981

To Vicka:

"Stay here so that Jakov will not be alone. Persevere (both of you) with patience. You will be rewarded." Our Lady also told Vicka that she had scolded Mirjana and Ivanka for a behavior which was not detailed.

Tuesday, September 15, 1981

"If this people are not converted very soon, bad things will happen to them."

Wednesday, September 16, 1981

"The militia will not stay here a long time. I will leave the sign. Be patient still. Don't pray for yourselves. You have been rewarded. Pray for others."

Thursday, September 17, 1981

Concerning a sick person: *"He will die very soon."*

Then the Blessed Virgin encouraged the children:
"Persevere, and you will be rewarded."

Sunday, September 20, 1981

To Vicka and Jakov:
"Do not relax in your prayers. I ask both of you to fast for a week on bread and water."

Wednesday, September 30, 1981

"Don't ask useless questions dictated by curiosity. The most important thing is to pray, my angels."

Thursday, October 1, 1981

"Are all religions the same?"

"Members of all faiths are equal before God. God rules over each faith just like a sovereign over his kingdom. In the world, all religions are not the same because all people have not complied with the commandments of God. They reject and disparage them." (See notations.)

"Are all churches the same?"

"In some, one prays to God more. In others, less. That depends on the priests who motivate others to pray. That also depends on the power which they have."

"Why are there so many apparitions, which repeat themselves so many times? Why does the Blessed Virgin appear to children who do not follow the way of God?" *"I appear to you often and in every place. To others, I appear from time to time and briefly. They do not yet follow completely the way of God. They are not aware of the gift which He has made them, that no one deserves. With time, they also will come to follow the right way."*

Tuesday, October 6, 1981

"The evening Mass must definitely be kept. The Mass of the sick must be celebrated on a specific day at a time which is most convenient. Father Tomislav must begin with the prayer group. It is very necessary. Have Father Tomislav pray with fervor."

Wednesday, October 7, 1981

The visionaries: "Are there, outside of Jesus, other intermediaries between God and man, and if so, what is their role?"
"There is only one mediator between God and man, and it is Jesus Christ."

On the request from Fr. Tomislav, "Should we found a community here just like that of Saint Francis of Assisi?"
"God has chosen Saint Francis as His elected one. It would be good to imitate his life. In the meantime, we must realize what God orders us to do."

59

Thursday, October 8, 1981

Marija humbly reports that the Gospa had scolded her for having stayed (during Mass) with her religious instruction school mates, who asked her about the apparitions:

"You would have done better to attend Mass rather than to satisfy human curiosity."

Saturday, October 10, 1981

"It is up to you to pray and to persevere. I have made promises to you; also be without anxiety. Faith will not know how to be alive without prayer. Pray more."

Sunday, October 11, 1981

The Virgin answers, as usual, questions on the subject of people who are sick or who have disappeared: *"Tomo Lovic* (an old man) *is dead."*

Monday, October 12, 1981

"Where are the Kingdom of God and paradise?" *"In Heaven."*

"Are you the Mother of God?"
"I am the Mother of God and the Queen of Peace."

"Did you go to Heaven before or after death?"
"I went to Heaven before death." (See notations.)

"When will you leave us the sign?"
"I will not yet leave the sign. I shall continue to appear. Father Jozo sends you greetings. He is experiencing difficulties, but he will resist, because he knows why he is suffering."

Saturday, October 17, 1981

Questioned on the subject of the visible sign, Our Lady responds,
"It is mine to realize the promise. With respect to the faithful, have them pray and believe firmly."

Monday, October 19, 1981

"Pray for Fr. Jozo and fast tomorrow on bread and water. Then you will fast for a whole week on bread and water. Pray, my angels. Now I will show you Fr. Jozo."

The visionaries have a vision of Fr. Jozo in prison. He tells them not to be afraid for him, and that everything was well.

With respect to Marinko who protected the visionaries:
"There are a few similar faithful. He has made a sufficient number of sacrifices for Jozo. He underwent many torments and sufferings. Continue, and do not let anyone take the Faith away from you."

Tuesday, October 20, 1981
Vicka: "Dear Gospa, have mercy on Fr. Jozo tomorrow during the trial. Paralyze someone; strike someone on the head. I know it is a sin to speak so, but what can we do?" The Gospa smiles at my words, then She sings, Jesus Christ, in Your Name. When we finished the song with Our Lady, She tells us, *"Go in the peace of God."* Then She leaves.

Wednesday, October 21, 1981
With respect to Fr. Jozo who is awaiting sentence from the court. Vicka: "Dear Gospa, I know that you do not have the spirit of vengeance, but try nevertheless to bring certain people to reason, so that they might judge impartially."
"Jozo looks well, and he greets you warmly. Do not fear for Jozo. He is a saint; I have already told you."

"Will Jozo be condemned?"
"Sentence will not be pronounced this evening. Do not be afraid; he will not be condemned to a severe punishment. Pray only, because Jozo asks from you prayer and perseverance. Do not be afraid because I am with you."

Thursday, October 22, 1981
"Jozo has been sentenced. Let us go to church to pray."

We were sad because of Jozo.
"You should rejoice!"

"Is the whiteness of the cross a supernatural phenomenon?"
"Yes, I confirm it."

After many people saw the cross on Mt. Krizevac transform itself into a light, and then into a silhouette of Our Lady, She said,

"All of these signs are designed to strengthen your faith until I leave you the visible and permanent sign."

Sunday, October 25, 1981

Three girls from Citluk are returning home after Mass and suddenly see a great light from which fifteen silhouettes, dressed in Franciscan frocks, are seen. They go down on their knees, and begin to pray and cry. The Blessed Virgin was asked about this and said:

"It was a supernatural phenomenon. I was among the saints."

Monday, October 26, 1981

The Blessed Virgin appeared smiling:

"Praised be Jesus. You are not to ask me any more questions on the subject of the sign. Do not be afraid, it will surely appear. I carry out my promises. As far as you are concerned, pray, persevere in prayer."

Wednesday, October 28, 1981

"Were you there at Krizevac yesterday for half an hour?"

"Yes, didn't you see me?"

Several hundred people saw, at the site of the first apparition, a fire which burned without consuming anything. In the evening, Our Lady tells the visionaries, *"The fire seen by the faithful was of a supernatural character. It is one of the signs, a forerunner of the great sign."*

Thursday, October 29, 1981

"You, my angels, be on your guard. There is enough mendacious news which people are spreading. Of course, I will show you my mercy. Be a little patient. Pray!"

Friday, October 30, 1981
"Praised be Jesus!"

Jakov and Vicka: "What was in the sealed envelope that they showed us at city hall?" (Someone told them they would believe in the apparitions, if they could read what was in the sealed envelope.)
"Do not respond to anything. It is a bad trick which they are playing on you. They have already given so much false news. Do not believe them. Continue to pray and to suffer! I will make the power of love appear."

"Should one celebrate Christmas Mass in the evening or at Midnight?"
"Have them celebrate it at midnight."

To the visionaries: *"Pray! Go in the peace of God!"*

To Ivanka: *"Pray more. The others are praying and suffering more than you."*

To the visionaries:
"Tell the young people not to allow themselves to be distracted from the true way. Let them remain faithful to their religion."

Saturday, October 31, 1981
Vicka's diary: "Mirjana arrives from Sarajevo, where she is studying at a professional school, and where she has had daily apparitions. Vicka reports: 'The Gospa advises as an attentive mother would.' She tells Mirjana twice whom she must distrust, which persons to avoid, how to conduct herself with those who reproach her and insult God. She also tells her to break a relationship with a girl who wanted to get her into drugs, and not to quarrel with anyone, and to answer a point when it is useful, or to remain silent and go on her way when that is better. She tells her also that Fr. Jozo will not spend more than four years in prison. She was happy because all five of us were together."

On the question of Danny Ljolje, the Gospa said:
"There is a lot of deception and erroneous information."

"Then Our Lady showed us a part of paradise. It was indescribably beautiful, with many people, particularly children. We were afraid. The Blessed Virgin told us not to be afraid."

"All those who are faithful to God will have that."

Ivanka saw her mother in paradise as well as another person who was an acquaintance.

October 1981
Regarding the conflict between the Franciscans and the Bishop of Mostar in Herzegovina: *"It is going to find a solution. We must have patience and pray."*

In response to a question posed by the visionaries: "What will become of Poland?" *"There will be great conflicts, but in the end, the just will take over."*

With respect to Russia:
"It is the people where God will be most glorified. The West has made civilization progress, but without God, as if they were their own creators."

Sunday, November 1, 1981
"Be persevering! Pray! Many people are beginning to convert."

Beginning of November 1981
The Virgin appears with a picture of John Paul II in her hand. She embraces the picture:
"He is our father, and the father of all. It is necessary to pray for him."

Monday, November 2, 1981
"Why did you show us paradise the day before yesterday?"
"I did it so that you could see the happiness which awaits those who love God."

Jesus appears to them crowned with thorns, and with injuries all over His body. The children are afraid.
"Do not be afraid. It is my Son. See how He has been martyred. In spite of all, He was joyful, and He endured all with patience."

Jesus tells them:

"Look at me. How I have been injured and martyred. In spite of all, I have gained the victory. You also, my angels, be persevering in your faith and pray so that you may overcome."

Tuesday, November 3, 1981

The Virgin begins the song, Come, Come to Us, Lord, and we continued it with her.

"I am often at Krizevac, at the foot of the cross, to pray there. Now I pray to my Son to forgive the world its sins. The world has begun to convert."

She smiles, and then leaves.

Friday, November 6, 1981

After twenty minutes, the Gospa disappears, and before us, Hell appears. Later she tells us:

"Do not be afraid! I have shown you Hell so that you may know the state of those who are there."

Sunday, November 8, 1981

The Blessed Virgin kisses an image of the Pope and says,

"It is your father, the spiritual father of all."

The visionaries have a vision of Fr. Jozo in prison. The Blessed Virgin tells them: *"Have you seen how our Fr. Jozo struggles for God?"*

Monday, November 9, 1981

Jakov and I were alone in the room. We were speaking of the militia which passed by. The Virgin arrived:

"Do not be afraid of the militia. Do not provoke anybody. Be polite with everybody."

Tuesday, November 10, 1981

"Do not give in. Keep your faith. I will accompany you at every step."

Friday, November 13, 1981

"Praised be Jesus!"

The visionaries answer: "Always Jesus and Mary."

"Then the Blessed Virgin shows us beautiful landscapes. The Baby Jesus was walking there, but we were not able to recognize Him." She said, *"It is Jesus. On my arrival and when I depart always sing the song, Come, Come to us, O Lord."*
"Then she blessed us."

Sunday, November 15, 1981

"We were in Fr. Jozo's room. The Gospa did not come. She appeared to us in the church after the prayers of seven Our Father's, Hail Mary's, and Glory Be's. We asked her why she had not appeared. She answered that She had not appeared because someone had installed something there."
"The world is on the point of receiving great favors from me and from my Son. May the world keep a strong confidence."

Monday, November 16, 1981

"The Devil is trying to conquer us. Do not permit him. Keep the Faith, fast and pray. I will be with you at every step."

To Jakov and Vicka, *"Persevere with confidence in prayer and in faith."*

Sunday, November 22, 1981

We asked the Blessed Virgin what the cross, the heart and the sun, seen during the apparition, meant.
"These are the signs of salvation: The cross is a sign of mercy, just like the heart. The sun is the source of light, which enlightens us."

A shining silhouette takes the place of the cross again on Krizevac. The visionaries ask Our Lady if it was She.
"Why do you ask me, my angels? Have you not seen me? The world must find salvation while there is time. Let it pray with fervor. May it have the spirit of faith."

Monday, November 23, 1981

The Gospa was all dressed in gold. Around her veil, and on her dress, everything shined and sparkled. It was indescribable. She was very, very beautiful.
"The people have begun to convert. Keep a solid faith. I need your prayers."

Thursday, November 26, 1981

This evening the Blessed Virgin was smiling. We prayed and sang with her. We asked her questions about the sick.

"Have a strong faith, pray, and fast, and they will be cured. Be confident and rest in joy. Go in the peace of God. Be patient and pray for the cure. Goodbye, my dear angels."

Saturday, November 28, 1981

There were five of us. Ivan was absent. Profound harmony reigned over us. The Virgin came at the moment when we began to say the Our Father. We conversed with her. Then She blessed religious objects. She looked at us with sweetness and said,

"Ah, it is so beautiful to see all of you together! Go in the peace of God, my angels. Goodbye."

Sunday, November 29, 1981

"It is necessary for the world to be saved while there is still time, for it to pray strongly, and to have the spirit of faith."

November 1981

"The Devil tries to impose his power on you. But you must remain strong and persevere in your faith. You must pray and fast. I will be always close to you."

Vicka: "This warning concerns everybody."

Wednesday, December 2, 1981

Marija, Vicka and Jakov: "We asked the Blessed Virgin on the matter of a young man who had suddenly lost his memory and stopped learning." She said, *"It is necessary to hospitalize him."*

"We still questioned her. She did not respond to some of the questions."

"It is not necessary to ask questions on every subject."

"She then greeted us as usual."

Thursday, December 3, 1981

"Pray, and persevere through prayer."

Sunday, December 6, 1981
"Be strong and persevering. My dear angels, go in the peace of God."

Monday, December 7, 1981
"The people are converting. It is true, but not yet all."
"She spoke while looking at the crowd."

Apparition at Jakov's home, "The blessed Virgin prayed all the time with us." She then said, *"Pray and persist in prayers."*

On the walls there was written in letters of gold "MIR LJUDIMA". (Peace to the people).

Tuesday, December 8, 1981 (Feast of the Immaculate Conception)
Responding to a question from the visionaries with respect to their future:
"I would like for all of you to become priests and religious, but only if you desire it. You are free. It is up to you to choose. If you are experiencing difficulties, or if you need something, come to me. If you do not have the strength to fast on bread and water, you can give up a number of things. It would be a good thing to give up television, because after seeing some programs, you are distracted and unable to pray. You can give up alcohol, cigarettes, and other pleasures. You yourselves know what you have to do."

"On this day of the Feast of the Immaculate Conception, the Gospa was serious; She knelt down with arms extended while praying."
"My beloved Son, I beseech you to be willing to forgive the world its great sin through which it offends you."

Wednesday, December 9, 1981
"While we were saying our prayers, the Blessed Virgin intervened:"
"Oh, My Son Jesus, forgive these sins; there are so many of them!"

"Then we were all silent."
"Continue to pray, because that is the salvation of this people."

Friday, December 11, 1981

Vicka: "I recommend to the Gospa my parents, who are in Germany."
"I promise to protect them. Everything will go well."

Saturday, December 12, 1981

As vacation approached, which allowed the visionaries to be back together, the Blessed Virgin was happy.
"Very soon you will all be united. You will be able to have a good time together."

Wednesday, December 16, 1981

"Kneel down, my children, and pray. Persevere in prayer."

Jakov and Vicka: "Every word of the Blessed Virgin invited us to be joyful."

Friday, December 18, 1981

"The Blessed Virgin did not respond to our questions. She sang, Jesus Christ, in Your Name. After the first verse, she said,"
"Come on, sing more joyfully. Why are you so pensive?"

"After the prayer, She began Queen of the Holy Rosary, and She departed."

Monday, December 21, 1981

"Be on your guard, my children. Prepare yourselves for difficult days. All kinds of people will come here."

Thursday, December 24, 1981

"Celebrate the days which are coming. Rejoice with my Son. Love your neighbor. May harmony reign among you."

Friday, December 25, 1981

"Love one another, my children. You are brothers and sisters. Don't argue among yourselves."
Our Lady then blesses them and leaves.

After having had a vision of Jesus,
"Give glory to God, glorify Him and sing, my angels."

Wednesday, December 30, 1981
In response to some questions concerning the sick, Our Lady began praying with the Our Father, then the song, The Queen of the Holy Rosary, and then she departed.

Thursday, December 31, 1981
Ivan: "How can one put priests, who do not believe in the apparitions, on the right track?"
"It is necessary to tell them that, from the very beginning, I have been conveying the message of God to the world. It is a great pity not to believe in it. Faith is a vital element, but one cannot compel a person to believe. Faith is the foundation from which everything flows."

"Is it really you who appears at the foot of the Cross?"
"Yes, it is true. Almost every day I am at the foot of the Cross. My Son carried the Cross. He has suffered on the Cross, and by it, He saved the world. Every day I pray to my Son to forgive the sins of the world."

The Apparitions in the Chapel
Opposite the Sacristy
(Jan-Feb 1982 To Apr 11, 1985)

1982

The apparitions since July 1981, often taking place in the church where they occurred spontaneously toward the end of the rosary, are transferred to the room serving as a storeroom. It is opposite the sacristy, and provided privacy from the curiosity of the pilgrims and every provocation on part of the police. This room was cleaned and decorated. Subsequently, it has since been called "chapel of the apparitions." Before the end of February this transfer was definitive, except for rare occasions.

Monday, January 11, 1982
"I invite you very specially to participate at Mass. Wait for me at church; that is the agreeable place."

Thursday, January 14, 1982
After the prayers, the songs, and the questions, Our Lady reprimanded two visionaries because of their behavior, and recommended to them not to behave in this manner again. In case of observation, the other visionaries did not understand what Our Lady told those she reprimanded, and observed only her expression and guessed what it was all about. Those whom She reprimanded say that at that moment, She was gentle and attentive in respect for them.

Monday, January 18, 1982
On the matter of a sick person with heart problems,
"There is little hope for her. I will pray for her."

After her departure, the children see the Cross, the heart, and the sun, signs which they perceive from time to time.

Wednesday, January 20, 1982
"Must the children from Lzbicno meet us tomorrow? They say that you told them of this meeting." *"It is not necessary for you to meet them."*

"They want to transfer Fr. Tomislav from here. What must he do?"
"If it is in God's design that he depart, as has been the case with Fr. Jozo, have him abandon himself to the will of God. He must think very much, and you must pray for him."

Thursday, January 21, 1982

The visionaries: "Why don't you leave a concrete sign, so that the priests are convinced, and that they be converted in order to be able to convert the others?" *"The sign will appear at the desired time."*

"Why are there apparitions in different places in Herzegovina?"
"My children, don't you see that faith begins to extinguish itself, and that it is necessary to awaken faith among men?"

"What must we do so that peace may reign among the priests?"
"Fast and pray!"

Friday, January 22, 1982

"Is the apparition at Lzbicno coming from God or from the devil?"
"It is coming from God."

Tuesday, February 2, 1982

"When must one celebrate the feast of The Queen of Peace?"
The Blessed Virgin smiled as she answered,
"I would prefer that it take place June 25th. The faithful have come for the first time on that day, on the hill."

Monday, February 8, 1982

Vicka: "Jakov and I were in the sacristy. When we began to pray the Our Father, the Gospa arrived. It was five minutes after six. We questioned her on the matter of a person who was sick emotionally."
"He must pray. I will help him within the limitation of my power."

To the Slovenes who were praying while she was with us,
"Persevere in prayer."
Then she blessed some religious articles.

72

Tuesday, February 9, 1982

At the fourth Our Father, the Blessed Virgin arrived. We always ask questions with respect to the sick.

"Pray for all the sick. Believe firmly. I will come to help. According to that which is in my power I will ask my Son, Jesus, to help them. The most important thing, in the meantime, is a strong faith. Numerous sick persons think that it is sufficient to come here in order to be quickly healed. Some of them do not even believe in God, and even less, in the apparitions, and then they ask for help from the Gospa!"

Wednesday, February 10, 1982

Vicka: "Jakov and I were alone. Just as every evening, we prayed, conversed with the Blessed Virgin, and asked many questions. To them she responded," *"Pray, Pray! It is necessary to believe firmly, to go to confession regularly, and likewise receive Holy Communion. It is the only salvation."*

"Her preferred prayer is the Creed. When we recite it, the Blessed Virgin does not cease to smile. I think that no one has seen her happier than during this prayer."

Thursday, February 11, 1982

"Just like every evening, except on Fridays, Saturdays, and Sundays, Jakov and I are alone. The Blessed Virgin begins first of all to pray the Our Father, then the Glory Be. We recommend the sick and then present her with questions." *"Pray my angels, persevere! Do not let the enemy take possession of you in anything. Be courageous. Go in the peace of God, my angels. Goodbye."*

Friday, February 12, 1982

"Be more calm, more poised. Do not take sides with other children. Be agreeable, well mannered, pious!"

"When Our Lady prays, she joins her hands. When she speaks she opens them and raises them toward Heaven, her palms turned upwards."

Saturday, February 13, 1982

To the seminarians who were present, *"Through prayer, one obtains everything."*

Sunday, February 14, 1982

"There are four of us today. When we are in a group, I feel a little happier and joyful in the presence of the Holy Virgin. The others agree."

"Be together like brothers and sisters. Do not argue. Satan exists! He seeks only to destroy. With regards to you, pray, and persevere in prayer. No one will be able to do anything against you."

Tuesday, February 16, 1982

"The Blessed Virgin began, Jesus in Your Name. Since she has appeared to us she hasn't been sad. Whatever she says, her countenance is smiling and filled with serenity. Her joy attracts us. She wants us to be joyful, wanting nothing to deceive us, no intrigues, or invented stories."

"Satan only says what he wants. He interferes in everything. You, my angels, be ready to endure everything. Here, many things will take place. Do not allow yourselves to be surprised by him."

Friday, February 19, 1982

"We asked if we could pray the Hail Mary. She said, 'Yes.' And while we prayed, She looked at us with a smile, but without praying with us. Truly, her beauty is indescribable. Since I have seen Our Lady, I have been filled with joy. Whatever her words may be, what She has told me, I have always done it. I have obeyed. She makes attentive remarks, as a mother."

"Listen attentively at Holy Mass. Be well mannered. Do not chatter during Holy Mass."

Sunday, February 21, 1982

"Be together, and do not argue; do not be disorderly. My angels, I will make you attentive. I will guide you on a sure way."

Tuesday, February 23, 1982

"When we asked Our Lady, She did not answer, but began immediately to pray. When we asked her if such a person were alive, She said,"

"Do not ask me any more questions! I know what there is in each sick person, or what there is in my power to help him. I will pray to my Son to put out His mercy on each one."

74

Thursday, February 25, 1982

"Be persevering and courageous. Do not fear anything. Pray, and do not pay attention to others."

We asked for news about Fr. Jozo. *"Do not fear for him."*

Sunday, February 28, 1982

"Thank Tomislav very much, for he is guiding you very well." Then she smiles, and begins to say the Glory Be. *"Go in the peace of God, my angels!"*

Monday, March 1, 1982

"All of you be happy, and may my blessing accompany you at each step."
She blessed many religious articles; She touched them with her hands.

Since the Yugoslavian authorities demanded that they put an end to the prayer meetings for the young people, the Blessed Virgin was questioned, and responded:
"It is better to temporarily suspend prayer meetings and those of meditation because of the authorities. Take them up later, when it will be possible."

Tuesday, March 2, 1982

A woman, who had come from Osijek, brought two large pictures of the Pope. The Blessed Virgin came at 6:00pm with her smile. I believed She was smiling at us; but it was because of the pictures on the table. She said:
"He is your father, my angels."

Then She began the Our Father. On leaving She said,
"Open the door well, follow the Mass well! Go in the peace of God, my angels! If you suffer for a just cause, blessings will be still more abundant for you."

Thursday, March 4, 1982

I asked questions with respect to a woman who had no children. She is not of our faith. Our Lady said:
"Let her believe firmly. God, who comes to help everyone, will likewise help her. Be patient, my angels; do not be afraid of anything. I am at your side and guard you. If you have any problems, whatever it be, call me. I will come immediately and help you in advising you on best resolving the difficulty. Go in peace, my angels. Goodbye."

75

Friday, March 5, 1982

"I questioned the Blessed Virgin on the matter of an Italian, who was very sick, and about another man who acquired cancer. She responded,

Tell them to pray and to put themselves in the hands of God. I, too, will call on the mercy of my Son. I will do everything in my power to help them. But it will be necessary to believe completely. Without a strong faith, nothing is possible. Goodbye, my angels.'"

Sunday, March 7, 1982

"The Blessed Virgin said that She has been with Ivan at the Seminary in Visoko." *"He prays well; he is obedient. He follows my instructions."*

Monday, March 8, 1982

"Concerning a boy named Bora (age 16), from Metkovic, who disappeared for a week,"

"He left because of many troubles. He himself created some of the problems."

Tuesday, March 9, 1982

"On the matter of a young man from Hadromilje, named Mladen, who disappeared from his home:"

"He has serious problems. It is necessary to pray for him very much, my angels. The people are beginning to be converted. Prayer has been taken up again in the homes, where people had no longer prayed."

Beginning of April 1982

Mirjana: "Do you wish the establishment of a special feast in your honor?"

"I wish a feast for the Queen of Peace, on the 25th of June, anniversary of the first apparition."

Easter Sunday, April 11, 1982

"Is it necessary to establish prayer groups, formed by priests, sisters, and laity in the parish?"

"It is necessary, but not only here. Communities of prayer are necessary in all parishes."

(It does not mean just Charismatic Groups, as the polemists, who are adversaries of this movement, have indicated.)

Wednesday, April 21, 1982

Fr. Vlasic questioned the visionaries and said, "They say that the Blessed Virgin continues to appear to them every day. The messages can be summarized thusly: Be patient! Everything is developing according to God's plan. His promises will be realized. May one continue to pray, to do penance, and to be converted."

Thursday, April 22, 1982

"Are the luminous signs at the cross on Krizevac natural, or do they come from God? What does the letter 'S' and the letter 'T', which appear on the cross mean?" *"They are signs of God, and not of natural phenomena. 'S' and 'T' are signs of salvation."*

Saturday, April 24, 1982

"What must one do in order to have more cures?"
"Pray! Pray and believe firmly. Say the prayers which have already been requested. (seven Our Father's, Hail Mary's, Glory Be's, and the Creed.) *Do more penance."*

Sunday, May 2, 1982

"I have come to call the world to conversion for the last time. Later, I will not appear any more on this earth."

Thursday, May 6, 1982

"May we write on a piece of paper the date of the great sign, describe it, seal it, and put it in the archives?" (as requested by the Commission).
"No! I have entrusted that only to you. You will unveil it when I will tell you. Many persons will not believe you, I know, and you will suffer very much for it. But you will endure everything, and you will finally be the happiest."

Thursday, May 13, 1982

After the attempt on the life of John Paul II:
"His enemies have wanted to kill him, but I protected him."

Spring, 1982
Question asked at the request of the pastor at Lzbicno, alleged place of other apparitions: "Why are there so many signs in Herzegovina?"
"It is God who gives them. My children, have you not observed that faith began to extinguish itself? There are many who do not come to church except through habit. It is necessary to awaken faith. It is a gift from God."

"People are surprised that you are appearing in so many places:"
"If it is necessary, I will appear in each home."

With respect to the little visionaries from Lzbicno, which is located thirty six miles from Medjugorje: "In 1982-83, eighteen persons, mostly females, said they received apparitions. The visionaries from Medjugorje were said to have received kind words from those in Lzbicno, but the Blessed Virgin reminded them strongly, that they must not have any contact with these persons, nor invite them to Medjugorje."
"Did I not tell you not to come together with those children? I am your mother, you must obey me."

For Jakov, who was crying to see Vicka ill:
"The cross is necessary because of the sins of the world."

Wednesday, June 23, 1982 (Possibly a few days preceding)
Just before the anniversary of June 24, Vicka answered some questions asked by Fr. Tomislav Vlasic, who reported them in the parish Chronicle in June. Our Lady said:
"The most important thing is that you, the visionaries, remain united. Let peace be among you. Pay very close attention to that. Obey, and do what the priests and your parents tell you. Go often to Holy Mass and receive Communion. Be very attentive these days. Some dishonest people will come to you, in numbers, in order to tempt you. Be careful of your statements. These days, I am expecting of you a very special discipline. Do not move around anywhere, or often, and do not separate from one another."
(Some of the visionaries understood that these words were directed specifically to them, and they began to cry).

"A number of those who have been very enthusiastic will cool off. But you, persist, and be proud of each of my words. Have the people pray very much. Have them pray more for salvation, and only for salvation. And let the people be converted so long as it is possible. There are many sins, vexations, curse words, lies, and other bad things. Let them be converted, go to confession, and receive Holy Communion. Let them not print books on the apparitions before the anniversary has passed, because that could have some undesirable consequences. You have asked me to keep in this parish good and faithful priests who will continue the work. Do not be afraid of anything. This grace will be given to you. From priests, I do not demand anything other than prayer, with perseverance, and preaching. May they be patient and wait for the promises of God."

With respect to a question from a theologian, "Does the Holy Spirit have two natures?" *"He has only one, the Divine nature."*

The visionaries: "They have said that these would be the last apparitions on earth? Is it true?" *"These apparitions are the last in the world."*

As far as I have understood, observes Fr. Tomislav Vlasic, her answer is not only given in Medjugorje, but also in other parts of the world.

Thursday, June 24 or Friday, June 25, 1982
Before the evening Mass, during the apparition, the Virgin told the priests, through the intermediary of the visionaries:
"Thank the people in my name for the prayers, the sacrifices, and the penance. Have them persevere in prayer, fasting, and conversion, and have them wait with patience for the realization of my promise. Everything is unfolding according to God's plan."

Monday, July 12, 1982
"Will there be a third world war?" *"The third world war will not take place."*

Wednesday, July 21, 1982
To the response conveyed by Fr. Tomislav Vlasic on Purgatory:
"There are many souls in Purgatory. There are also persons who have been consecrated to God: some priests, some religious. Pray for their intentions, at least seven Our Father's, Hail Mary's and Glory Be's and the Creed. I recommend it to you. There is a large number of souls who have been in Purgatory for a long time because no one prays for them."

A response to a question on fasting:

"The best fast is on bread and water. Through fasting and prayer, one can stop wars, one can suspend the laws of nature. Charity cannot replace fasting. Those who are not able to fast can sometime replace it with prayer, charity and a confession; but everyone, except the sick, must fast."

Saturday, July 24, 1982

Answer to some questions which were asked:

"We go to Heaven in full conscience: that which we have now. At the moment of death, we are conscious of the separation of the body and the soul. It is false to teach people that we are re-born many times and that we pass to different bodies. One is born only once. The body, drawn from the earth, decomposes after death. It never comes back to life again. Man receives a transfigured body. Whoever has done very much evil during his life can go straight to Heaven if he confesses, is sorry for what he has done, and received Communion at the end of his life."

Sunday, July 25, 1982

A response to questions asked regarding Hell:

"Today many persons go to Hell. God permits His children to suffer in Hell due to the fact that they have committed grave unpardonable sins. Those who are in Hell no longer have a chance to know a better lot."

Response to questions regarding cures:

"For the cure of the sick, it is important to say the following prayers: the Creed, seven Our Father's, Hail Mary's and Glory Be's, and to fast on bread and water. It is good to impose one's hands on the sick and to pray. It is good to anoint the sick with holy oil. All priests do not have the gift of healing. In order to revive this gift, the priest must pray with perseverance and believe firmly."

Friday, August 6, 1982 (Feast of the Transfiguration)

A response to questions which were asked concerning Confession:

"One must invite people to go to confession each month, especially the first Saturday. Here I have not spoken about it yet. I have invited people to frequent confession. I will give you yet some concrete messages for our time. Be patient because the time has not yet come. Do what I have told you. They are numerous who do not observe it. Monthly confession will be a remedy for the Church in the West. One must convey this message to the West."

That night Our Lady gave a sign to a group of young people who prayed with Ivan Dragicevic. Two luminary signs descended on Krizevac and the church. This phenomenon was observed by Fr. Tomislav Vlasic near the church.

Sunday, August 15, 1982
The vision lasted about seven minutes. The Gospa entrusted a new secret to Vicka and Ivanka. The other visionaries saw that it was about a secret, but they did not understand anything.

Monday, August 16, 1982
No special message. Our Lady only corrected the very resonant and very rapid prayer of the visionaries, and the people in church.

Mirjana says that at the time of the apparition, she sometimes sees heavenly persons: Jesus, Mary, and angels in three dimensions, and earthly persons in two dimensions.

Wednesday, August 18, 1982
Mirjana reports to Fr. Tomislav Vlasic what the Gospa has told her concerning the sick:
"Have them believe and pray; I cannot help those who do not pray and do not sacrifice. The sick, just like those who are in good health, must pray and should offer their sufferings for the sick. The more you believe firmly, the more you pray and fast for the same intention, the greater is the grace and the mercy of God."

Question asked with regard to a marriage planned between a Catholic and an Orthodox, *"In my eyes and in the sight of God, everything is equal. But for you, it is not the same thing because you are divided. If it is possible, it is better if she were not to marry this man because she will suffer and her children also. She will be able to live and follow only with difficulty, the way of her Faith."*

Sunday, August 29, 1982

With reference to the critiques on the apparitions, which have divided the priests in Herzegovina:

"I have not desired your division. On the contrary, I desire that you be united. Do not ignore the fact that I am the Queen of Peace. If you desire practical advice: I am the Mother who has come from the people; I cannot do anything without the help of God. I, too, must pray like you. It is because of that, that I can only say to you: Pray, fast, do penance, and help the weak. I am sorry if my preceding answer was not agreeable to you. Perhaps you do not want to understand it."

Tuesday, August 31, 1982

"I do not dispense all graces. I receive from God what I obtain through prayer. God has placed His complete trust in me. I protect particularly those who have been consecrated to me. The great sign has been granted. It will appear independently of the conversion of the people." (See notations.)

End of August 1982

Ivan is on the hill of Bijakovici with his friends. The Virgin appears to him. *"Now, I am going to give you a sign in order to strengthen your faith."*
They see two rays of light, one on the church, the other on the Cross at Krizevac.

Saturday, September 4, 1982

"Jesus prefers that you address yourselves directly to Him rather than through an intermediary. In the meantime, if you wish to give yourselves completely to God and if you wish that I be your protector, then confide to me all your intentions, your fasts, and your sacrifices so that I can dispense them according to the will of God."

Sunday, September 26, 1982

For a religious who had come from Rome:
"Have her strengthen the faith of those who have been entrusted to her."

For Fr. Faricy and Fr. Forrest: *"They are on the good path; have them persist."*

For Pope John Paul II:
"Have him consider himself the father of all mankind and not only of Christians. Have him spread untiringly and with courage the message of peace and love among all mankind."

Friday, October 1, 1982
"I am happy because you have begun to prepare the monthly feast of the sacrament of reconciliation. That will be good for the whole world. Persevere in prayer. It is the true way which leads you toward my Son."

Thursday, November 4, 1982
Regarding a vision seen by Andja from Mostar one evening during prayer: She saw thirteen persons coming from the East, and another evening six persons: *"It is about a true vision. They were some souls of his close family from purgatory. It is necessary to pray for them."*

Saturday, November 6, 1982
Frightened by the eighth secret, Mirjana prayed to the Blessed Virgin to preserve humanity from this calamity:
"I have prayed; the punishment has been softened. Repeated prayers and fasting reduce punishments from God, but it is not possible to avoid entirely the chastisement. Go on the streets of the city, count those who glorify God and those who offend Him. God can no longer endure that."

Monday, November 8, 1982
Fr. Tomislav has the visionaries ask Our Lady if it is necessary to write to the Bishop and to priests, so that they can call the faithful to intensify their prayers, or if it is better to wait for other events:
"It is better to wait than to precipitate that."

Monday, November 15, 1982
Jakov: "Must Vicka take the prescribed medicines, or must she have herself admitted to a hospital in Zagreb?" *"It is necessary to send Vicka to Zagreb."*

Vicka refused to question the Blessed Mother on this subject. She said that she wanted to accept whatever God sent her.

Saturday, December 18, 1982
With respect to the article from the Bishop of Mostar in the journal, Vijesnik, on the events of Medjugorje, Fr. Tomislav Vlasic had the visionaries ask: "Must we respond to the Bishop in writing?"
"Yes, respond!"

Monday, December 20, 1982
With respect to the same article (Dec. 18, 1982), the visionaries ask, "Is it necessary to give the faithful of Mostar objective information concerning the case in Herzegovina?" *"No!"*

"Is it better for the visionaries to pray with you, and for the pilgrims to ask their questions to the priests instead?"
"Yes, it is better that the children pray with me, and that the pilgrims ask the priests and look for solutions with them. In the meanwhile I will continue to answer the questions which they ask me."

Thursday, December 23, 1982
To Mirjana, *"On Christmas I will appear to you for the last time."*
(On a daily basis)

Saturday, December 25, 1982
To Mirjana after she had received the tenth secret,
"Now you will have to turn to God in faith like any other person. I will appear to you on the day of your birthday and when you will experience difficulties in life. Mirjana, I have chosen you, I have confided in you everything that is essential. I have also shown you many terrible things. You must now bear it all with courage. Think of Me, and think of the tears I must shed for that. You must remain courageous. You have quickly grasped the messages. You must also understand now that I have to go away. Be courageous."

Monday, December 27, 1982
Today the statue of the Queen of Peace was finished. It was sculptured by Vipotnik, a sculptor from Slovenia, and painted by Luka Stojaknac, and Florijan Mickovic, who wanted to maintain anonymity. This statue has been a source of grace for Luka, who is Orthodox.

The Visionaries ask, "May we put the statue in church?" *"Yes, you may!"*

It is this statue which had been venerated for a long time in the nave. It was removed from there on orders from the bishop on March 25, 1985. It then found itself consigned to the small chapel of the apparitions.

Friday, December 31, 1982
On Vicka's request, the Blessed Virgin gives this message for the New Year: *"Pray as much as possible and fast!"*

In the evening, to the visionaries:
"You must persevere in prayer and fasting. I wish that the New Year will be spent in prayer and penance. Persevere in prayer and in sacrifice, and I will protect you and will hear your prayers."

Saturday, January 1, 1983
Ivanka: "Are you still appearing to Mirjana?"
"After Christmas, I am no longer appearing to her for the present."

Wednesday, January 5, 1983
Fr. Tomislav receives from the four visionaries present (Ivan, Jakov, Marija and Vicka), the following information: Marija has received 7 secrets, Vicka 8, Jakov, Ivanka and Ivan 9, and Mirjana 10. We do not know how long the apparitions will last, or why she no longer appears to Mirjana after Christmas. The Gospa invites us constantly to prayer, to fasting, to conversion. She confirms her promises.

Questioned with respect to the time of the sign: Which month? Which year?, Ivan says: "It is forecast."

Friday, January 7, 1983
Our Lady begins to tell her life to the visionaries. They are invited to write down her testimony. They will not be able to make it public until they have received her authorization.

This dictation of her life lasted for Jakov until April, for Ivanka until May 22, and for Marija until July 17.

Marija, who was still attending a school for hairdressers in Mostar, received only an abridged account on the days when she was in Medjugorje. For Vicka, it lasted until April 10, 1985, and is a long account which filled three notebooks. Up to this day, the visionaries have not received authorization to reveal the contents.

Monday, January 10, 1983

Confidences from Mirjana to Fr. Tomislav Vlasic: "During the 18 months that I saw the Gospa, a great intimacy was established between us. I felt her maternal love. I could ask her all kinds of questions. Thus I asked her why God was so merciless in sending sinners to Hell for eternity."

"Men who go to Hell no longer want to receive any benefit from God. They do not repent; nor do they cease to swear and to blaspheme. They make up their mind to live in Hell and do not at all contemplate leaving it."

(Man's refusal is an irreversible choice.)

Questioned on the subject of Purgatory, the Blessed Virgin says:

"There are different levels of which the lowest are close to Hell and the highest gradually draw near to Heaven. It is not on All Souls day, but at Christmas, that the greatest numbers of souls leave Purgatory. Those in Purgatory are the souls who pray ardently to God, but for whom no relative or friend prays for them on earth. God makes them benefit from the prayers of other people. It happens that God permits them to manifest themselves in different ways, close to their relatives on earth, in order to remind men of the existence of Purgatory, and to solicit their prayers close to God who is just, but good. The majority go to Purgatory. Many go to Hell. A small number go directly to Heaven."

Wednesday, January 12, 1983

Regarding an American television team: "Will they be able to finish without difficulties?"

"There will be some difficulties, but it will be for the glory of God."

Thursday, April 21, 1983

"You (the visionaries), *must behave well; be pious and set a good example for the faithful."*

Jakov admits that the Blessed Virgin has made remarks to him several times concerning his conduct. She has taught him how to participate at Mass, to pray, and to behave around others.

Sunday, April 24, 1983

Message for an Italian doctor who is present:

"I bless him just as those who work with him at the hospital in Milan, for everything they are doing. Have them continue, and pray. I bless the sick of this hospital, just like the sick for whom you have prayed this evening, and those for whom you will pray."

Thursday, May 5, 1983

With respect to a sick person from Vienna: "The doctor has diagnosed schizophrenia. Some priests think it is a question of diabolical possession." *"It is a diabolical possession. One can succeed only through prayer."*

Wednesday, June 1, 1983

"Dear Children: I hoped that the world would begin to be converted on its own. Do now everything you can so that the world can be converted."

Thursday, June 2, 1983

"Read what has been written about Jesus. Meditate on it, and convey it to others."

Friday, June 3, 1983

Fr. Vlasic has begun to form a prayer group requested by the Virgin on May 25. Jakov, Vicka, and Ivanka, "What do you expect of Fr. Tomislav? Has he begun well?" *"Yes, it is good. Have him continue."*

"What should one do so that people will not drive away from here the priests who work with faith and love?"

"Pray and fast for this intention. I will tell you when the moment comes what you must do."

"Fr. Tomislav wants to call the parish to prayer and fasting, so that the Church recognizes that the events here are supernatural. Is it a good way?"

"Yes, it is a good way. Have the parish pray for this gift. Have them pray also for the gift of the Holy Spirit so that all those who come here will feel the presence of God."

Sunday, June 12, 1983

Ivan: "May the priests begin new work around the church, or must they request authorization from the authorities?"

"Do not begin the work until receiving permission from the authorities. Otherwise, someone will inform the latter, and the works would be forbidden. Go, and kindly request the authorization. It will be given to you."

Tuesday, June 14, 1983

Ivan: "What do you wish that the priests preach during the ten anniversary days of the first apparitions?"

"Have them do what they think is best. It would be good to remind the faithful of the events which have been revealed here in relation to my coming. Have them remind them the reasons for my coming here."

Spring 1983

"Hasten your conversion. Do not await the sign, which has been announced, for those who do not believe. It will be too late. You who believe, be converted, and deepen your faith."

Friday, June 24, 1983

"The sign will come; you must not worry about it. The only thing that I would want to tell you is to be converted. Make that known to all my children as quickly as possible. No pain, no suffering is too great for me in order to save you. I will pray to my Son not to punish the world; but I beseech you, be converted. You cannot imagine what is going to happen or what the Eternal Father will send to earth. That is why you must be converted! Renounce everything. Do penance. Express my acknowledgement to all my children who have prayed and fasted. I carry all this to my Divine Son in order to obtain an alleviation of His justice against the sins of mankind. I thank the people who have prayed and fasted. Persevere and help me to convert the world."

Sunday, June 26, 1983
"Love your enemies. Pray for them and bless them."

Friday, July 1, 1983 (Toward 11:00pm on Krizevac)
"I thank all those who have responded to my call. I bless all of you. I bless each of you. In these days, I ask you to pray for my intentions. Go in the peace of God."

Beginning of July 1983
Concerning the tensions within the diocese:
"Fast two days a week for the intentions of the Bishop, who bears a heavy responsibility. If there is a need to, I will ask for a third day. Pray each day for the Bishop."

Saturday, August 6, 1983
On orders from the Bishop, Fr. Pervan, the parish priest, put an end to the custom which called for the visionaries beginning the prayers of the Rosary and the seven Our Father's, Hail Mary's and Glory Be's. Jakov questioned the Blessed Virgin on this subject:
"If it is so, then do not go against it so as not to provoke any quarrels. If it is possible, talk about it tomorrow among yourselves. All of you come to an agreement beforehand."

Friday, August 12, 1983
This was an exceptionally long apparition (thirty-eight minutes). The Blessed Virgin gives the visionaries instructions to guide their lives which only concerned them:
"Pray more for your spiritual life. Do your utmost in this sense. Pray for your Bishop."

Monday, August 15, 1983
To the young people who are returning to school,
"Be careful not to diminish the spirit of prayer. Satan is enraged against those who fast and those who are converted."

Tuesday, August 23, 1983
With respect to Fr. Emilien Tardif, the Canadian priest of the charismatic renewal,
"Have him announce my messages to the whole world. Let Jesus, only Jesus, be at the center of his efforts."

Thursday, August 25, 1983

Fr. Tardif, Fr. Raucourt, and Dr. Phillippe Madre have been arrested and expelled by the Yugoslavian authorities.

"Do not worry for them. Everything is in God's plan."

Monday, August 29, 1983

For the intention of a group of young people before their departure on their pilgrimage to Brijeg:

"I wish that you pray throughout your trip, and that you glorify God. There you will be able to meet other young people. Convey the messages which I have given you. Do not hesitate to speak to them about it. Some begin to pray and to fast just as they have been told, but they get tired very quickly, and thus loose the graces which they have acquired."

Monday, September 5, 1983

The mother of Jakov (twelve years old) dies. The Blessed Virgin consoles him and reveals to him, *"Your mother is with me in Heaven."*

Monday, September 12, 1983

"Pray. When I give you this message, do not be content to just listen to it. Increase your prayer and see how it makes you happy. All graces are at your disposal. All you have to do is to gain them. In order to do that, I tell you again, 'Pray!'"

Friday, September 16, 1983

"Pray, pray, pray! Do not be discouraged. Be in peace because God gives you the grace to defeat Satan."

"In my messages I recommend to everyone, and to the Holy Father in particular, to spread the message which I have received from my Son here at Medjugorje. I wish to entrust to the Pope, the word with which I came here: 'MIR', (peace in Croatian), which he must spread everywhere. And here is a message which is especially for him: That he bring together the Christian people, through his words and his preaching; that he spread particularly among the young people the messages which he has received from the Father in his prayers, when God inspires him."

90

Monday, September 26, 1983

"My Son suffers very much because the world is not converting. May the world be converted and make peace."

Thursday, September 29, 1983

For three priests from Liverpool,

"Preach my messages. Speak about the events at Medjugorje. Continue to increase your prayers."

Sometime in September 1983

"I have already said many times that the peace of the world is in a state of crisis. Become brothers among yourselves; increase prayer and fasting in order to be saved."

Saturday, October 15, 1983

To Jakov:

"My Son suffers very much because men do not want to be reconciled. They have not listened to me. Be converted; be reconciled."

Thursday, October 20, 1983

For the parish:

"Have all the families consecrate themselves to the Sacred Heart each day. I am very happy when the entire family meets to pray each morning for half an hour."

Friday, October 21, 1983

"The important thing is to pray to the Holy Spirit, so that He may descend on you. When one has Him, one has everything. People make a mistake when they turn only to the saints to request something."

Advent 1983

"Begin by calling on the Holy Spirit each day. The most important thing is to pray to the Holy Spirit. When the Holy Spirit descends on earth, then everything becomes clear, and everything is transformed."

Saturday, November 26, 1983

Our Lady only said, *"Prayer and fasting."*

Wednesday, November 30, 1983

To Marija, for a priest,

"You must warn the Bishop very soon, and the Pope, with respect to the urgent and the great importance of the message for all humanity."

Thursday, December 1, 1983

"Thanks to all of you who have come here, so numerous during this year, in spite of snow, ice, and bad weather, to pray to Jesus. Continue; hold on in your suffering. You know well that when a friend asks you for something, you give it to him. It is thus with Jesus. When you pray without ceasing, and you come in spite of your fatigue, He will give you all that you ask from Him. For that, pray."

Wednesday, December 14, 1983

"Pray and fast! I am asking you for prayer."

Thursday, December 15, 1983

"Fast on Thursday and Friday for the Bishop."

Friday, December 16, 1983

"Pray and fast only!"

Monday, December 26, 1983

To a question from Fr. Laurentin, Ivan conveys this answer from Our Lady: *"Our Lady prays for that. May he who undertakes it, do it in prayer. It is there that he will find his inspiration."*

Wednesday, December 28, 1983

"My children, understand that the most important thing in our lives is prayer."

December 1983

"There are many Christians who are no longer faithful, because they do not pray anymore. Have them begin again to recite each day, at least seven Our Father's, seven Hail Mary's, seven Glory Be's, and the Creed. Above all, abstain from certain television programs. They represent a great peril for your families. After you have seen them, you cannot pray any more. Give up likewise alcohol, cigarettes, and pleasure of this kind."

"The fasting which you are doing in eating fish, instead of meat, is not fasting but abstinence. The true fast consists in giving up all our sins, but one must also renounce himself and make the body participate in it."

"Monthly confession will be a remedy for the Church in the West. Whole sections of the Church could be cured, if the believers would go to confession once a month."

Sunday, January 1, 1984
"My children, pray! I say again, pray, because prayer is indispensable to life."

Beginning of 1984
For the intention of the pilgrims:
"When you are in the room of the apparitions or at the church, you should not preoccupy yourself with taking pictures. You should rather use the time to pray to Jesus, especially in those moments of particular grace during the apparitions."

Monday, January 2, 1984
"Why have you stopped saying the prayer to the Holy Spirit? I have asked you to pray always and at all times so that the Holy Spirit may descend over all of you. Begin again to pray for that."
The visionaries had stopped saying the prayer to the Holy Spirit, thinking that it was said only until Christmas.

Tuesday, January 3, 1984
"My children, pray; I say it again, pray! Know that in your life the most important thing is prayer."

Wednesday, January 4, 1984
"Before all, pray! That I do not cease to ask you for."

Sunday, January 8, 1984 (Feast of the Epiphany)
"My children, pray! I say it again, pray! I will say it to you again. Do not think that Jesus is going to manifest Himself again in the manger, friends. He is born again in your hearts."

Sunday, January 15, 1984

"I know that I speak to you very often about prayer, but know that there are many people in the world who do not pray, who do not even know what to say in prayer."

Tuesday, January 17, 1984

"Pray and fast! I wish that in your hearts prayer and fasting flourish."

Wednesday, January 18, 1984

"I wish to engrave in every heart the sign of love. If you love all mankind, then there is peace in you. If you are at peace with all men, it is the kingdom of love."

Thursday, January 19, 1984

"Pray and fast, because without prayer you cannot do anything."

Saturday, January 21, 1984

"Pray and fast. Do not give up on meditation. At home meditate at least half an hour."

Sunday, January 22, 1984

"Pray and fast. I permit all those who mortify themselves to do it at the most three times a week. May they not prolong it."

Monday, January 23, 1984

"Pray and fast. You have not understood well what it means to pray: If you can understand that, I desire it very much."

Tuesday, January 24, 1984

"Pray very much. I desire to permeate you with prayer."

Wednesday, January 25, 1984

"Pray and fast. You need enthusiasm in your prayer. May you pray in meditation for a long time and fervently."

Thursday, January 26, 1984

"Thank you for adoring my Son in the Sacred Host. That touches me very much. With respect to you, pray! I desire to see you happy."

Friday, January 27, 1984

"Pray and fast. I wish that you deepen and continue your life in prayer. Every morning say the prayer of consecration to the Heart of Mary. Do it in the family. Recite each morning the Angelus, five Our Father's, Hail Mary's, and Glory Be's in honor of the Holy Passion and a sixth one for our Holy Father, the Pope. Then say the Creed and the prayer to the Holy Spirit. And, if it is possible, it would be well to pray a Rosary."

Saturday, January 28, 1984

"I wish that all of you pray and that my heart extend to the whole world. I wish to be with you."

Sunday, January 29, 1984

"Pray and fast! I wish for you to purify your hearts. Purify them, and open them to me."

Monday, January 30, 1984

"Pray! I desire to purify your hearts. Prayer is indispensable, because God gives you the greatest graces when you pray."

Wednesday, February 1, 1984

"It is raining at this time, and you say: 'It is not reasonable to go to church in this slush. Why is it raining so much? Why doesn't the rain stop?' Do not ever speak like that. You have not ceased to pray so that God may send you rain, which makes the earth rich. Then, do not turn against the blessing from God. Above all, thank Him through prayer and fasting."

Thursday, February 2, 1984

"Pray, because I need many prayers. Be reconciled, because I desire reconciliation among you and more love for each other, like brothers. I wish that prayer, peace, and love bloom in you."

Saturday, February 4, 1984

"Pray, because prayer is very necessary for you. With prayer, your body and soul will find peace. There are some young people who have consecrated themselves to me. But there are in the parish some persons who have not entirely given themselves. As soon as Mass has ended, they are in a hurry to leave the church. That is not good. That way

95

they will never be able to give themselves completely. It is not good for them to linger about the church. One must be pious and set a good example for others in order to awaken in them faith. It is necessary to pray as much as possible while offering your heart. They should consecrate themselves in order to become truly better."

Sunday, February 5, 1984
"Pray and fast. I desire to live in your hearts."

Monday, February 6, 1984
"Pray, pray, I ask of you."

Thursday, February 9, 1984
"Pray, pray! How many persons have followed other beliefs or sects and have abandoned Jesus Christ! They create their own gods; they adore idols. How that hurts me! If they could be converted! Like the unbelievers, they are many. That will change only if you help me with your prayers."

Friday, February 10, 1984
"Pray and fast! I desire humility from you. But you can become humble only through prayer and fasting."

Saturday, February 11, 1984
"Open your hearts to me; I desire to bless them fully."

Sunday, February 12, 1984
"Pray and fast! I ask of you. Pray for the peace and humility of your hearts."

Tuesday, February 14, 1984
"Pray and fast! I desire to purify your hearts completely. I wish to make you happy."

Wednesday, February 15, 1984
In very cold weather and an icy wind:
"The wind is my sign. I will come in the wind. When the wind blows, know that I am with you. You have learned that the Cross represents Christ; it is a sign of Him. It is the same for the crucifix you have in your home. For me, it is not the same. When it is cold, you come to church, you want to offer everything to God. I am then with you. I am with you in the wind. Do not be afraid."

Friday, February 17, 1984

"My children, pray! The world has been drawn into a great whirlpool. It does not know what it is doing. It does not realize in what sense it is sinking. It needs your prayers so that I can pull it out of this danger."

Monday, February 20, 1984

"Pray and fast! I desire to purify you and to save you. For that, help me with your prayers."

Tuesday, February 21, 1984

"Pray and fast! I expect generosity and prayers from your hearts."

Thursday, February 23, 1984

"I hold all of you in my arms. You are mine. I need your prayers so that you may be mine. I desire to be all yours and for you to be all mine. I receive all your prayers. I receive them with joy."

Friday, February 24, 1984

"Pray and fast! I desire to be with you always. I desire to stay in your hearts always and for you to stay in mine."

Saturday, February 25, 1984

"Know that I love all of you. Know that you are all mine. To no one do I desire to give more than to you. Come to me all of you. Stay with me. I want to be your Mother. Come, I desire all of you."

Sunday, February 26, 1984

"Pray and fast! Know that I love you. I hold all of you on my knees."

Monday, February 27, 1984

"Do not be tired. I desire to be with you."

Tuesday, February 28, 1984

"Pray and fast! Love everyone on earth, just as you love yourselves."

Wednesday, February 29, 1984

"Pray! It may seem strange to you that I always speak of prayer. And yet I say: pray! Why do you hesitate? In Holy Scripture you have heard it said: 'Do not worry about tomorrow; each day will have its own worries.' Then do not worry about the other days. Be content with prayer. I, your Mother, will take care of the rest."

Thursday, March 1, 1984

"Dear children, today I ask you to read the Bible in your homes every day. Put it in a very visible place in your home; that way it will encourage all to prayer. May each one find his way to fast; he who smokes may abstain from smoking; he who drinks alcohol, have him not drink. Have each one give up something which is dear to him. May these recommendations be conveyed to the parish."

Lent 1984 (March 7 - April 22)

"Do not be afraid for yourselves; you are already saved. Pray rather for those who are in sin and who do not believe."

Wednesday, March 14, 1984

"Pray and fast so that the kingdom of God may come among you. Let my Son set you aglow with His fire."

Thursday, March 15, 1984

"Dear children, pray! All agitation comes from Satan. Your prayer should lead to peace."

Monday, March 19, 1984

"Dear children, sympathize with me! Pray, pray, pray!"

Thursday, March 22, 1984

"Pray each day the Veni Creator Spiritus (Come Holy Spirit) and the Angelus. God has given each one the will to decide for himself. My wish is for all to be converted, but I do not want to force anyone."

Sunday, March 25, 1984 (Annunciation)

The 1,000th apparition in Medjugorje.

"Rejoice with me and with my angels because a part of my plan has already been realized. Many have been converted, but many do not want to be converted. Pray."

After these words, the Blessed Virgin began to cry.

Wednesday, March 28, 1984

"Many persons come here out of curiosity and not as pilgrims."

Friday, March 30, 1984

"I wish that your hearts would be united to mine, like my heart is united to that of my Son."

Sunday, April 8, 1984

"I ask you to pray for the conversion of everyone. For that I need your prayers."

Easter Sunday, April 22, 1984

"We all rejoice in Heaven. Rejoice with us."

Monday, April 23, 1984

"There is no need to give more information to the people; they already know what they are supposed to do."

Tuesday, April 24, 1984

With sadness and with tears:

"So many people, after they have begun here to pray, to be converted, to fast, and do penance, quickly forget when they return home, and return to their bad habits."

"The information suffices. People already know enough. Tell them this place is a place of prayer. Pray as much as you can; pray however you can, but pray more always. Each of you could pray even four hours a day. But I know that many do not understand because they think only of living for their work."

Fr. Tomislav Vlasic then had this conveyed to Our Lady, "If I tell this to the people, then they will go away completely."

"Even you do not understand. It is hardly a sixth of your day."

Monday, June 4, 1984

"Dear children, I am happy that you have begun to pray as I requested of you. Continue."

Saturday, June 9, 1984 (Vigil of Pentecost)

"Tomorrow evening, pray to receive the spirit of truth. More particularly, you, members of this parish. The spirit of truth is indispensable to you in order to convey the messages, such as I give them to you, without adding or deleting whatever it may be. Pray, so that the Holy Spirit inspires you with a spirit of prayer, so that you may pray more. I, your mother, find that you pray too little."

Wednesday, June 13, 1984

"Dear children, I invite you to pray more, you and the entire parish, until the day of the anniversary. Let your prayer become a sign of offering to God. Dear children, I know that you are all tired. You do not know how to offer yourselves to me. Offer yourselves completely to me these days."

Saturday, June 23, 1984

"Dear children, I am very happy that there are so many people here this evening. Thank God alone."

Sunday, June 24, 1984 (Feast of Corpus Christi)

The third anniversary of the apparitions.
"My Children, I thank you for each sacrifice that you have made during these days. Be converted, forgive each other, fast, pray, pray, pray!"

Monday June 25, 1984

"Thank you for all your sacrifices."

Tuesday, June 26, 1984

"When I say pray, pray, pray, I do not want to say to only increase the number of hours of prayer, but also to reinforce the desire for prayer, and to be in contact with God. Place yourself permanently in a state of spirit bathed in prayer."

Thursday, July 5, 1984

"Always pray before your work, and end it with prayer. If you do that, God will bless you and your work. These last days you have prayed little and worked very much. Pray more. In prayer you will find repose."

Monday, July 16, 1984

"I pray for the priests and the parishioners, that no one may be troubled. I know the changes which will take place soon, (in the parish clergy). At the time of the changes, I will be there. Also, do not be afraid; there will be in the future signs concerning sinners, unbelievers, alcoholics, and young people. They will accept me again."

Friday, July 20, 1984

Late in the evening, on the hill of the apparitions:
"Open your hearts to me; come close. Say in a loud voice your intentions and your prayers."

The Blessed Virgin paid close attention to the prayers of the visionaries. When they prayed for the Bishop of Mostar, her eyes were filled with tears. While crying, she tells them,
"You are my little flowers. Continue to pray; my task is lighter because of it."

Our Lady disappeared into Heaven, still crying, after having blessed everyone with a crucifix.

Sunday, August 5, 1984

The celebration of the second millennium of Mary's birthday was preceded by three days of fasting and continuous prayer. Seventy priests heard confessions without rest; there were a great number of conversions.
"Never in my life have I cried with sorrow, as I have cried this evening with joy. Thank you!"

In anticipation of this day Our Lady had said,
"The priest who will hear confession will have great joy on that day."

During these three days of fasting and continuous prayer the visionaries say the Blessed Virgin was very joyful. Our Lady repeated,
"I am very happy; continue, continue. Continue to pray and to fast."

Her joy seemed to have reached a peak Sunday, August 5. Like a flower when it blooms, and full of joy, Our Lady said:
"Continue, continue, open your hearts, ask God, and I will ask for you."

Monday, August 6, 1984
"Continue, and make me happy each day."

Thursday, August 9, 1984
"Dear children, Satan continues to hinder my plans. Pray, pray, pray! In prayer abandon yourselves to God. Pray with the heart. Thank you for your response to my call."

Saturday, August 25, 1984
To Mirjana:
"Wait for me September 13; I will speak to you about the future."

Friday, August 31, 1984
"I love very specially the Cross which you have providentially erected on Mount Krizevac. Go there more often and pray."

Saturday, October 13, 1984
For the priests of the Marian Movement of Priests:
"A message to you and to all those who love me. Dear children, pray unceasingly and ask the Holy Spirit to inspire you always. In everything that you ask, in everything that you do, look only for the will of God. Live according to your convictions and respect others."

Saturday, October 20, 1984
"When you pray, you must feel more. Prayer is a conversation with God. To pray means to listen to God. Prayer is useful for you because after prayer everything is clear. Prayer makes one know happiness. Prayer can teach you how to cry. Prayer can teach you how to blossom. Prayer is not a joke. Prayer is a dialogue with God."

Wednesday, October 24, 1984

At 10:00pm in the evening at Krizevac,

"My dear children, I am so happy to see you pray. Pray with me so that God's plan may be realized, thanks to your prayers and to mine. Pray more and more intensely."

Sometime in October 1984

"I would like to guide you spiritually, but I would not know how to help you, if you are not open. It suffices for you to think, for example, where you were with your thoughts yesterday during Mass. When you go to Mass, your trip from home to church should be a time of preparation for Mass. You should also receive Holy Communion with an open and pure heart, purity of heart, and openness. Do not leave the church without an appropriate act of thanksgiving. I can help you only if you are accessible to my suggestions; I cannot help you if you are not open. The most important thing in spiritual life is to ask for the gift of the Holy Spirit. When the Holy Spirit comes, then peace will be established. When that occurs, everything changes around you. Things will change."

Monday, December 17, 1984

Message conveyed by the visionaries to Monsignor Franic, Archbishop of Split, during a retreat which he was making in Medjugorje:

"You will have to suffer more."

Tuesday, December 25, 1984

The Virgin did not give a message, but she appeared holding the Child Jesus in her arms.

Wednesday, January 2, 1985

At 11:30pm at night at Krizevac, the Virgin appeared surrounded by five angels:

"I am very happy to have been able to come here for three years, thanks to the prayers of believers. Continue to pray thusly. A part of my plan has been realized. God blesses in a special way all those who are here. You can return happily to your homes. You do not immediately understand the reasons. Offer your prayers of thanksgiving for next week."

Wednesday, January 9, 1985
"I thank the faithful for having come to church in very bad and cold weather."

Sometime in January or February 1985
To Vicka, at the time of a prayer meeting on the mountain,
"My dear children, Satan is strong. He wishes, with all his strength, to destroy my plans. Pray only, and do not stop doing it. I will also pray to my Son, so that all the plans that I have begun will be realized. Be patient and persevere in prayer. Do not permit Satan to take away your courage. He works very hard in the world. Be on your guard."

Sunday, February 3, 1985
"I wish for Father Slavko to stay here, for him to guide life, and to assemble all the news, so that when I leave there will be a complete image of everything that has happened here. I am also praying now for Slavko and for all those who work in this parish."

Sunday, February 17, 1985
"Pray, dear children, so that God's plan may be accomplished, and all the works of Satan be changed in favor of the glory of God."

Monday, February 25, 1985
"For next week, I invite you to say these words: 'I love God in everything'. With love, one obtains everything. You can receive many things, even the most impossible. The Lord wishes for all the parishes to surrender to Him, and I, too, in Him. I desire it. Each evening make your examination of conscience, but only to give thanks in acknowledgment for everything that His love offers us at Medjugorje."

February - March 1985
"Dear children! You have always prayed that I not abandon you. Now I ask of you, in turn, not to abandon me. Satan wants especially during these days to disperse you. For that, pray very much these days."

"Dear children, I came again to thank you. You have not yet understood what that means, to give joy to my heart. It is a very great thing. I ask you only to persevere in prayer. As long as you pray, I will have words for you. Good-bye. I thank you, dear children. My love for you is unlimited; be happy with me, because I am happy with you."

Saturday, March 9, 1985

"You can receive a grace immediately, or in a month, or in ten years. I do not need a hundred or two hundred Our Father's. It is better to pray only one, but with a desire to encounter God. You should do everything out of love. Accept all annoyances, all difficulties, everything, with love. Dedicate yourselves to love."

Wednesday, March 13, 1985

Message addressed to Vicka, when a mistake by Ivan, who was frightened, caused a stir:

"Pray, pray, pray! It is only with prayer that you will be able to avoid Ivan's error. He should not have written. And after that he had to clearly acknowledge it so as not to plant any doubts."

Monday, March 18, 1985

To Mirjana:

"The rosary is not an ornament for the home, as one often time-limits himself to using it. Tell everyone to pray it."

"Right now, many are greatly seeking money, not only in the parish, but in the whole world. Woe to those who seek to take everything from those who come, and blessed are those from whom they take everything."

(This relates to the exploitation of some pilgrims.)

"May the priests help you because I have entrusted to you a heavy burden, and I suffer from your difficulties. Ivan did not make a big mistake. I have sufficiently reprimanded him for the error. It is not necessary to scold him anymore."

Monday, March 25, 1985 (Feast of the Annunciation)

"Through my joy and the joy of this people, I say to all of you this evening, 'I love you,' and I wish you well."

Apparitions in the Rectory
(Apr 11, 1985 To Sep 1987)

On orders from the Bishop (letter of March 25), the apparitions are
forbidden in every room contiguous to the Church itself, which are then
transferred to the rectory.

Monday, April 15, 1985

*"You must begin to work in your hearts as you work in the field. Work and change
your hearts so that the new spirit of God can dwell there."*

Tuesday, May 7, 1985

Ivanka has a vision at home, which lasts about an hour: "The Blessed
Virgin was more beautiful than ever and was accompanied by two angels.
She asks me what I wished. I prayed to her to let me see my mother. The
Blessed Virgin smiled and approved with a nod. My mother appeared to
me very soon. She was smiling. Our Lady told me to stand up. My mother
embraced me, and said: *'My child, I am so proud of you.'* She embraced me
again and disappeared. Our Lady then said to me,"

*"My dear child, today is our last meeting; do not be sad. I will return to see you at each
anniversary of the first apparition (June 25), beginning next year. Dear child, do not
think that you have done anything bad, and that this would be the reason why I'm not
returning near to you. No, it is not that. With all your heart you have accepted the
plans which my Son and I formulated, and you have accomplished everything. No one
in the world has had the grace which you, your brothers, and sisters have received. Be
happy because I am your Mother and I love you from the bottom of my heart. Ivanka,
thank you for the response to the call of my Son; thank you for persevering and
remaining always with Him as long as He will ask you. Dear child, tell all your
friends that my Son and I are always with them when they call on us. What I have told
you during these years concerning the secrets, do not speak to anyone about them."*

Ivanka: "Dear Gospa, may I embrace you? The Blessed Virgin gives an
affirmative sign with her head. I then embraced her. I asked her to bless
me. She did it with a smile and added,"
"Go in the peace of God."
"Then she left slowly with the two angels."

Tuesday, May 28, 1985

"Love is a gift from God. Pray so that God may grant you the gift to be able to love."

Sunday, June 2, 1985

"Dear children, this evening I would like to tell you to pray more during the novena for an outpouring of the Holy Spirit on your families and your parish. Pray, and you will not be sorry for it. God will present you with gifts for which you are going to glorify Him all your earthly life."

Thursday, June 27, 1985

"Today I invite you to humility. These days all of you have felt a great joy because of all the people who came here, and to whom you spoke with love about your experience. With humility and an opening of the heart, continue to speak with all those who come."

Monday, July 1, 1985

On the hill of the apparitions:
"I thank all those who have responded to my call. I bless all of you; I bless each of you. These days I ask you to pray for my intentions. Go in the peace of God."

Monday, August 5, 1985

Message to Ivan, during an apparition in the evening, on the mountain of Krizevac, where Our Lady came dressed in gold vestments.
"Praised be Jesus Christ. My children, I'm happy to be with you this evening, and to see you so numerous. I bless you with a special blessing."

After having prayed for a long time and having listened to Ivan who recommended the persons present, Our Lady concluded with,
"Make progress in holiness through the messages. I will help you. Give your utmost, and we will go together, sensitive to the sweetness of life, light, and joy."

After having blessed them, Our Lady left in the sign of the radiant Cross while saying:
"Go in the peace of God, my children, my little children."

Wednesday, August 14, 1985

To Ivan:

"Observe the complete fasts on Wednesdays and Fridays. Pray at least an entire Rosary: Joyous, Sorrowful, and Glorious mysteries."

Thursday, August 15, 1985 (Feast of the Assumption)

To Mirjana:

"My angel, pray for unbelievers. People will tear their hair; brother will plead with brother; he will curse his past life lived without God. They will repent, but it will be too late. Now is the time for conversion. I have been exhorting you for the past four years. Pray for them. Invite everyone to pray the Rosary."

September 1985

"I have given you my love so that you may give it to others."

Friday, October 25, 1985

Mirjana: "When she appeared, the Blessed Virgin greeted me, '*Praised be Jesus.*' Then she spoke of unbelievers:"

"They are my children. I suffer because of them. They do not know what awaits them. You must pray more for them."

"We prayed with her for the weak, the unfortunate, and the forsaken. After the prayer, She blessed us. Then She showed me, as in a film, the realization of the first secret. The earth was desolate. It is the upheaval of a region of the world. She was precise. I cried. Why so soon?, I asked."

"In the world, there are so many sins. What can I do, if you do not help me. Remember, that I love you."

"How can God have such a hard heart?"

"God does not have a hard heart. Look around you, and see what men do; then you will no longer say that God has a hard heart. How many people come to church, to the house of God, with respect, a strong faith, and love of God? Very few! Here you have a time of grace and conversion. It is necessary to use it well."

To Mirjana:

"Pray very much for Father Petar, to whom I send a special blessing. I am a mother; that is why I come. You must not fear, for I am there."

Fr. Petar Ljubicic had been chosen by Mirjana to unveil to the world the first three warnings, three days before each event.

Monday, January 6, 1986

To Vicka: *"If you agree to it, I will not appear to you anymore for fifty days."*
Vicka accepts this sacrifice.

Thursday, January 9, 1986

"I invite you to help Jesus through your prayer for the realization of all His plans, which He has already begun here. Offer your sacrifices to Jesus, so that He will realize everything that He has planned, and that Satan will not be able to do anything."

Monday, March 24, 1986

"Dear children, receive all that the Lord offers you. Do not have your hands paralyzed and do not repeat: 'Jesus, give me'. But open your hands, and take everything that the Lord offers you."

Tuesday, June 24, 1986

Marija and Ivan met with the prayer group on Mt. Krizevac, *"You are on a Thabor. You receive blessings, strength, and love. Carry them into your families and into your homes. To each one of you, I grant a special blessing. Continue in joy, prayer, and reconciliation."*

The Weekly Messages 1984-1987

March 1, 1984 *"Dear children! I have chosen this parish in a special way, and I wish to lead it. I am guarding it in love, and I want everyone to be mine. Thank you for having responded tonight. I wish you always to be with me and my Son in ever greater numbers. I shall speak a message to you every Thursday."*

March 8, 1984 *"Thank you for having responded to my call! Dear children, you in the parish, be converted. This is my other wish. That way all those who shall come here shall be able to convert."*

March 15, 1984 *"Tonight also, dear children, I am grateful to you in a special way for being here. Unceasingly adore the Most Blessed Sacrament of the Altar. I am always present when the faithful are adoring. Special graces are then being received."*

March 22, 1984 *"Dear children! In a special way this evening I am calling you during Lent to honor the wounds of my Son, which He received from the sins of this parish. Unite yourselves with my prayers for the parish so that His sufferings may be bearable. Thank you for having responded to my call. Try to come in ever greater numbers."*

March 29, 1984 *"Dear children! In a special way this evening I am calling you to perseverance in trials. Consider how the Almighty is still suffering today on account of your sins. So when sufferings come, offer them up as a sacrifice to God. Thank you for having responded to my call."*

April 5, 1984 *"Dear children! This evening I pray you especially to venerate the Heart of my Son, Jesus. Make reparation for the wound inflicted on the Heart of my Son. That Heart is offended by all kinds of sins. Thank you for coming this evening."*

April 12, 1984 *"Dear children! Today I beseech you to stop slandering and to pray for the unity of the parish, because I and my Son have a special plan for this parish. Thank you for having responded to my call."*

April 19, 1984 (Holy Thursday) *"Dear children! Sympathize with me! Pray, pray, pray!"*

April 30, 1984 (Monday) Marija asked Our Lady, "Dear Madonna, why didn't you give me a message for the parish on Thursday?" Our Lady replied,

"I do not wish to force anyone to do that which he/she neither feels nor desires, even though I had special messages for the parish by which I wanted to awaken the faith of every believer. But only a really small number has accepted my Thursday messages. In the beginning there were quite a few. But it's become a routine affair for them. And now recently some are asking for the message out of curiosity, and not out of faith and devotion to my Son and me."

May 10, 1984 Many of the faithful felt shaken by the last message of Our Lady. Some had the feeling that Our Lady would not give any more messages to the parish, but this evening She said,

"I am speaking to you and I wish to speak further. You just listen to my instructions!"

May 17, 1984 *"Dear children! Today I am very happy because there are many who want to consecrate themselves to me. Thank you. You have not made a mistake. My Son Jesus Christ wishes to bestow on you special graces through me. My Son is happy because of your dedication. Thank you for having responded to my call."*

May 24, 1984 *"Dear children! I have told you already that I have chosen you in a special way, just the way you are. I, the Mother, love you all. And in any moment that is difficult for you, do not be afraid because I love you even then when you are far from me and my Son. Please, do not let my heart weep with tears of blood because of the souls who are lost in sin. Therefore, dear children, pray, pray, pray! Thank you for having responded to my call."*

May 31, 1984 (Ascension Thursday) There were many people present from abroad. Our Lady did not give a message for the parish. She told Marija that she would give a message on Saturday to be announced at the Sunday parish Mass.

June 2, 1984 (Saturday) *"Dear children! Tonight I wish to tell you during the days of this Novena to pray for the outpouring of the Holy Spirit on your families and on your parish. Pray, and you shall not regret it. God will give you gifts by which you will glorify Him till the end of your life on this earth. Thank you for having responded to my call."*

June 9, 1984 (Saturday) *"Dear children! Tomorrow night pray for the Spirit of Truth! Especially, you from the parish, because you need the Spirit of Truth to be able to convey the messages just the way they are, neither adding anything to them, nor taking anything whatsoever away from them, but just the way I said them. Pray for the Holy Spirit to inspire you with the spirit of prayer, so you will pray more. I, your Mother, tell you that you are praying little. Thank you for having responded to my call."*

June 21, 1984 *"Pray, pray, pray! Thank you for having responded to my call."*

July 12, 1984 *"Dear children! These days Satan wants to frustrate my plans. Pray that his plan not be realized. I will pray my Son Jesus to give you the grace to experience the victory of Jesus in the temptations of Satan. Thank you for having responded to my call."*

July 19, 1984 *"Dear children! These days you have been experiencing how Satan is working. I am always with you, and don't you be afraid of temptations because God is always watching over us. Also I have given myself to you, and I sympathize with you even in the smallest temptation. Thank you for having responded to my call."*

July 26, 1984 *"Dear children! Today also I wish to call you to persistent prayer and penance. Especially, let the young people of this parish be more active in their prayers. Thank you for having responded to my call."*

August 2, 1984 *"Dear children! Today I am joyful and I thank you for your prayers. Pray still more these days for the conversion of sinners. Thank you for having responded to my call."*

August 11, 1984 (Saturday) *"Dear children! Pray, because Satan wishes to complicate my plans still further. Pray with the heart and surrender yourselves to Jesus in prayer."*

August 14, 1984 (Tuesday) This apparition was unexpected. Ivan was praying at home. After that he started to get ready to go to church for the evening services. By surprise Our Lady appeared to him and told him to relate to the people,

"I would like the people to pray along with me these days. And to pray as much as possible! And to fast strictly on Wednesdays and Fridays, and every day to pray at least one Rosary: the joyful, sorrowful and glorious mysteries." Our Lady asked that we accept this message with a firm will. She especially requested this of the parishioners and the faithful of the surrounding places.

August 16, 1984 *"Dear children! I beseech you, especially those from this parish, to live my messages and convey them to others, to whomever you meet. Thank you for having responded to my call."*

August 23, 1984 *"Dear children! Pray, pray!"*
Marija said that she also invited the people, and especially the young people, to keep order during the Mass.

August 30, 1984 *"Dear children! The Cross was also in God's plan when you built it. These days, especially, go on the mountain and pray before the Cross. I need your prayers. Thank you for having responded to my call."*

September 6, 1984 *"Dear children! Without prayer there is no peace. Therefore I say to you, dear children, pray at the foot of the Cross for peace. Thank you for having responded to my call."*

September 13, 1984 *"Dear children! I still need your prayers. You wonder why all these prayers? Look around you, dear children, and you will see how greatly sin has dominated the world. Pray, therefore, that Jesus conquers. Thank you for having responded to my call."*

September 20, 1984 *"Dear children! Today I call on you to begin fasting with the heart. There are many people who are fasting, but only because everyone else is fasting. It has become a custom which no one wants to stop. I ask the parish to fast out of gratitude because God has allowed me to stay this long in this parish. Dear children, fast and pray with the heart. Thank you for having responded to my call."*

113

September 27, 1984 *"Dear children! You have helped me along by your prayers to realize my plans. Keep on praying that my plans are completely fulfilled. I request the families of the parish to pray the family rosary. Thank you for having responded to my call."*

October 4, 1984 *"Dear children! Today I want to tell you that again and again you make me happy by your prayer, but there are enough of those in this very parish who do not pray, and my heart is saddened. Therefore, pray that I can bring all your sacrifices and prayers to the Lord. Thank you for having responded to my call."*

October 8, 1984 (Monday) (Jakov was sick and received this message at home.) *"Dear children, Let all the prayers you say in your homes in the evening be for the conversion of sinners, because the world is in great sin. Every evening pray the Rosary."*

October 11, 1984 *"Dear children! Thank you for dedicating all your hard work to God even now when He is testing you through the grapes you are picking. Be assured, dear children, that He loves you and, therefore, He tests you. You just always offer up all your burdens to God and do not be anxious. Thank you for having responded to my call."*

October 18, 1984 *"Dear children! Today I call on you to read the Bible every day in your homes and let it be in a visible place so as always to encourage you to read it and to pray. Thank you for having responded to my call."*

October 25, 1984 *"Dear children! Pray during this month. God allows me every day to help you with graces to defend yourselves against evil. This is my month. I want to give it to you. You just pray, and God will give you the graces you are seeking. I will help along with it. Thank you for having responded to my call."*

November 1, 1984 *"Dear children! Today I call you to the renewal of prayer in your homes. The work in the fields is over. Now devote yourselves to prayer. Let prayer take the first place in your families. Thank you for having responded to my call."*

November 8, 1984 *"Dear children! You are not conscious of the messages which God is sending you through me. He is giving you great graces and you do not comprehend them. Pray to the Holy Spirit for enlightenment. If you only knew how great are the graces God is granting you, you would be praying without ceasing. Thank you for having responded to my call."*

November 15, 1984 *"Dear children! You are a chosen people, and God has given you great graces. You are not conscious of every message which I am giving you. Now I just want to say, 'Pray, pray, pray!' I don't know what else to tell you, because I love you, and I want you to comprehend my love and God's love through prayer. Thank you for having responded to my call."*

November 22, 1984 *"Dear children! These days live all the main messages and keep rooting them in your hearts till Thursday. Thank you for having responded to my call."*

November 29, 1984 *"Dear children! No, you don't know how to love, and you don't know how to listen with love to the words I am saying to you. Be conscious, my beloved, that I am your Mother, and I have come on earth to teach you to listen out of love, to pray out of love and not be compelled by the fact that you are carrying a cross. By means of the Cross God is glorified through every person. Thank you for having responded to my call."*

December 6, 1984 *"Dear children! These days I am calling you to family prayer. In God's Name many times I have been giving you messages, but you have not listened to me. This Christmas will be unforgettable for you only if you accept the messages which I am giving you. Dear children, don't allow that day of joy to become my most sorrowful day. Thank you for having responded to my call."*

December 13, 1984 *"Dear children! You know that the season of joy is getting closer, but without love you will achieve nothing. So first of all, begin to love your own family, everyone in the parish, and then you'll be able to love and accept all who are coming over here. Now let these seven days be a week when you need to learn to love. Thank you for having responded to my call."*

December 20, 1984 *"Dear children! Today I am inviting you to do something concrete for Jesus Christ. As a sign of dedication to Jesus I want each family of the parish to bring a single flower before that happy day. I want every member of the family to have a single flower by the crib so Jesus can come and see your dedication to Him! Thank you for having responded to my call."*

December 27, 1984 *"Dear children! This Christmas Satan wanted in a special way to spoil God's plans. You, dear children, have discerned Satan even on Christmas day itself. But God is winning in all your hearts. So let your hearts keep on being happy. Thank you for having responded to my call."*

January 3, 1985 *"Dear children! These days the Lord has bestowed upon you great graces. Let this week be one of thanksgiving for all the graces which God has granted you. Thank you for having responded to my call."*

January 10, 1985 *"Dear children! Today I want to thank you for all your sacrifices, but special thanks to those who have become dear to my heart and come here gladly. There are enough parishioners who are not listening to the messages, but because of those who are in a special way close to my heart, because of them I am giving messages for the parish. And I will go on giving them because I love you, and I want you to spread my messages with your heart. Thank you for having responded to my call."*

January 14, 1985 (Monday) *"My dear children! Satan is so strong and with all his might wants to disturb my plans which I have begun with you. You pray, just pray, and don't stop for a minute! I will pray to my Son for the realization of all the plans I have begun. Be patient and constant in your prayers. And don't let Satan discourage you. He is working hard in the world. Be on your guard!"* (Message conveyed by Vicka from Our Lady.)

January 17, 1985 *"Dear children! These days Satan is working underhandedly against this parish, and you, dear children, have fallen asleep in prayer, and only some are going to Mass. Withstand the days of temptation! Thank you for having responded to my call."*

January 24, 1985 *"Dear children! These days you have experienced God's sweetness through the renewals which have been in this parish. Satan wants to work still more fiercely to take away your joy from each one of you. By prayer you can completely disarm him and ensure your happiness. Thank you for having responded to my call."*

January 31, 1985 *"Dear children! Today I wish to tell you to open your hearts to God like the spring flowers which crave for the sun. I am your Mother, and I always want you to be closer to the Father and that He will always give abundant gifts to your hearts. Thank you for having responded to my call."*

February 7, 1985 *"Dear children! These days Satan is manifesting himself in a special way in this parish. Pray, dear children, that God's plan is brought into effect and that every work of Satan ends up for the glory of God. I have stayed with you this long so I might help you along in your trials. Thank you for having responded to my call."*

February 14, 1985 *"Dear children! Today is the day when I give you a message for the parish, but the whole parish is not accepting the messages and is not living them. I am saddened, and I want you, dear children, to listen to me and to live my messages. Every family must pray family prayer and read the Bible! Thank you for having responded to my call."*

February 21, 1985 *"Dear children! From day to day I have been inviting you to renewal and prayer in the parish, but you are not accepting it. Today I am calling you for the last time! Now it's Lent, and you as a parish can turn to my messages during Lent out of love. If you do not do that, I do not wish to keep on giving messages. God is permitting me that. Thank you for having responded to my call."*

February 28, 1985 *"Dear children! Today I call you to live the word this week: 'I love God!' Dear children, through love you will achieve everything and even what you think is impossible. God wants this parish to belong completely to Him. And that's what I want, too. Thank you for having responded to my call."*

March 7, 1985 *"Dear children! Today I call you to renew prayer in your families. Dear children, encourage the very young to prayer and the children to go to Holy Mass. Thank you for having responded to my call."*

March 14, 1985 *"Dear children! In your life you have all experienced light and darkness. God grants to every person to recognize good and evil. I am calling you to the light which you should carry to all the people who are in darkness. People who are in darkness daily come into your homes. Dear children, give them the light! Thank you for having responded to my call."*

March 21, 1985 *"Dear children! I wish to keep on giving messages, and therefore today I call you to live and accept my messages! Dear children, I love you, and in a special way I have chosen this parish, one more dear to me than the others, in which I have gladly remained when the Almighty sent me. Therefore, I call on you; accept me, dear children, that it might go well with you. Listen to my messages! Thank you for having responded to my call."*

March 24, 1985 (Sunday) *"Today I wish to call you all to confession, even if you have confessed a few days ago. I wish that you all experience my feast day within yourselves. But you cannot experience it unless you abandon yourselves completely to God. Therefore, I am inviting you all to reconciliation with God!"*

March 28, 1985 *"Dear children! Today I wish to call you to pray, pray, pray! In prayer you shall perceive the greatest joy and the way out of every situation that has no exit. Thank you for starting up prayer. Each individual is dear to my heart. And I thank all who have urged prayer in their families. Thank you for having responded to my call."*

April 4, 1985 (Holy Thursday) *"Dear children! I thank you for having started to think more about God's glory in your hearts. Today is the day when I wished to stop giving the messages because some individuals did not accept me. The parish has been moved, and I wish to keep on giving you messages as it has never been in history from the beginning of the world. Thank you for having responded to my call."*

April 5, 1985 (Good Friday) *"You parishioners have a great and heavy cross, but don't be afraid to carry it. My Son is here Who will help you."* (Message given through Ivanka)

Apparitions in the Rectory
(Apr 11, 1985 To Sep 1987)

April 11, 1985 *"Dear children! Today I wish to say to everyone in the parish to pray in a special way to the Holy Spirit for enlightenment. From today God wishes to test the parish in a special way in order that He might strengthen it in faith. Thank you for having responded to my call."*

April 18, 1985 *"Dear children! Today I thank you for every opening of your hearts. Joy overtakes me for every heart that is opened to God, especially from the parish. Rejoice with me! Pray all the prayers for the opening of sinful hearts. I desire that. God desires that through me. Thank you for having responded to my call."*

April 25, 1985 *"Dear children! Today I wish to tell you to begin to work in your hearts as you are working in the fields. Work and change your hearts so that a new spirit from God can take its place in your hearts. Thank you for having responded to my call."*

May 2, 1985 *"Dear children! Today I call you to prayer with the heart, and not just from habit. Some are coming but do not wish to move ahead in prayer. Therefore, I wish to warn you like a Mother. Pray that prayer prevails in your hearts in every moment. Thank you for having responded to my call."*

May 9, 1985 *"Dear children! No, you do not know how many graces God is giving you. You do not want to move ahead during these days when the Holy Spirit is working in a special way. Your hearts are turned toward the things of earth and they preoccupy you. Turn your hearts toward prayer and seek the Holy Spirit to be poured out on you. Thank you for having responded to my call."*

May 16, 1985 *"Dear children! I am calling you to a more active prayer and attendance at Holy Mass. I wish your Mass to be an experience of God. I wish especially to say to the young people: Be open to the Holy Spirit because God wishes to draw you to Himself in these days when Satan is at work. Thank you for having responded to my call."*

May 23, 1985 *"Dear children! These days I call you especially to open your hearts to the Holy Spirit. Especially during these days the Holy Spirit is working through you. Open your hearts and surrender your life to Jesus so that He works through your hearts and strengthens you in faith. Thank you for having responded to my call."*

May 30, 1985 *"Dear children! I call you again to prayer with the heart. Let prayer, dear children, be your everyday food in a special way when your work in the fields is so wearing you out that you cannot pray with the heart. Pray, and then you shall overcome even every weariness. Prayer will be your joy and your rest. Thank you for having responded to my call."*

June 6, 1985 *"Dear children! During these days people from all nations will be coming into the parish. And now I am calling you to love. Love first of all your own household members, and then you will be able to accept and love all who are coming. Thank you for having responded to my call."*

June 13, 1985 *"Dear children! Until the anniversary day I am calling you, the parish, to pray more and to let your prayer be a sign of surrender to God. Dear children, I know that you are all tired, but you don't know how to surrender yourselves to me. During these days surrender yourselves completely to me! Thank you for having responded to my call."*

June 20, 1985 *"Dear children! For this Feast Day I wish to tell you to open your hearts to the Master of all hearts. Give me all your feelings and all your problems! I wish to comfort you in all your trials. I wish to fill you with peace, joy, and love of God. Thank you for having responded to my call."*

June 25, 1985 (Tuesday) *"I invite you to call on everyone to pray the Rosary. With the Rosary you shall overcome all the adversities which Satan is trying to inflict on the Catholic Church. All you priests, pray the Rosary! Dedicate your time to the Rosary!"* (This message Our Lady gave in response to the question of Marija Pavlovic, "Our Lady, what do you wish to recommend to priests?")

June 28, 1985 (Friday) *"Dear children! Today I am giving you a message through which I desire to call you to humility. These days you have felt great joy because of all the people who have come and to whom you could tell your experiences with love. Now I invite you to continue in humility and with an open heart speak to all who are coming. Thank you for having responded to my call."*

July 4, 1985 *"Dear children! I thank you for every sacrifice you have offered. And now I urge you to offer every sacrifice with love. I wish you, the helpless ones, to begin helping with confidence, and the Lord will keep on giving to you in confidence. Thank you for having responded to my call."*

July 11, 1985 *"Dear children! I love the parish, and with my mantle I protect it from every work of Satan. Pray that Satan retreats from the parish and from every individual who comes into the parish. In that way you shall be able to hear every call of God and answer it with your life. Thank you for having responded to my call."*

July 18, 1985 *"Dear children! Today I call you to place more blessed objects in your homes and that everyone put some blessed objects on their person. Bless all the objects, and thus Satan will attack you less because you will have armor against him. Thank you for having responded to my call."*

July 25, 1985 *"Dear children! I desire to lead you, but you do not wish to listen to my messages. Today I am calling you to listen to the messages, and then you will be able to live everything which God tells me to convey to you. Open yourselves to God, and God will work through you and keep on giving you everything you need. Thank you for having responded to my call."*

August 1, 1985 *"Dear children! I wish to tell you that I have chosen this parish and that I am guarding it in my hands like a little flower that does not want to die. I call you to surrender to me so that I can keep on presenting you to God, fresh and without sin. Satan has taken part of the plan and wants to possess it. Pray that he does not succeed in that, because I wish you for myself so I can keep on giving you to God. Thank you for having responded to my call."*

August 8, 1985 *"Dear children! Today I call you especially now to advance against Satan by means of prayer. Satan wants to work still more now that you know he is at work. Dear children, put on the armor for battle, and with the Rosary in your hand defeat him! Thank you for having responded to my call."*

August 15, 1985 *"Dear children! Today I am blessing you, and I wish to tell you that I love you and that I urge you to live my messages. Today I am blessing you with the solemn blessing that the Almighty grants me. Thank you for having responded to my call."*

August 22, 1985 *"Dear children! Today I wish to tell you that God wants to send you trials which you can overcome by prayer. God is testing you through daily chores. Now pray to peacefully withstand every trial. From everything through which God tests you come out more open to God and approach Him with love. Thank you for having responded to my call."*

August 29, 1985 *"Dear children! I am calling you to prayer, especially since Satan wishes to take advantage of the yield of your vineyards. Pray that Satan does not succeed in his plan. Thank you for having responded to my call."*

September 5, 1985 *"Dear children! Today I thank you for all the prayers. Keep on praying all the more so that Satan will be far away from this place. Dear children, Satan's plan has failed. Pray for fulfillment of what God plans in this parish. I especially thank the young people for the sacrifices they have offered up. Thank you for having responded to my call."*

September 12, 1985 *"Dear children! I wish to tell you that the Cross should be central these days. Pray especially before the Cross from which great graces are coming. Now in your homes make a special consecration to the Cross. Promise that you will neither offend Jesus nor abuse the Cross. Thank you for having responded to my call."*

121

September 19, 1985 *"Dear children! Today I invite you to live in humility all the messages which I am giving you. Do not become arrogant living the messages and saying 'I am living the messages.' If you shall bear and live the messages in your heart, everyone will feel it so that words, which serve those who do not obey, will not be necessary. For you, dear children, it is necessary to live and witness by your lives. Thank you for having responded to my call."*

September 26, 1985 *"Dear children! I thank you for all the prayers. Thank you for all the sacrifices. I wish to tell you, dear children, to renew the messages which I am giving you. Especially live the fast, because by fasting you will achieve and permit me the joy of the whole plan, which God is planning here in Medjugorje, to be fulfilled. Thank you for having responded to my call."*

October 3, 1985 *"Dear children! I wish to tell you to thank God for all the graces which God has given you. For all the fruits thank the Lord and glorify Him! Dear children, learn to give thanks in little things, and then you will be able to give thanks also for the big things. Thank you for having responded to my call."*

October 10, 1985 *"Dear children! I wish also today to call you to live the messages in the parish. Especially I wish to call the youth of the parish, who are dear to me. Dear children, if you live the messages, you are living the seed of holiness. I, as the Mother, wish to call you all to holiness so that you can bestow it on others. You are a mirror to others! Thank you for having responded to my call."*

October 17, 1985 *"Dear children! Everything has its own time. Today I call you to start working on your own hearts. Now that all the work in the field is over, you are finding time for cleaning even the most neglected areas, but you leave your heart aside. Work more and clean with love every part of your heart. Thank you for having responded to my call."*

October 24, 1985 *"Dear children! From day to day I wish to clothe you in holiness, goodness, obedience and God's love, so that from day to day you become more beautiful and more prepared for your Master. Dear children, listen to and live my messages. I wish to guide you. Thank you for having responded to my call."*

October 31, 1985 *"Dear children! Today I wish to call you to work in the Church. I love all the same, and I desire from each one to work as much as is possible. I know, dear children, that you can, but you do not wish to because you feel small and humble in these things. You need to be courageous and with little flowers do your share for the Church and for Jesus so that everyone can be satisfied. Thank you for having responded to my call."*

November 7, 1985 *"Dear children! I am calling you to the love of neighbor and love toward the one from whom evil comes to you. In that way with love you will be able to discern the intentions of hearts. Pray and love, dear children! By love you are able to do even that which you think is impossible. Thank you for having responded to my call."*

November 14, 1985 *"Dear children! I, your Mother, love you and wish to urge you to prayer. I am tireless, dear children, and I am calling you even then, when you are far away from my heart. I am a Mother, and even though I feel pain for each one who goes astray, I forgive easily and am happy for every child who returns to me. Thank you for having responded to my call."*

November 21, 1985 *"Dear children! I want to tell you that this season is especially for you from the parish. When it is summer, you see that you have a lot of work. Now you don't have work in the fields; work on your own self personally! Come to Mass because this is the season given to you. Dear children, there are enough of those who come regularly despite bad weather because they love me and wish to show their love in a special way. What I want from you is to show me your love by coming to Mass, and the Lord will reward you abundantly. Thank you for having responded to my call."*

November 28, 1985 *"Dear children! I want to thank everyone for all you have done for me, especially the youth. I beseech you, dear children, come to prayer with awareness. In prayer you shall come to know the greatness of God. Thank you for having responded to my call."*

December 5, 1985 *"Dear children! I am calling you to prepare yourselves for Christmas by means of penance, prayer, and works of charity. Dear children, do not look toward material things, because then you will not be able to experience Christmas. Thank you for having responded to my call."*

December 12, 1985 *"Dear children! For Christmas my invitation is that together we glorify Jesus. I present Him to you in a special way on that day, and my invitation to you is that on that day we glorify Jesus and His nativity. Dear children, on that day pray still more and think more about Jesus. Thank you for having responded to my call."*

December 19, 1985 *"Dear children! Today I wish to call you to love of neighbor. The more you love your neighbor, the more you shall experience Jesus, especially on Christmas Day. God will bestow great gifts on you if you surrender yourselves to Him. I wish in a special way on Christmas Day to give mothers my own special motherly blessing, and Jesus will bless the rest with His own blessing. Thank you for having responded to my call."*

December 26, 1985 *"Dear children! I wish to thank all who have listened to my messages and who on Christmas Day have lived what I said. Undefiled by sin from now on, I wish to lead you further in love. Abandon your hearts to me! Thank you for having responded to my call!"*

January 2, 1986 *"Dear children! I call you to decide completely for God. I beseech you, dear children, to surrender yourselves completely, and you shall be able to live everything I am telling you. It shall not be difficult for you to surrender yourselves completely to God. Thank you for having responded to my call."*

January 9, 1986 *"Dear children! I call you by your prayers to help Jesus along in the fulfillment of all the plans which He is forming here. And offer your sacrifices to Jesus in order that everything is fulfilled the way He has planned it and that Satan can accomplish nothing. Thank you for having responded to my call."*

January 16, 1986 *"Dear children! Today also I am calling you to prayer. Your prayers are necessary to me so that God may be glorified through all of you. Dear children, I pray you, obey and live the Mother's invitation, because only out of love am I calling you in order that I might help you. Thank you for having responded to my call."*

January 23, 1986 *"Dear children! Again I call you to prayer with the heart. If you pray with the heart, dear children, the ice of your brothers will melt, and every barrier shall disappear. Conversion will be easy for all who desire to accept it. That is the gift which by prayer you must obtain for your neighbor. Thank you for having responded to my call."*

January 30, 1986 *"Dear children! Today I call you all to pray that God's plans for us may be realized and also everything that God desires through you! Help others to be converted, especially those who are coming to Medjugorje. Dear children, do not allow Satan to get control of your hearts, so you would be an image of Satan and not of me. I call you to pray for how you might be witnesses of my presence. Without you, God cannot bring to reality that which He desires. God has given a free will to everyone, and it's in your control. Thank you for having responded to my call."*

February 6, 1986 *"Dear children! This parish, which I have chosen, is special and different from others. And I am giving great graces to all who pray with the heart. Dear children, I am giving the messages first of all to the residents of the parish, and then to all the others. First of all you must accept the messages, and then the others. You shall be answerable to me and my Son, Jesus. Thank you for having responded to my call."*

February 13, 1986 *"Dear children! This Lent is a special incentive for you to change. Start from this moment. Turn off the television and renounce various things that are of no value. Dear children, I am calling you individually to conversion. This season is for you. Thank you for having responded to my call."*

February 20, 1986 *"Dear children! The second message of these Lenten days is that you renew prayer before the Cross. Dear children, I am giving you special graces, and Jesus is giving you special gifts from the Cross. Take them and live! Reflect on Jesus' Passion, and in your life be united with Jesus! Thank you for having responded to my call."*

February 27, 1986 *"Dear children! In humility live the messages which I am giving you. Thank you for having responded to my call."*

March 6, 1986 *"Dear children! Today I call you to open yourselves more to God, so that He can work through you. The more you open yourselves, the more you receive the fruits. I wish to call you again to prayer. Thank you for having responded to my call."*

March 13, 1986 *"Dear children! Today I call you to live Lent by means of your little sacrifices. Thank you for every sacrifice you have brought me. Dear children, live that way continuously, and with your love help me to present the sacrifice. God will reward you for that. Thank you for having responded to my call."*

March 20, 1986 *"Dear children! Today I call you to approach prayer actively. You wish to live everything I am telling you, but you are not succeeding because you are not praying. Dear children, I beseech you to open yourselves and begin to pray. Prayer will be your joy. If you make a start, it won't be boring to you because you will be praying out of joy. Thank you for having responded to my call."*

March 27, 1986 *"Dear children! I wish to thank you for all the sacrifices, and I invite you to the greatest sacrifice, the sacrifice of love. Without love, you are not able to accept either me or my Son. Without love, you cannot give an account of your experiences to others. Therefore, dear children, I call you to begin to live love within yourselves. Thank you for having responded to my call."*

April 3, 1986 *"Dear children! I wish to call you to a living of the Holy Mass. There are many of you who have sensed the beauty of the Holy Mass, but there are also those who come unwillingly. I have chosen you, dear children, but Jesus gives you His graces in the Mass. Therefore, consciously live the Holy Mass and let your coming to it be a joyful one. Come to it with love and make the Mass your own. Thank you for having responded to my call."*

April 10, 1986 *"Dear children! I desire to call you to grow in love. A flower is not able to grow normally without water. So also you, dear children, are not able to grow without God's blessing. From day to day you need to seek His blessing so you will grow normally and perform all your actions in union with God. Thank you for having responded to my call."*

April 17, 1986 *"Dear children! You are absorbed with material things, but in the material you lose everything that God wishes to give you. I call you, dear children, to pray for the gifts of the Holy Spirit, which are necessary for you now in order to be able to give witness to my presence here and to all that I am giving you. Dear children, let go so I can lead you completely. Don't be absorbed with material things. Thank you for having responded to my call."*

April 24, 1986 *"Dear children! Today my invitation is that you pray. Dear children, you are forgetting that you are all important. The elderly are especially important in the family. Urge them to pray. Let all the young people be an example to others by their life and let them witness to Jesus. Dear children, I beseech you, begin to change through prayer, and you will know what you need to do. Thank you for having responded to my call."*

May 1, 1986 *"Dear children! I beseech you to start changing your life in the family. Let the family be a harmonious flower that I wish to give to Jesus. Dear children, let every family be active in prayer for I wish that the fruits in the family be seen one day. Only in that way shall I give you all, like petals, as a gift to Jesus in fulfillment of God's plans. Thank you for having responded to my call."*

May 8, 1986 *"Dear children! You are the ones responsible for the messages. The source of grace is here, but you, dear children, are the vessels which transport the gifts. Therefore, dear children, I am calling you to do your job with responsibility. Each one shall be responsible according to his own ability. Dear children, I am calling you to give the gifts to others with love, and not to keep them for yourselves. Thank you for having responded to my call."*

May 15, 1986 *"Dear children! Today I call you to give me your heart so I can change it to be like mine. You are wondering, dear children, why you cannot respond to that which I am seeking from you. You are not able to because you have not given me your heart so I can change it. You are talking, but you are not doing. I call on you to do everything that I am telling you. That way I will be with you. Thank you for having responded to my call."*

May 22, 1986 *"Dear children! Today I wish to give you my own love. You do not know, dear children, how great my love is, and you do not know how to accept it. In various ways I wish to show it to you, but you, dear children, do not recognize it. You do not understand my words with your heart, and neither are you able to comprehend my love. Dear children, accept me in your life, and so you will be able to accept all I am saying to you and to which I am calling you. Thank you for having responded to my call."*

May 29, 1986 *"Dear children! Today my call to you is that in your life you live love toward God and neighbor. Without love, dear children, you can do nothing. Therefore, dear children, I am calling you to live in mutual love. Only in that way will you be able to love and accept both me and all those around you who are coming into your parish. Everyone will sense my love through you. Therefore, I beseech you, dear children, to start loving from today with an ardent love, the love with which I love you. Thank you for having responded to my call."*

June 5, 1986 *"Dear children! Today I am calling on you to decide whether or not you wish to live the messages which I am giving you. I wish you to be active in living and spreading the messages. Especially, dear children, I wish that you all be the reflection of Jesus, which will enlighten this unfaithful world walking in darkness. I wish all of you to be the light for everyone and that you give witness in the light. Dear children, you are not called to darkness, but you are called to light. Therefore, live the light with your own life. Thank you for having responded to my call."*

June 12, 1986 *"Dear children! Today I call you to begin to pray the Rosary with a living faith. In that way I will be able to help you. You, dear children, wish to obtain graces, but you are not praying. I am not able to help you because you do not want to get started. Dear children, I am calling you to pray the Rosary and that your Rosary be an obligation which you shall fulfill with joy. In that way you shall understand the reason I am with you this long. I desire to teach you to pray. Thank you for having responded to my call."*

June 19, 1986 *"Dear children! During these days my Lord is allowing me to be able to intercede for more graces for you. Therefore, I wish to urge you once more to pray, dear children! Pray without ceasing! In that way I will give you the joy which the Lord gives to me. With these graces, dear children, I want your sufferings to be a joy. I am your Mother, and I desire to help you. Thank you for having responded to my call."*

June 26, 1986 *"Dear children! God is allowing me along with Himself to bring about this oasis of peace. I wish to call on you to protect it and that the oasis always be unspoiled. There are those who by their carelessness are destroying peace and prayer. I am inviting you to give witness and by your own life to help to preserve the peace. Thank you for having responded to my call."*

July 3, 1986 *"Dear children! Today I am calling you all to prayer. Without prayer, dear children, you are not able to experience either God or me or the graces which I am giving you. Therefore, my call to you is that the beginning and end of your day always be prayer. Dear children, I wish to lead you daily more and more in prayer, but you are not able to grow because you do not desire it. My call, dear children, is that for you prayer be in first place. Thank you for having responded to my call."*

July 10, 1986 *"Dear children! Today I am calling you to holiness. Without holiness you cannot live. Therefore, with love overcome every sin and with love overcome all the difficulties which are coming to you. Dear children, I beseech you to live love within yourselves. Thank you for having responded to my call."*

July 17, 1986 *"Dear children! Today I am calling you to reflect upon why I am with you this long. I am the Mediatrix between you and God. Therefore, dear children, I desire to call you to live always out of love all that which God desires of you. For that reason, dear children, in your own humility live all the messages which I am giving you. Thank you for having responded to my call."*

July 24, 1986 *"Dear children! I rejoice because of all of you who are on the way to holiness, and I beseech you, by your own testimony to help those who do not know how to live in holiness. Therefore, dear children, let your family be a place where holiness is birthed. Help everyone to live in holiness, but especially your own family. Thank you for having responded to my call."*

July 31, 1986 *"Dear children! Hatred gives birth to dissensions and does not regard anyone or anything. I call you always to bring harmony and peace. Especially, dear children, in the place where you live, act with love. Let your only instrument always be love. By love turn everything into good, which Satan desires to destroy and possess. Only in that way shall you be completely mine, and I shall be able to help you. Thank you for having responded to my call."*

August 7, 1986 *"Dear children! You know that I promised you an oasis of peace, but you don't know that beside an oasis stands the desert, where Satan is lurking and wanting to tempt each one of you. Dear children, only by prayer are you able to overcome every influence of Satan in your place. I am with you, but I cannot take away your freedom. Thank you for having responded to my call."*

August 14, 1986 *"Dear children! My call to you is that your prayer be the joy of an encounter with the Lord. I am not able to guide you as long as you yourselves do not experience joy in prayer. From day to day I desire to lead you more and more in prayer, but I do not wish to force you. Thank you for having responded to my call."*

August 21, 1986 *"Dear children! I thank you for the love which you are showing me. You know, dear children, that I love you immeasurably, and daily I pray the Lord to help you to understand the love which I am showing you. Therefore, you, dear children, pray, pray, pray!"*

August 28, 1986 *"Dear children! My call is that in everything you would be an image for others, especially in prayer and witnessing. Dear children, without you I am not able to help the world. I desire that you cooperate with me in everything, even in the smallest things. Therefore, dear children, help me by letting your prayer be from the heart and with all of you surrendering completely to me. In that way I shall be able to teach and lead you on this way which I have begun with you. Thank you for having responded to my call."*

September 4, 1986 *"Dear children! Today again I am calling you to prayer and fasting. You know, dear children, that with your help I am able to accomplish everything and force Satan from seducing to evil and to remove himself from this place. Dear children, Satan is lurking for each individual. Especially in everyday affairs he wants to spread confusion among each one of you. Therefore, dear children, my call to you is that your day would be only prayer and complete surrender to God. Thank you for having responded to my call."*

September 11, 1986 *"Dear children! For these days while you are joyfully celebrating the Cross, I desire that your cross also would be a joy for you. Especially, dear children, pray that you may be able to accept sickness and suffering with love the way Jesus accepted them. Only in that way shall I be able with joy to give out to you the graces and healings which Jesus is permitting me. Thank you for having responded to my call."*

September 18, 1986 *"Dear children! Today again I thank you for all that you have accomplished for me in these days. Especially, dear children, I thank you in the Name of Jesus for the sacrifices which you offered this past week. Dear children, you are forgetting that I desire sacrifices from you so I can help you and drive Satan away from you. Therefore, I am calling you again to offer sacrifices with a special reverence toward God. Thank you for having responded to my call."*

September 25, 1986 *"Dear children! By your own peace I am calling you to help others to see and begin to seek peace. You, dear children, are at peace and not able to comprehend lack of peace. Therefore, I am calling you, so that by your prayer and your life you may help to destroy everything that is evil in people and uncover the deception that Satan makes use of. You pray that the truth prevails in all hearts. Thank you for having responded to my call."*

October 2, 1986 *"Dear children! Today again I am calling you to pray. You, dear children, are not able to understand how great the value of prayer is as long as you yourselves do not say: 'Now is the time for prayer; now nothing else is important to me; now not one person is important to me but God.' Dear children, consecrate yourselves to prayer with a special love so that God will be able to render graces back to you. Thank you for having responded to my call."*

October 9, 1986 *"Dear children! You know that I desire to lead you on the way of holiness, but I do not want to compel you to be saints by force. I desire that each of you by your own little self-denials help yourself and me so that I can lead you from day to day closer to holiness. Therefore, dear children, I do not desire to force you to observe the messages. But rather this long time that I am with you is a sign that I love you immeasurably, and what I desire of each individual is to become holy. Thank you for having responded to my call."*

October 16, 1986 *"Dear children! Today again I want to show you how much I love you, but I am sorry that I am not able to help each one to understand my love. Therefore, dear children, I am calling you to prayer and complete surrender to God, because Satan wants to sift you through everyday affairs, and in your life he wants to snatch the first place. Therefore, dear children, pray without ceasing! Thank you for having responded to my call."*

October 23, 1986 *"Dear children! Today again I am calling you to pray. Especially, dear children, do I call you to pray for peace. Without your prayers, dear children, I cannot help you to fulfill the message which the Lord has given me to give to you. Therefore, dear children, pray, so that in prayer you realize what God is giving you. Thank you for having responded to my call."*

October 30, 1986 *"Dear children! Today again I desire to call you to take seriously and carry out the messages which I am giving you. Dear children, it is for your sake that I have stayed this long so I could help you to fulfill all the messages which I am giving you. Therefore, dear children, out of love for me carry out all the messages which I am giving you. Thank you for having responded to my call."*

November 6, 1986 *"Dear children! Today I wish to call you to pray daily for souls in Purgatory. For every soul prayer and grace are necessary to reach God and the love of God. By doing this, dear children, you obtain new intercessors who will help you in life to realize that all the earthly things are not important for you, that only Heaven is that for which it is necessary to strive. Therefore, dear children, pray without ceasing that you may be able to help yourselves and the others to whom your prayers will bring joy. Thank you for having responded to my call."*

November 13, 1986 *"Dear children! Today again I am calling you to pray with your whole heart and day by day to change your life. Especially, dear children, I am calling that by your prayers and sacrifices you begin to live in holiness, because I desire that each one of you who has been to this fountain of grace will come to Paradise with the special gift which you shall give me, and that is holiness. Therefore, dear children, pray and daily change your life in order to become fully holy. I shall always be close to you. Thank you for having responded to my call."*

November 20, 1986 *"Dear children! Today also I am calling you to live and follow with a special love all the messages which I am giving you. Dear children, God does not want you lukewarm and undecided, but that you totally surrender to Him. You know that I love you and that out of love I long for you. Therefore, dear children, you also decide for love so that you will long for and daily experience God's love. Dear children, decide for love so that love prevails in all of you, but not human love, rather God's love. Thank you for having responded to my call."*

November 27, 1986 *"Dear children! Again today I call you to consecrate your life to me with love, so I am able to guide you with love. I love you, dear children, with a special love, and I desire to bring you all to Heaven unto God. I want you to realize that this life lasts briefly compared with the one in Heaven. Therefore, dear children, decide again today for God. Only in that way will I be able to show how much you are dear to me and how much I desire all to be saved and to be with me in Heaven. Thank you for having responded to my call."*

December 4, 1986 *"Dear children! Today I call you to prepare your hearts for these days when the Lord particularly desires to purify you from all the sins of your past. You, dear children, are not able to do this by yourselves; therefore I am here to help you. You pray, dear children! Only in that way shall you be able to recognize all the evil that is in you and to surrender it to the Lord so that the Lord may completely purify your hearts. Therefore, dear children, pray without ceasing, and prepare your hearts in penance and fasting. Thank you for having responded to my call."*

December 11, 1986 *"Dear children! I am calling you to pray especially at this time in order to experience the joy of meeting with the new-born Jesus. Dear children, I desire that you experience these days just as I experience them. With joy I wish to guide you and show you the joy into which I desire to bring each one of you. Therefore, dear children, pray and surrender completely to me. Thank you for having responded to my call."*

December 18, 1986 *"Dear children! Once again I desire to call you to prayer. When you pray, you are much more beautiful, like flowers, which after the snow, show all their beauty, and all their colors become indescribable. So also you, dear children, after prayer show before God all so much more what is beautiful and loved by Him. Therefore, dear children, pray and open your inner self to the Lord so that He makes of you a harmonious and beautiful flower for Paradise. Thank you for having responded to my call."*

December 25, 1986 (Christmas Day) *"Dear children! Today also I give thanks to the Lord for all that He is doing for me, especially for this gift that I am able to be with you also today. Dear children, these are the days in which the Father grants special graces to all who open their hearts. I bless you, and I desire that you too, dear children, become alive to graces and that you place everything at God's disposal so that He may be glorified through you. My heart carefully follows your progress. Thank you for having responded to my call."*

January 1, 1987 *"Dear children! Today I wish to call on all of you that in the New Year you live the messages which I am giving you. Dear children, you know that for your sake I have remained a long time so I might teach you how to make progress on the way to holiness. Therefore, dear children, pray without ceasing and live the messages which I am giving you, for I am doing it with great love toward God and toward you. Thank you for having responded to my call."*

133

January 8, 1987 *"Dear children! I desire to thank you for every response to the messages. Especially, dear children, thank you for all the sacrifices and prayers which you have presented to me. Dear children, I desire to keep on giving you still further messages, only not every Thursday, dear children, but on each 25th of the month. The time has come when what my Lord desired has been fulfilled. Now I will give you fewer messages, but I am still with you. Therefore, dear children, I beseech you, listen to my messages and live them, so I can guide you. Dear children, thank you for having responded to my call."*

The Monthly Messages 1987-2017

January 25, 1987 The first apparition of the 25th of the month, given to Marija, for the parish:

"Today I want to appeal to all of you to start living a new life from this day on. Dear children, I wish that you would understand that God has chosen each one of you to have a part in the great plan for the salvation of mankind. You cannot fully understand how great your role is in God's design. For that reason, pray, dear children, so that through prayer, you may be able to know your role in God's plan. I am with you, so that you may be able to realize it fully."

January 28, 1987 To Mirjana, at Sarajevo:

"My dear children! I came to you in order to lead you to purity of soul, and then to God. How did you receive me? At the beginning you were fearful, suspicious of the children I had chosen. Later on, the majority received me in their heart. They began to put into practice my maternal recommendation. Unfortunately, that did not last a long time. Whatever be the place where I appear, and with me also my Son, Satan also comes. You permitted him to subdue you without realizing that you were being led by him."

"It is up to you to realize that your behavior is not permitted by God, but that you immediately stifle the thought. Do not give in dear children. Wipe away from my face the tears which I shed on seeing you act in this manner. Look around you. Take the time to come to God in the church. Come into your Father's house. Take the time to meet for family prayer in order to obtain grace from God. Remember your deceased; make them happy by offering the Mass. Do not look with scorn on the poor man who is begging a morsel of bread. Do not send him away from your abundant table. Help him, and God will help you. It could very well happen that the blessing he leaves you as a sign of gratitude will be fulfilled for you. God may listen to him."

"You have forgotten all of that, my children. Satan has influenced you in that. Do not give in. Pray with me! Do not deceive yourselves in thinking, 'I am good, but my brother, who lives next to me, is not good.' You will be mistaken. I love you because I am your mother, and I warn you. There are the secrets, my children. One does not know what they are; when they learn, it will be too late. Return to prayer! Nothing is more necessary. I would like it if the Lord would have permitted me to show you just a little about the secrets, but, He already gives you enough graces."

"Think! What do you offer to Him in return? When was the last time you gave up something for the Lord? I will not blame you further, but once again call you to prayer, fasting, and to penance. If you wish to obtain a grace from the Lord by fasting, then let no one know that you are fasting. If you wish to obtain the grace of God through a gift to the poor, let no one know it except you and the Lord. Listen to me, my children! Meditate on my message in prayer."

February 25, 1987 *"Dear children! Today I want to wrap you all in my mantle and lead you all along the way of conversion. Dear children, I beseech you, surrender to the Lord your entire past, all the evil that has accumulated in your hearts. I want each one of you to be happy, but in sin nobody can be happy. Therefore, dear children, pray, and in prayer you shall realize a new way of joy. Joy will manifest in your hearts, and thus you shall be joyful witnesses of that which I and My Son want from each one of you. I am blessing you. Thank you for having responded to my call."*

March 25, 1987 *"Dear children! Today I am grateful to you for your presence in this place, where I am giving you special graces. I call each one of you to begin to live as of today that life which God wishes of you and to begin to perform good works of love and mercy. I do not want you, dear children, to live the message and be committing sin which is displeasing to me. Therefore, dear children, I want each of you to live a new life without destroying all that God produces in you and is giving you. I give you my special blessing, and I am remaining with you on your way of conversion. Thank you for having responded to my call."*

April 25, 1987 *"Dear children! Today also I am calling you to prayer. You know, dear children, that God grants special graces in prayer. Therefore, seek and pray in order that you may be able to comprehend all that I am giving here. I call you, dear children, to prayer with the heart. You know that without prayer you cannot comprehend all that God is planning through each one of you. Therefore, pray! I desire that through each one of you God's plan may be fulfilled, that all which God has planted in your heart may keep on growing. So pray that God's blessing may protect each one of you from all the evil that is threatening you. I bless you, dear children. Thank you for having responded to my call."*

May 25, 1987 *"Dear children! I am calling every one of you to start living in God's love. Dear children, you are ready to commit sin, and to put yourselves in the hand of Satan without reflecting. I call on each one of you to consciously decide for God and against Satan. I am your Mother and, therefore, I want to lead you all to perfect holiness. I want each one of you to be happy here on earth and to be with me in Heaven. That is, dear children, the purpose of my coming here and it's my desire. Thank you for having responded to my call."*

June 24, 1987 – The prelude to the sixth anniversary of the apparitions: Marija invited the pilgrims to climb Krizevac at 11:30pm at night. A crowd of thousands of people climbed the rocky foot path without accident. After reciting the Rosary, toward midnight Marija confided to those who surrounded her: "The Blessed Virgin was joyful. First of all, she prayed over all of us. We asked her to bless us. She did. Then She gave us, in substance, this message:"

"Dear children! I want to lead you on the road to conversion. I desire that you convert the world and that your life be a conversion for others. Do not fall into infidelity. Let each one of you be completely submissive to my will and to the will of God. Beginning this day, I give you special graces, and in particular the gift of conversion. Let each one of you take home my blessing and motivate the others to a real conversion."

Through Our Lady, Marija concluded: "God gives us this gift this evening. Before leaving us, Our Lady prayed again over all of us for a moment. We prayed with Her for all our needs, for all your needs, for each of you here present. Finally the Blessed Virgin said: *'Go in the peace of God!'"*

June 25, 1987 *"Dear children! Today I thank you, and I want to invite you all to God's peace. I want each one of you to experience in your heart that peace which God gives. I want to bless you all today. I am blessing you with God's blessing, and I beseech you, dear children, to follow and to live my way. I love you, dear children, and so not even counting the number of times, I go on calling you, and I thank you for all that you are doing for my intentions. I beg you, help me to present you to God and to save you. Thank you for having responded to my call."*

July 25, 1987 *"Dear children! I beseech you to take up the way of holiness beginning today. I love you and, therefore, I want you to be holy. I do not want Satan to block you on that way. Dear children, pray and accept all that God is offering you in a way which is bitter. But at the same time, God will reveal every sweetness to whoever begins to go on that way, and that person will gladly answer every call of God. Do not attribute importance to petty things. Long for Heaven. Thank you for having responded to my call."*

August 25, 1987 *"Dear children! Today also I am calling you all in order that each one of you decides to live my messages. God has permitted me also in this year, which the Church has dedicated to me, to be able to speak to you and to be able to spur you on to holiness. Dear children, seek from God the graces which He is giving you through me. I am ready to intercede with God for all that you seek so that your holiness may be complete. Therefore, dear children, do not forget to seek, because God has permitted me to obtain graces for you. Thank you for having responded to my call."*

The Apparitions Are Forbidden in the Rectory, In Search of a Discreet Place (Beginning Sep 1987-1989)

The solution: The choir loft in the church.

September 25, 1987 *"Dear children! Today also I want to call you all to prayer. Let prayer be your life. Dear children, dedicate your time only to Jesus, and He will give you everything that you are seeking. He will reveal Himself to you in fullness. Dear children, Satan is strong and is waiting to test each one of you. Pray, and in that way he will neither be able to injure you nor block you on the way of holiness. Dear children, through prayer grow toward God from day to day all the more. Thank you for having responded to my call."*

October 25, 1987 *"My dear children! Today I want to call all of you to decide for Paradise. The way is difficult for those who have not decided for God. Dear children, decide and believe that God is offering Himself to you in His fullness. You are invited, and you need to answer the call of the Father, who is calling you through me. Pray, because in prayer each one of you will be able to achieve complete love. I am blessing you, and I desire to help you so that each one of you might be under my motherly mantle. Thank you for having responded to my call."*

November 25, 1987 *"Dear children! Today also I call each one of you to decide to surrender again everything completely to me. Only in that way will I be able to present each of you to God. Dear children, you know that I love you immeasurably and that I desire each of you for myself, but God has given to all a freedom which I lovingly respect and humbly submit to. I desire, dear children, that you help so that everything God has planned in this parish shall be realized. If you do not pray, you shall not be able to recognize my love and the plans which God has for this parish and for each individual. Pray that Satan does not entice you with his pride and deceptive strength. I am with you, and I want you to believe me, that I love you. Thank you for having responded to my call."*

December 25, 1987 *"Dear children! Rejoice with me! My heart is rejoicing because of Jesus, and today I want to give Him to you. Dear children, I want each one of you to open your heart to Jesus, and I will give Him to you with love. Dear children, I want Him to change you, to teach you, and to protect you. Today I am praying in a special way for each one of you, and I am presenting you to God so He will manifest Himself in you. I am calling you to sincere prayer with the heart so that every prayer of yours may be an encounter with God. In your work and in your everyday life, put God in first place. I call you today with great seriousness to obey me and to do as I am calling you. Thank you for having responded to my call."*

1988

January 25, 1988 *"Dear children! Today again I am calling you to complete conversion, which is difficult for those who have not chosen God. God can give you everything that you seek from Him. But you seek God only when sicknesses, problems, and difficulties come to you, and you think that God is far from you and is not listening and does not hear your prayers. No, dear children, that is not the truth. When you are far from God, you cannot receive graces because you do not seek them with a firm faith. Day by day, I am praying for you, and I want to draw you ever more near to God, but I cannot if you don't want it. Therefore, dear children, put your life in God's hands. I bless you all. Thank you for having responded to my call."*

February 25, 1988 *"Dear children! Today again I am calling you to prayer to complete surrender to God. You know that I love you and am coming here out of love so I could show you the path to peace and salvation for your souls. I want you to obey me and not permit Satan to seduce you. Dear children, Satan is very strong and, therefore, I ask you to dedicate your prayers to me so that those who are under his influence can be saved. Give witness by your life. Sacrifice your lives for the salvation of the world. I am with you, and I am grateful to you, but in heaven you shall receive the Father's reward which He has promised to you. Therefore, dear children, do not be afraid. If you pray, Satan cannot injure you even a little bit because you are God's children, and He is watching over you. Pray and let the rosary always be in your hand as a sign to Satan that you belong to me. Thank you for having responded to my call."*

March 25, 1988 *"Dear children! Today also I am inviting you to a complete surrender to God. Dear children, you are not conscious of how God loves you with such a great love because He permits me to be with you so I can instruct you and help you to find the way of peace. In this way, however, you cannot discover if you do not pray. Therefore, dear children, forsake everything and consecrate your time to God, and God will bestow gifts upon you and bless you. Little children, don't forget that your life is fleeting like a spring flower, which today is wondrously beautiful but tomorrow has vanished. Therefore, pray in such a way that your prayer, your surrender to God, may become like a road sign. In that way, your witness will not only have value for yourselves but for all eternity. Thank you for having responded to my call."*

April 25, 1988 *"Dear children! God wants to make you holy. Therefore, through me He is inviting you to complete surrender. Let Holy Mass be your life. Understand that the church is God's palace, the place in which I gather you and want to show you the way to God. Come and pray. Neither look at others nor slander them, but rather, let your life be a testimony on the way of holiness. Churches deserve respect, and are set apart as holy because God, who became man, dwells in them day and night. Therefore, little children, believe and pray that the Father increase your faith, and then ask for whatever you need. I am with you, and I am rejoicing because of your conversion, and I am protecting you with my motherly mantle. Thank you for having responded to my call."*

May 25, 1988 *"Dear children! I am inviting you to a complete surrender to God. Pray, little children, that Satan may not carry you about like the branches in the wind. Be strong in God. I desire that through you the whole world may get to know the God of joy. By your life bear witness for God's joy. Do not be anxious or worried. God Himself will help you and show you the way. I desire that you love all men with my love. Only in that way can love reign over the world. Little children, you are mine. I love you and want you to surrender to me so that I can lead you to God. Never cease praying so that Satan cannot take advantage of you. Pray for the knowledge that you are mine. I bless you with blessings of joy. Thank you for having responded to my call."*

June 25, 1988 *"Dear children! I am calling you to that love which is loyal and pleasing to God. Little children, love bears everything bitter and difficult for the sake of Jesus, who is love. Therefore, dear children, pray that God come to your aid, not however according to your desire, but according to His love. Surrender yourself to God so that He may hear you, console you and forgive everything inside you which is a hindrance on the way of love. In this way God can move your life, and you will grow in love. Dear children, glorify God with a hymn of love so that God's love may be able to grow in you day by day to its fullness. Thank you for having responded to my call."*

July 25, 1988 *"Dear children! Today I am calling you to a complete surrender to God. Everything you do and everything you possess give over to God so that He can take control of your life as King of all that you possess. In that way, through me, God can lead you into the depths of the spiritual life. Little children, do not be afraid, because I am with you, even if you think there is no way out and that Satan is in control. I am bringing peace to you. I am your Mother, the Queen of Peace. I am blessing you with the blessings of joy so that for you God may be everything in your life. Thank you for having responded to my call."*

August 25, 1988 *"Dear children! Today I invite you all to rejoice in the life which God gives you. Little children, rejoice in God, the Creator, because He has created you so wonderfully. Pray that your life be a joyful thanksgiving which flows out of your heart like a river of joy. Little children, give thanks unceasingly for all that you possess, for each little gift which God has given you, so that a joyful blessing always comes down from God upon your life. Thank you for having responded to my call."*

September 25, 1988 *"Dear children! Today I am inviting all of you, without exception, to the way of holiness in your life. God gave you the grace, the gift of holiness. Pray that you may, more and more, comprehend it, and in that way, you will be able, by your life, to bear witness for God. Dear children, I am blessing you, and I intercede to God for you so that your way and your witness may be a complete one and a joy for God. Thank you for having responded to my call."*

October 25, 1988 *"Dear children! My invitation that you live the messages which I am giving you is a daily one, especially, little children, because I want to draw you closer to the Heart of Jesus. Therefore, little children, I am inviting you today to the prayer of consecration to Jesus, my dear Son, so that each of you may be His. And then I am inviting you to the consecration of my Immaculate Heart. I want you to consecrate yourselves as parents, as families, and as parishioners so that all belong to God through my heart. Therefore, little children, pray that you comprehend the greatness of this message which I am giving you. I do not want anything for myself, rather all for the salvation of your soul. Satan is strong, and therefore, you, little children, by constant prayer, press tightly against my motherly heart. Thank you for having responded to my call."*

November 25, 1988 *"Dear children! I call you to prayer, to have an encounter with God in prayer. God gives Himself to you, but He wants you to answer in your own freedom to His invitation. That is why, little children, during the day, find yourself a special time when you can pray in peace and humility, and have this meeting with God, the Creator. I am with you, and I intercede for you in front of God; so watch in vigil, so that every encounter in prayer be the joy of your contact with God. Thank you for having responded to my call."*

December 25, 1988 *"Dear children! I call you to peace. Live it in your heart and all around you, so that all will know peace, peace that does not come from you but from God. Little children, today is a great day. Rejoice with me. Glorify the Nativity of Jesus through the peace that I give you. It is for this peace that I have come as your Mother, Queen of Peace. Today I give you my special blessing. Bring it to all creation, so that all creation will know peace. Thank you for having responded to my call."*

The Apparitions
Now Take Place Privately
(Sometime in 1989-Present)

1989

January 25, 1989 *"Dear children! Today I am calling you to the way of holiness. Pray that you may comprehend the beauty and the greatness of this way, where God reveals Himself to you in a special way. Pray that you may be open to everything that God does through you so that in your life you may be enabled to give thanks to God and to rejoice over everything that He does through each individual. I give you my blessing. Thank you for having responded to my call."*

February 25, 1989 *"Dear children! Today I invite you to prayer of the heart. Throughout this season of grace I wish each of you to be united with Jesus, but without unceasing prayer you cannot experience the beauty and greatness of the grace which God is offering you. Therefore, little children, at all times fill your heart with even the smallest prayers. I am with you and unceasingly keep watch over every heart which is given to me. Thank you for having responded to my call."*

March 25, 1989 *"Dear children! I am calling you to a complete surrender to God. I am calling you to great joy and peace, which only God can give. I am with you, and I intercede for you every day before God. I call you, little children, to listen to me and to live the messages that I am giving you. Already for years you are invited to holiness, but you are still far away. I am blessing you. Thank you for having responded to my call."*

April 25, 1989 *"Dear children! I am calling you to a complete surrender to God. Let everything that you possess be in the hands of God. Only in that way shall you have joy in your heart. Little children, rejoice in everything that you have. Give thanks to God, because everything is God's gift to you. In that way in your life you shall be able to give thanks for everything and discover God in everything, even in the smallest flower. Thank you for having responded to my call."*

May 25, 1989 *"Dear children! I invite you now to be open to God. See, children, how nature is opening herself and is giving life and fruits. In the same way I invite you to live with God and to surrender completely to Him. Children, I am with you, and I want to introduce you continuously to the joy of life. I desire that everyone may discover the joy and love which can be found only in God and which only God can give. God*

144

doesn't want anything from you, only your surrender. Therefore, children, decide seriously for God because everything else passes away. Only God doesn't pass away. Pray to be able to discover the greatness and joy of life which God gives you. Thank you for having responded to my call."

June 25, *1989* "Dear children! Today I am calling you to live the messages I have been giving you during the past eight years. This is the time of grace, and I desire the grace of God be great for every single one of you. I am blessing you, and I love you with a special love. Thank you for having responded to my call."

July 25, 1989 "Dear children! Today I am calling you to renew your hearts. Open yourselves to God and surrender to Him all your difficulties and crosses so God may turn everything into joy. Little children, you cannot open yourselves to God if you do not pray. Therefore, from today decide to consecrate a time in the day only for an encounter with God in silence. In that way you will be able, with God, to witness my presence here. Little children, I do not wish to force you. Rather freely give God your time, like children of God. Thank you for having responded to my call."

August 25, 1989 "Dear children! I call you to prayer. By means of prayer, little children, you obtain joy and peace. Through prayer you are richer in the mercy of God. Therefore, little children, let prayer be the life of each one of you. Especially I call you to pray so that all those who are far away from God may be converted. Then our hearts shall be richer because God will rule in the hearts of all men. Therefore, little children, pray, pray, pray! Let prayers begin to rule in the whole world. Thank you for having responded to my call."

September 25, 1989 "Dear children! Today I invite you to give thanks to God for all the gifts you have discovered in the course of your life and even for the least gift that you have received. I give thanks with you and want all of you to experience the joy of these gifts. And I want God to be everything for each one of you. And then, little children, you can grow continuously on the way of holiness. Thank you for responding to my call."

October 25, 1989 *"Dear children! Today also I am inviting you to prayer. I am always inviting you, but you are still far away. Therefore, from today decide seriously to dedicate time to God. I am with you, and I wish to teach you to pray with the heart. In prayer with the heart you shall encounter God. Therefore, little children, pray, pray, pray! Thank you for having responded to my call."*

November 25, 1989 *"Dear children! I am inviting you for years by these messages which I am giving you. Little children, by means of the messages I wish to make a very beautiful mosaic in your hearts, so I may be able to present each one of you to God like the original image. Therefore, little children, I desire that your decisions be free before God, because He has given you freedom. Therefore, pray, so that, free from any influence of Satan, we may decide only for God. I am praying for you before God, and I am seeking your surrender to God. Thank you for having responded to my call."*

December 25, 1989 *"Dear children! Today I bless you in a special way with my motherly blessing, and I am interceding for you before God that He gives you the gift of conversion of the heart. For years I am calling you and exhorting you to a deep spiritual life in simplicity, but you are so cold. Therefore, little children, I ask you to accept and live the messages with seriousness, so that your soul will not be sad when I will no longer be with you, and when I will no longer lead you like insecure children in their first steps. Therefore, little children, every day read the messages that I have given you and transform them into life. I love you, and therefore I am calling you all to the way of salvation with God. Thank you for having responded to my call."*

146

1990

January 25, 1990 *"Dear children! Today I invite you to decide for God once again and to choose Him before everything and above everything, so that He may work miracles in your life and that day by day your life may become joy with Him. Therefore, little children, pray, and do not permit Satan to work in your life through misunderstandings, the non-understanding and non-acceptance of one another. Pray that you may be able to comprehend the greatness and the beauty of the gift of life. Thank you for having responded to my call."*

February 25, 1990 *"Dear children! I invite you to surrender to God. In this season I especially want you to renounce all the things to which you are attached which are hurting your spiritual life. Therefore, little children, decide completely for God, and do not allow Satan to come into your life through those things that hurt both you and your spiritual life. Little children, God is offering Himself to you in fullness, and you can discover and recognize Him only in prayer. Therefore, make a decision for prayer. Thank you for having responded to my call."*

March 25, 1990 *"Dear children! I am with you even if you are not conscious of it. I want to protect you from everything that Satan offers you and through which he wants to destroy you. As I bore Jesus in my womb, so also, dear children, do I wish to bring you into holiness. God wants to save you and sends you messages through men, nature, and so many things which can only help you to understand that you must change the direction of your life. Therefore, little children, understand also the greatness of the gift which God is giving you through me, so that I may protect you with my mantle and lead you to the joy of life. Thank you for having responded to my call."*

April 25, 1990 *"Dear children! Today I invite you to accept with seriousness and to live the messages which I am giving you. I am with you and I desire, dear children, that each one of you be ever closer to my heart. Therefore, little children, pray and seek the will of God in your everyday life. I desire that each one of you discover the way of holiness and grow in it until eternity. I will pray for you and intercede for you before God that you understand the greatness of this gift which God is giving me that I can be with you. Thank you for having responded to my call."*

May 25, 1990 *"Dear children! I invite you to decide with seriousness to live this novena. Consecrate the time to prayer and to sacrifice. I am with you, and I desire to help you to grow in renunciation and mortification, so that you may be able to understand the beauty of the life of people who go on giving themselves to me in a special way. Dear children, God blesses you day after day and desires a change in your life. Therefore, pray that you may have the strength to change your life. Thank you for having responded to my call."*

June 25, 1990 *"Dear children! Today I desire to thank you for all your sacrifices and for all your prayers. I am blessing you with my special motherly blessing. I invite you all to decide for God, so that from day to day you will discover His will in prayer. I desire, dear children, to call all of you to a full conversion so that joy will be in your hearts. I am happy that you are here today in such great numbers. Thank you for having responded to my call."*

July 25, 1990 *"Dear children! Today I invite you to peace. I have come here as the Queen of Peace, and I desire to enrich you with my motherly peace. Dear children, I love you, and I desire to bring all of you to the peace which only God gives and which enriches every heart. I invite you to become carriers and witnesses of my peace to this unpeaceful world. Let peace reign in the whole world, which is without peace and longs for peace. I bless you with my motherly blessing. Thank you for having responded to my call."*

August 25, 1990 *"Dear children! I desire to invite you to take with seriousness and put into practice the messages which I am giving you. You know, little children, that I am with you, and I desire to lead you along the same path to heaven, which is beautiful for those who discover it in prayer. Therefore, little children, do not forget that those messages which I am giving you have to be put into your everyday life in order that you might be able to say: 'There, I have taken the messages and tried to live them.' Dear children, I am protecting you before the heavenly Father by my own prayers. Thank you for having responded to my call."*

September 25, 1990 *"Dear children! I invite you to pray with the heart in order that your prayer may be a conversation with God. I desire each one of you to dedicate more time to God. Satan is strong and wants to destroy and deceive you in many ways. Therefore, dear children, pray every day that your life will be good for yourselves and for all those you meet. I am with you, and I am protecting you, even though Satan wishes to destroy my plans and to hinder the desires which the Heavenly Father wants to realize here. Thank you for having responded to my call."*

October 25, 1990 *"Dear children! Today I call you to pray in a special way that you offer up sacrifices and good deeds for peace in the world. Satan is strong and with all his strength desires to destroy the peace which comes from God. Therefore, dear children, pray in a special way with me for peace. I am with you, and I desire to help you with my prayers, and I desire to guide you on the path of peace. I bless you with my motherly blessing. Do not forget to live the messages of peace. Thank you for having responded to my call."*

November 25, 1990 *"Dear children! Today I invite you to do works of mercy with love and out of love for me and for your and my brothers and sisters. Dear children, all that you do for others, do it with great joy and humility for God. I am with you, and day after day I offer your sacrifices and prayers to God for the salvation of the world. Thank you for having responded to my call."*

December 25, 1990 *"Dear children! Today I invite you in a special way to pray for peace. Dear children, without peace you cannot experience the birth of the little Jesus either today or in your daily lives. Therefore, pray the Lord of Peace that He may protect you with His mantle and that He may help you to comprehend the greatness and the importance of peace in your heart. In this way you shall be able to spread peace from your heart throughout the whole world. I am with you, and I intercede for you before God. Pray, because Satan wants to destroy my plans of peace. Be reconciled with one another, and by means of your lives help peace reign in the whole earth. Thank you for having responded to my call."*

1991

January 25, 1991 *"Dear children! Today, like never before, I invite you to prayer. Let your prayer be a prayer for peace. Satan is strong and desires to destroy not only human life, but also nature and the planet on which you live. Therefore, dear children, pray that through prayer you can protect yourselves with God's blessing of peace. God has sent me among you so that I may help you. If you so wish, grasp for the rosary. Even the rosary alone can work miracles in the world and in your lives. I bless you and I remain with you for as long as it is God's will. Thank you for not betraying my presence here, and I thank you because your response is serving the good and the peace."*

February 25, 1991 *"Dear children! Today, I invite you to decide for God, because distance from God is the fruit of the lack of peace in your hearts. God is only peace. Therefore, approach Him through your personal prayer and then live peace in your hearts, and in this way peace will flow from your hearts like a river into the whole world. Do not talk about peace, but make peace. I am blessing each of you and each good decision of yours. Thank you for having responded to my call."*

March 25, 1991 *"Dear children! Again today I invite you to live the passion of Jesus in prayer, and in union with Him. Decide to give more time to God, who gave you these days of grace. Therefore, dear children, pray and in a special way renew the love for Jesus in your hearts. I am with you, and I accompany you with my blessing and my prayers. Thank you for having responded to my call."*

April 25, 1991 *"Dear children! Today I invite you all so that your prayer will be prayer with the heart. Let each of you find time for prayer so that in prayer you discover God. I do not desire you to talk about prayer, but to pray. Let your everyday be filled with prayer of gratitude to God for life and for all that you have. I do not desire your life to pass by in words but that you glorify God with deeds. I am with you, and I am grateful to God for every moment spent with you. Thank you for having responded to my call."*

May 25, 1991 *"Dear Children! Today I invite all of you who have heard my message of peace to realize it with seriousness and with love in your life. There are many who think that they are doing a lot by talking about the messages, but who do not live them. Dear children, I invite you to life and to change all that is negative in you, so that it all turns into the positive and life. Dear children, I am with you, and I desire to help each of you to live and by living, to witness the good news. I am here, dear children, to help you and to lead you to heaven, and heaven is the joy which you can already live now. Thank you for having responded to my call!"*

June 25, 1991 *"Dear children! Today on this great day which you have given to me, I desire to bless all of you and to say: 'These days while I am with you are days of grace.' I desire to teach you and help you to walk the way of holiness. There are many people who do not desire to understand my messages and to accept with seriousness what I am saying. But you I therefore call and ask that by your lives and by your daily living you witness my presence. If you pray, God will help you to discover the true reason for my coming. Therefore, little children, pray and read the Sacred Scriptures so that through my coming you discover the message in Sacred Scripture for yourselves. Thank you for having responded to my call."*

July 25, 1991 *"Dear Children! Today I invite you to pray for peace. At this time peace is being threatened in a special way, and I am asking you to renew fasting and prayer in your families. Dear children, I desire you to grasp the seriousness of the situation and that much of what will happen depends on your prayers. You are praying a little bit. Dear children, I am with you, and I am inviting you to begin to pray and fast seriously as in the first days of my coming. Thank you for having responded to my call."*

August 25, 1991 *"Dear Children! Today also I invite you to prayer, now as never before when my plan has begun to be realized. Satan is strong and wants to sweep away my plans of peace and joy and make you think that my Son is not strong in His decisions. Therefore, I call all of you, dear children, to pray and fast still more firmly. I invite you to self-renunciation for nine days so that, with your help, everything that I desire to realize through the secrets I began in Fatima, may be fulfilled. I call you, dear children, to now grasp the importance of my coming and the seriousness of the situation. I want to save all souls and present them to God. Therefore, let us pray that everything I have begun be fully realized. Thank you for having responded to my call."*

September 25, 1991 *"Dear children! Today in a special way I invite you all to prayer and renunciation. For now as never before Satan wants to show the world his shameful face by which he wants to seduce as many people as possible onto the way of death and sin. Therefore, dear children, help my Immaculate Heart to triumph in the sinful world. I beseech all of you to offer prayers and sacrifices for my intentions so I can present them to God for what is most necessary. Forget your desires, dear children, and pray for what God desires and not for what you desire. Thank you for having responded to my call."*

October 25, 1991 *"Dear children! Pray! Pray! Pray!"*

November 25, 1991 *"Dear Children! This time also I am inviting you to prayer. Pray that you might be able to comprehend what God desires to tell you through my presence and through the messages I am giving you. I desire to draw you ever closer to Jesus and to His wounded heart that you might be able to comprehend the immeasurable love which gave itself for each one of you. Therefore, dear children, pray that from your heart will flow a fountain of love to every person, both to the one who hates you and to the one who despises you. In that way you will be able through Jesus' love to overcome all the misery in this world of sorrows, which is without hope for those who do not know Jesus. I am with you, and I love you with the immeasurable love of Jesus. Thank you for all your sacrifices and prayers. Pray so I might be able to help you still more. Your prayers are necessary for me. Thank you for having responded to my call."*

December 25, 1991 *"Dear children! Today in a special way I bring the little Jesus to you so that He may bless you with His blessing of peace and love. Dear children, do not forget that this is a grace which many people neither understand nor accept. Therefore, you who have said that you are mine, and seek my help, give all of yourself. First of all, show your love and example in your families. You say that Christmas is a family feast. Therefore, dear children, put God in first place in your families, so that He may give you peace and may protect you not only from war, but also in peace protect you from every satanic attack. When God is with you, you have everything. But when you do not want Him, then you are miserable and lost, and you do not know on whose side you are. Therefore, dear children, decide for God. Then you will get everything. Thank you for having responded to my call."*

1992

January 25, 1992 *"Dear Children! Today I am inviting you to a renewal of prayer in your families so in that way every family will become a joy to my son Jesus. Therefore, dear children, pray and seek more time for Jesus, and then you will be able to understand and accept everything, even the most difficult sicknesses and crosses. I am with you, and I desire to take you into my heart and protect you, but you have not yet decided. Therefore, dear children, I am entreating you to pray, so that through prayer you would allow me to help you. Pray, my dear little children, so prayer becomes your daily bread. Thank you for having responded to my call."*

February 25, 1992 *"Dear children! Today I invite you to draw still closer to God through prayer. Only in that way will I be able to help you and to protect you from every attack of Satan. I am with you, and I intercede for you with God, that He protect you. But I need your prayers and your – 'Yes.' You get lost easily in material and human things and forget that God is your greatest friend. Therefore, my dear little children, draw close to God so He may protect you and guard you from every evil. Thank you for having responded to my call!"*

March 25, 1992 *"Dear children! Today as never before I invite you to live my messages and to put them into practice in your life. I have come to you to help you and, therefore, I invite you to change your life because you have taken a path of misery, a path of ruin. When I told you to convert, pray, fast, and be reconciled, you took these messages superficially. You started to live them, and then you stopped, because it was difficult for you. No, dear children, when something is good, you have to persevere in the good and not think, 'God does not see me, He is not listening, He is not helping.' And so you have gone away from God and from me because of your miserable interest. I wanted to create of you an oasis of peace, love, and goodness. God wanted you, with your love and with His help, to do miracles and, thus, give an example. Therefore, here is what I say to you, 'Satan is playing with you and with your souls, and I cannot help you because you are far away from my heart.' Therefore, pray, live my messages, and then you will see the miracles of God's love in your everyday life. Thank you for having responded to my call."*

April 25, 1992 *"Dear children! Today also I invite you to prayer. Only by prayer and fasting can war be stopped. Therefore, my dear little children, pray, and by your life give witness that you are mine and that you belong to me, because Satan wishes in these turbulent days to seduce as many souls as possible. Therefore, I invite you to decide for God, and He will protect you and show you what you should do and which path to take. I invite all those who have said 'yes' to me to renew their consecration to my Son Jesus and to His Heart and to me so we can take you more intensely as instruments of peace in this unpeaceful world. Medjugorje is a sign to all of you and a call to prayer and to live the days of grace that God is giving you. Therefore, dear children, accept the call to prayer with seriousness. I am with you, and your suffering is also mine. Thank you for having responded to my call."*

May 25, 1992 *"Dear children! Today also I invite you to prayer, so that through prayer you come still nearer to God. I am with you, and I desire to lead you on the path to salvation that Jesus gives you. From day to day, I am nearer to you, although you are not aware of it, and you do not want to admit that you are only linked to me in a small way with your few prayers. When trials and problems arise, you say, 'O God! O Mother! Where are you?' As for me, I only wait for your 'Yes' to present to Jesus for Him to fill you with His grace. That is why, once more, please accept my call and start to pray in a new way until prayer becomes joy to you. Then you will discover that God is all-powerful in your daily life. I am with you, and I am waiting for you. Thank you for having responded to my call."*

June 25, 1992 *"Dear children! Today I am happy, even if in my heart there is still a little sadness for all those who have started on this path and then have left it. My presence here is to take you on a new path, the path to salvation. This is why I call you, day after day, to conversion. But if you do not pray, you cannot say that you are on the way to being converted. I pray for you, and I intercede to God for peace, first peace in your hearts and also peace around you, so that God may be your peace. Thank you for having responded to my call."*

July 25, 1992 *"Dear children! Today also I invite you to prayer, a prayer of joy so that in these sad days no one amongst you may feel sadness in prayer, but a joyful meeting with God His Creator. Pray, little children, to be able to come closer to me and to feel through prayer what it is I desire from you. I am with you, and each day I bless you with my maternal blessing so that Our Lord may fill you abundantly with His grace for your daily life. Give thanks to God for the grace of my being able to be with you, because I assure you it is a great grace. Thank you for having responded to my call."*

August 25, 1992 *"Dear children! Today I desire to tell you that I love you. I love you with my maternal love, and I invite you to open yourselves completely to me so that, through each one of you, I may convert and save this world, which is full of sin and bad things. That is why, my dear little children, you should open yourselves completely to me so that I may carry you always further toward the marvelous love of God the Creator, who reveals Himself to you from day to day. I am with you, and I wish to reveal to you and show you the God who loves you. Thank you for having responded to my call."*

September 25, 1992 *"Dear children! Today again I would like to say to you that I am with you also in these troubled days during which Satan wishes to destroy all that my Son Jesus and I are building. He desires especially to destroy your souls. He wants to take you away as far as possible from the Christian life and from the commandments that the Church calls you to live. Satan wishes to destroy everything that is holy in you and around you. This is why, little children, pray, pray, pray to be able to grasp all that God is giving you through my coming. Thank you for having responded to my call."*

October 25, 1992 *"Dear children! I invite you to prayer now when Satan is strong and wishes to make as many souls as possible his own. Pray, dear children, and have more trust in me because I am here in order to help you and to guide you on a new path toward a new life. Therefore, dear little children, listen and live what I tell you, because it is important for you when I shall not be with you any longer that you remember my words and all that I told you. I call you to begin to change your life from the beginning and that you decide for conversion not with words but with your life. Thank you for having responded to my call."*

November 25, 1992 *"Dear Children! Today, more than ever, I am calling you to pray. May your life become a continuous prayer. Without love you cannot pray. That is why I am calling you to love God, the Creator of your lives, above everything else. Then you will come to know God and will love Him in everything, as He loves you. Dear children, it is a grace that I am with you. That is why you should accept and live my messages for your own good. I love you, and that is why I am with you, in order to teach you and to lead you to a new life of conversion and renunciation. Only in this way will you discover God and all that which now seems so far away from you. Therefore, my dear children, pray. Thank you for having responded to my call."*

December 25, 1992 *"Dear children! I desire to place all of you under my mantle and protect you from all satanic attacks. Today is a day of peace, but in the whole world there is a great lack of peace. That is why I call you all to build a new world of peace with me through prayer. This I cannot do without you, and this is why I call all of you with my motherly love, and God will do the rest. So, open yourselves to God's plan and to His designs to be able to cooperate with Him for peace and for everything that is good. Do not forget that your life does not belong to you, but is a gift with which you must bring joy to others and lead them to eternal life. May the tenderness of the little Jesus always accompany you. Thank you for having responded to my call."*

1993

January 25, 1993 *"Dear children! Today I call you to accept and live my messages with seriousness. These days are the days when you need to decide for God, for peace, and for the good. May every hatred and jealousy disappear from your life and your thoughts, and may there only dwell love for God and for your neighbor. Thus, and only thus shall you be able to discern the signs of the time. I am with you, and I guide you into a new time, a time which God gives you as grace so that you may get to know him more. Thank you for having responded to my call."*

February 25, 1993 *"Dear children! Today I bless you with my motherly blessing and I invite you all to conversion. I wish that each of you decide for a change of life and that each of you work more in the Church, not through words and thoughts, but through example, so that your life may be a joyful testimony for Jesus. You cannot say that you are converted, because your life must become a daily conversion. In order to understand what you have to do, little children, pray, and God will give you what you completely have to do, and where you have to change. I am with you and place you all under my mantle. Thank you for having responded to my call."*

March 25, 1993 *"Dear children! Today like never before I call you to pray for peace, for peace in your hearts, peace in your families, and peace in the whole world, because Satan wants war, wants lack of peace, wants to destroy all which is good. Therefore, dear children, pray, pray, pray. Thank you for having responded to my call."*

April 25, 1993 *"Dear children! Today I invite you all to awaken your hearts to love. Go into nature and look how nature is awakening, and it will be a help to you to open your hearts to the love of God, the Creator. I desire you to awaken love in your families so that where there is unrest and hatred, love will reign, and when there is love in your hearts, then there is also prayer. And, dear children, do not forget that I am with you, and I am helping you with my prayer that God may give you the strength to love. I bless and love you with my motherly love. Thank you for having responded to my call."*

May 25, 1993 *"Dear children! Today I invite you to open yourselves to God by means of prayer so the Holy Spirit may begin to work miracles in you and through you. I am with you, and I intercede before God for each one of you, because, dear children, each one of you is important in my plan of salvation. I invite you to be bearers of good and peace. God can give you peace only if you convert and pray. Therefore, my dear little children, pray, pray, pray and do that which the Holy Spirit inspires you. Thank you for having responded to my call."*

June 25, 1993 *"Dear children! Today I also rejoice at your presence here. I bless you with my motherly blessing and intercede for each one of you before God. I call you anew to live my messages and to put them into life and practice. I am with you and bless all of you day by day. Dear children, these are special times and, therefore, I am with you to love and protect you, to protect your hearts from Satan and to bring you all closer to the heart of my Son Jesus. Thank you for having responded to my call."*

July 25, 1993 *"Dear children! I thank you for your prayers and for the love you show toward me. I invite you to decide to pray for my intentions. Dear children, offer novenas, making sacrifices for that to which you feel the most bound. I want your life to be bound to me. I am your Mother, little children, and I do not want Satan to deceive you, for He wants to lead you the wrong way, but he cannot if you do not permit him. Therefore, little children, renew prayer in your hearts, and then you will understand my call and my desire to help you. Thank you for having responded to my call."*

August 25, 1993 *"Dear children! I want you to understand that I am your Mother, that I want to help you and call you to prayer. Only by prayer can you understand and accept my messages and practice them in your life. Read Sacred Scripture, live it, and pray to understand the signs of the times. This is a special time; therefore, I am with you to draw you close to my heart and the heart of my Son Jesus. Dear little children, I want you to be children of the light and not of darkness. Therefore, live what I am telling you. Thank you for having responded to my call."*

September 25, 1993 *"Dear children! I am your Mother and I invite you to come closer to God through prayer because only He is your peace, your savior. Therefore, little children, do not seek comfort in material things, but rather seek God. I am praying for you, and I intercede before God for each individual. I am looking for your prayers that you accept me and accept my messages as in the first days of the apparitions, and only then, when you open your hearts and pray, will miracles happen. Thank you for having responded to my call."*

October 25, 1993 *"Dear children! These years I have been calling you to pray, to live what I am telling you, but you are living my messages a little. You talk, but do not live; that is why, little children, this war is lasting so long. I invite you to open yourselves to God and in your hearts to live with God, living the good and giving witness to my messages. I love you and wish to protect you from every evil, but you do not desire it. Dear children, I cannot help you if you do not live God's commandments, if you do not live the Mass, if you do not give up sin. I invite you to be apostles of love and goodness. In this world of unrest give witness to God and God's love, and God will bless you and give you what you seek from Him. Thank you for having responded to my call."*

November 25, 1993 *"Dear children! I invite you in this time like never before to prepare for the coming of Jesus. Let little Jesus reign in your hearts, and only then when Jesus is your friend will you be happy. It will not be difficult for you either to pray or to offer sacrifices or to witness Jesus' greatness in your life because He will give you strength and joy in this time. I am close to you by my intercession and prayer, and I love and bless all of you. Thank you for having responded to my call."*

December 25, 1993 *"Dear children! Today I rejoice with the little Jesus, and I desire that Jesus' joy may enter into every heart. Little children, with the message I give you a blessing with my Son Jesus, so that in every heart peace may reign. I love you, little children, and I invite all of you to come closer to me by means of prayer. You talk and talk but do not pray. Therefore, little children, decide for prayer. Only in this way will you be happy, and God will give you what you seek from Him. Thank you for having responded to my call."*

1994

January 25, 1994 *"Dear children! You are all my children. I love you. But, little children, you must not forget that without prayer you cannot be close to me. In these times Satan wants to create disorder in your hearts and in your families. Little children, do not give in. You should not allow him to lead you and your life. I love you and intercede before God for you. Little children, pray. Thank you for having responded to my call."*

February 25, 1994 *"Dear children! Today I thank you for your prayers. All of you have helped me so that this war may end as soon as possible. I am close to you, and I pray for each one of you, and I beg you to pray, pray, pray. Only through prayer can we defeat evil and protect all that Satan wants to destroy in your lives. I am your Mother, and I love you all equally, and I intercede for you before God. Thank you for having responded to my call."*

March 25, 1994 *"Dear children! Today I rejoice with you, and I invite you to open yourselves to me and become an instrument in my hands for the salvation of the world. I desire, little children, that all of you who have felt the odor of holiness through these messages which I am giving you to carry, to carry it into this world, hungry for God and God's love. I thank you all for having responded in such a number, and I bless you all with my motherly blessing. Thank you for having responded to my call."*

April 25, 1994 *"Dear children! Today I invite you to decide to pray according to my intention. Little children, I invite each one of you to help my plan to be realized through this parish. Now I invite you in a special way, little children, to decide to go along the way of holiness. Only in this way will you be close to me. I love you, and I desire to conduct you all with me to Paradise. But, if you do not pray, and if you are not humble and obedient to the messages which I am giving you, I cannot help you. Thank you for having responded to my call."*

May 25, 1994 *"Dear children! I invite you all to have more trust in me and to live my messages more deeply. I am with you, and I intercede before God for you, but also I wait for your hearts to open up to my messages. Rejoice because God loves you and gives you the possibility to convert every day and to believe more in God the Creator. Thank you for having responded to my call."*

June 25, 1994 *"Dear children! Today I rejoice in my heart in seeing you all present here. I bless you, and I call you all to decide to live my messages which I give you here. I desire, little children, to guide you all to Jesus because He is your salvation. Therefore, little children, the more you pray, the more you will be mine and of my Son Jesus. I bless you all with my motherly blessing, and I thank you for having responded to my call."*

July 25, 1994 *"Dear children! Today I invite you to decide to give time patiently for prayer. Little children, you cannot say you are mine and that you have experienced conversion through my messages if you are not ready to give time to God every day. I am close to you, and I bless you all. Little children, do not forget that if you do not pray, you are not close to me; nor are you close to the Holy Spirit, who leads you along the path to holiness. Thank you for having responded to my call."*

August 25, 1994 *"Dear children! Today I am united with you in prayer in a special way, praying for the gift of the presence of my most beloved son in your home country. Pray, little children, for the health of my most beloved son, who suffers, and whom I have chosen for these times. I pray and intercede before my Son Jesus, so that the dream that your fathers had may be fulfilled. Pray, little children, in a special way, because Satan is strong and wants to destroy hope in your heart. I bless you. Thank you for having responded to my call."* (See notations.)

September 25, 1994 *"Dear children! I rejoice with you, and I invite you to prayer. Little children, pray for my intention. Your prayers are necessary to me, through which I desire to bring you closer to God. He is your salvation. God sends me to help you and to guide you towards Paradise, which is your goal. Therefore, little children, pray, pray, pray. Thank you for having responded to my call."*

October 25, 1994 *"Dear children! I am with you, and I rejoice today because the Most High has granted me to be with you and to teach you and to guide you on the path of perfection. Little children, I wish you to be a beautiful bouquet of flowers which I wish to present to God for the day of All Saints. I invite you to open yourselves and to live, taking the saints as an example. Mother Church has chosen them, that they may be an impulse for your daily life. Thank you for having responded to my call!"*

November 25, 1994 *"Dear children! Today I call you to prayer. I am with you, and I love you all. I am your Mother, and I wish that your hearts be similar to my heart. Little children, without prayer you cannot live and say that you are mine. Prayer is joy. Prayer is what the human heart desires. Therefore, get closer, little children, to my Immaculate Heart, and you will discover God. Thank you for having responded to my call."*

December 25, 1994 *"Dear children! Today I rejoice with you, and I am praying with you for peace, peace in your hearts, peace in your families, peace in your desires, peace in the whole world. May the King of Peace bless you today and give you peace. I bless you, and I carry each one of you in my heart. Thank you for having responded to my call."*

1995

January 25, 1995 *"Dear children! I invite you to open the door of your heart to Jesus as the flower opens itself to the sun. Jesus desires to fill your hearts with peace and joy. You cannot, little children, realize peace if you are not at peace with Jesus. Therefore, I invite you to confession so Jesus may be your truth and peace. So, little children, pray to have the strength to realize what I am telling you. I am with you, and I love you. Thank you for having responded to my call."*

February 25, 1995 *"Dear children! Today I invite you to become missionaries of my messages, which I am giving here through this place that is dear to me. God has allowed me to stay this long with you, and, therefore, little children, I invite you to live with love the messages I give and to transmit them to the whole world, so that a river of love flows to people who are full of hatred and without peace. I invite you, little children, to become peace where there is no peace and light where there is darkness, so that each heart accepts the light and the way of salvation. Thank you for having responded to my call."*

March 25, 1995 *"Dear Children! Today I invite you to live peace in your hearts and families. There is no peace, little children, where there is no prayer, and there is no love, where there is no faith. Therefore, little children, I invite you all to decide again today for conversion. I am close to you, and I invite you all, little children, into my embrace to help you, but you are not willing, and in this way, Satan is tempting you, and in the smallest way, your faith disappears. This is why, little children, pray and through prayer, you will have blessing and peace. Thank you for having responded to my call."*

April 25, 1995 *"Dear children! Today I call you to love. Little children, without love you can neither live with God nor with brother. Therefore, I call all of you to open your hearts to the love of God that is so great and open to each one of you. God, out of love for man, has sent me among you to show you the path of salvation, the path of love. If you do not first love God, then you will neither be able to love our neighbor nor the one you hate. Therefore, little children, pray and through prayer you will discover love. Thank you for having responded to my call."*

May 25, 1995 *"Dear Children! I invite you, little children, to help me through your prayers so that as many hearts as possible come close to my Immaculate Heart. Satan is strong, and with all his forces he wants to bring closer as many people as possible to himself and to sin. That is why he is on the prowl to snatch more every moment. I beg you, little children, pray and help me to help you. I am your mother, and I love you, and that is why I wish to help you. Thank you for having responded to my call."*

June 25, 1995 *"Dear Children! Today I am happy to see you in such great numbers, that you have responded and have come to live my messages. I invite you, little children, to be my joyful carriers of peace in this troubled world. Pray for peace so that as soon as possible a time of peace, which my heart waits impatiently for, may reign. I am near to you, little children, and intercede for every one of you before the Most High. I bless you with my motherly blessing. Thank you for having responded to my call."*

July 25, 1995 *"Dear children! Today I invite you to prayer because only in prayer can you understand my coming here. The Holy Spirit will enlighten you to understand that you must convert. Little children, I wish to make of you a most beautiful bouquet prepared for eternity but you do not accept the way of conversion, the way of salvation that I am offering you through these apparitions. Little children, pray, convert your hearts, and come closer to me. May good overcome evil. I love you and bless you. Thank you for having responded to my call."*

August 25, 1995 *"Dear children! Today I invite you to prayer. Let prayer be life for you. A family cannot say that it is in peace if it does not pray. Therefore, let your morning begin with morning prayer, and evening end with thanksgiving. Little children, I am with you, and I love you, and I bless you, and I wish for every one of you to be in my embrace. You cannot be in my embrace if you are not ready to pray every day. Thank you for having responded to my call."*

September 25, 1995 *"Dear Children! Today I invite you to fall in love with the Most Holy Sacrament of the Altar. Adore Him, little children, in your parishes, and in this way you will be united with the entire world. Jesus will become your friend, and you will not talk of Him like someone whom you barely know. Unity with Him will be a joy for you, and you will become witnesses to the love of Jesus that He has for every creature. Little children, when you adore Jesus, you are also close to me. Thank you for having responded to my call."*

October 25, 1995 *"Dear Children! Today I invite you to observe nature because there you will meet God the Creator. Today I invite you, little children, to thank God for all that He gives you. In thanking Him you will discover the Most High and all the goods that surround you. Little children, God is great, and His love for every creature is great. Therefore, pray to be able to understand the love and goodness of God. In the goodness and the love of God the Creator, I also am with you as a gift. Thank you for having responded to my call."*

November 25, 1995 *"Dear Children! Today I invite you so that each of you begins again to love, in the first place, God who saved and redeemed each of you, and then brothers and sisters in your proximity. Without love, little children, you cannot grow in holiness and cannot do good deeds. Therefore, little children, pray without ceasing that God reveals His love to you. I have invited all of you to unite yourselves with me and to love. Today I am with you and invite you to discover love in your hearts and in families. For God to live in your hearts, you must love. Thank you for having responded to my call."*

December 25, 1995 *"Dear Children! Today I also rejoice with you, and I bring you little Jesus so that He may bless you. I invite you, dear children, so that your life may be united with Him. Jesus is the King of Peace, and only He can give you the peace that you seek. I am with you, and I present you to Jesus in a special way, now in this new time in which one should decide for Him. This time is the time of grace. Thank you for having responded to my call."*

1996

January 25, 1996 *"Dear Children! Today I invite you to decide for peace. Pray that God give you true peace. Live peace in your hearts, and you will understand, dear children, that peace is the gift of God. Dear children, without love you cannot live peace. The fruit of peace is love, and the fruit of love is forgiveness. I am with you, and I invite all of you, little children, before all else to forgive in the family, and then you will be able to forgive others. Thank you for having responded to my call."*

February 25, 1996 *"Dear children! Today I invite you to conversion. This is the most important message that I have given you here. Little children, I wish that each of you become a carrier of my messages. I invite you, little children, to live the messages that I have given you over these years. This time is a time of grace, especially now, when the Church also is inviting you to prayer and conversion. I also, little children, invite you to live my messages that I have given you during the time I appeared here. Thank you for having responded to my call."*

March 25, 1996 *"Dear children! I invite you to decide again to love God above all else. In this time when due to the spirit of consumerism one forgets what it means to love and to cherish true values, I invite you again, little children, to put God in first place in your life. Do not let Satan attract you through material things, but, little children, decide for God, who is freedom and love. Choose life and not death of the soul, little children, and in this time when you meditate upon the suffering and death of Jesus, I invite you to decide for life, which blossomed through the Resurrection, and that your life may be renewed today through conversion, that shall lead you to eternal life. Thank you for having responded to my call."*

April 25, 1996 *"Dear children! Today I invite you again to put prayer in first place in your families. Little children, when God is in first place, then you will, in all that you do, seek the will of God. In this way your daily conversion will become easier. Little children, seek with humility that which is not in order in your hearts, and you shall understand what you have to do. Conversion will become a daily duty that you will do with joy. Little children, I am with you, I bless you all, and I invite you to become my witnesses by prayer and personal conversion. Thank you for having responded to my call."*

166

May 25, 1996 *"Dear children! Today I wish to thank you for all your prayers and sacrifices that you, during this month which is consecrated to me, have offered to me. Little children, I also wish that you all become active during this time that through me is connected to Heaven in a special way. Pray in order to understand that you all, through your life and your example, ought to collaborate in the work of salvation. Little children, I wish that all people convert and see me and my Son Jesus in you. I will intercede for you and help you to become the light. In helping others, your soul will also find salvation. Thank you for having responded to my call."*

June 25, 1996 *"Dear children! Today I thank you for all the sacrifices you have offered me these days. Little children, I invite you to open yourselves to me and to decide for conversion. Your hearts, little children, are still not completely open to me, and therefore, I invite you again to open to prayer so that in prayer the Holy Spirit will help you, so that your hearts be of flesh and not of stone. Little children, thank you for having responded to my call and for having decided to walk with me toward holiness."*

July 25, 1996 *"Dear children! Today I invite you to decide every day for God. Little children, you speak much about God, but you witness little with your life. Therefore, little children, decide for conversion, that your life may be true before God, so that in the truth of your life you witness the beauty God gave you. Little children, I invite you again to decide for prayer, because through prayer, you will be able to live conversion. Each one of you shall become simple, like a child which is open to the love of the Father. Thank you for having responded to my call."*

August 25, 1996 *"Dear children! Listen, because I wish to speak to you and to invite you to have more faith and trust in God, who loves you immeasurably. Little children, you do not know how to live in the grace of God; that is why I call you all anew, to carry the word of God in your heart and in your thoughts. Little children, place the Sacred Scripture in a visible place in your family, and read and live it. Teach your children, because if you are not an example to them, children fall into godlessness. Reflect and pray, and then God will be born in your heart, and your heart will be joyous. Thank you for having responded to my call."*

September 25, 1996 *"Dear children! Today I invite you to offer your crosses and suffering for my intentions. Little children, I am your mother, and I wish to help you by seeking for you the grace from God. Little children, offer your sufferings as a gift to God so they become a most beautiful flower of joy. That is why, little children, pray that you may understand that suffering can become joy and the cross the way of joy. Thank you for having responded to my call."*

October 25, 1996 *"Dear children! Today I invite you to open yourselves to God the Creator, so that He changes you. Little children, you are dear to me. I love you all, and I call you to be closer to me and that your love towards my Immaculate Heart be more fervent. I wish to renew you and lead you with my Heart to the Heart of Jesus, which still today suffers for you and calls you to conversion and renewal. Through you, I wish to renew the world. Comprehend, little children, that you are today the salt of the earth and the light of the world. Little children, I invite you, and I love you and in a special way implore: 'Convert!' Thank you for having responded to my call."*

November 25, 1996 *"Dear children! Today, again, I invite you to pray, so that through prayer, fasting, and small sacrifices you may prepare yourselves for the coming of Jesus. May this time, little children, be a time of grace for you. Use every moment and do good, for only in this way will you feel the birth of Jesus in your hearts. If with your life you give an example and become a sign of God's love, joy will prevail in the hearts of men. Thank you for having responded to my call."*

December 25, 1996 *"Dear children! Today I am with you in a special way, holding little Jesus in my lap, and I invite you, little children, to open yourselves to His call. He calls you to joy. Little children, joyfully live the messages of the Gospel, which I am repeating since I have been with you. Little children, I am your Mother, and I desire to reveal to you the God of love and the God of peace. I do not desire for your life to be in sadness but that it be realized in joy for eternity, according to the Gospel. Only in this way will your life have meaning. Thank you for having responded to my call."*

1997

January 25, 1997 *"Dear children! I invite you to reflect about your future. You are creating a new world without God, with your own strength only, and that is why you are unsatisfied and without joy in your heart. This time is my time, and that is why, little children, I invite you again to pray. When you find unity with God, you will feel hunger for the Word of God, and your heart, little children, will overflow with joy. You will witness God's love wherever you are. I bless you, and I repeat to you that I am with you to help you. Thank you for having responded to my call."*

February 25, 1997 *"Dear children! Today I invite you in a special way to open yourselves to God the Creator and to become active. I invite you, little children, to see at this time who needs your spiritual or material help. By your example, little children, you will be the extended hands of God, which humanity is seeking. Only in this way will you understand that you are called to witness and to become joyful carriers of God's Word and of His love. Thank you for having responded to my call."*

March 25, 1997 *"Dear children! Today in a special way I invite you to take the cross in your hands and to meditate on the wounds of Jesus. Ask Jesus to heal your wounds, which you, dear children, during your life sustained because of your sins or the sins of your parents. Only in this way, dear children, you will understand that the world is in need of a healing faith in God the Creator. By Jesus' passion and death on the cross, you will understand that only through prayer you, too, can become true apostles of faith when, in simplicity and in prayer, you live faith, which is a gift. Thank you for having responded to my call."*

April 25, 1997 *"Dear children! Today I call you to have your life connected with God the Creator, because only in this way will your life have meaning, and you will comprehend that God is love. God sends me to you out of love, that I may help you to comprehend that without Him there is no future or joy and, above all, there is no eternal salvation. Little children, I call you to leave sin and to accept prayer at all times, that you may in prayer come to know the meaning of your life. God gives Himself to him who seeks Him. Thank you for having responded to my call."*

169

May 25, 1997 *"Dear children! Today I invite you to glorify God and for the Name of God to be holy in your hearts and in your life. Little children, when you are in the holiness of God, He is with you and gives you peace and joy, which come from God only through prayer. That is why, little children, renew prayer in your families, and your heart will glorify the Holy Name of God, and heaven will reign in your heart. I am close to you, and I intercede for you before God. Thank you for having responded to my call."*

June 25, 1997 *"Dear children! Today I am with you in a special way, and I bring you my motherly blessing of peace. I pray for you, and I intercede for you before God, so that you may comprehend that each of you is a carrier of peace. You cannot have peace if your heart is not at peace with God. That is why, little children, pray, pray, pray, because prayer is the foundation of your peace. Open your heart and give time to God so that He will be your friend. When true friendship with God is realized, no storm can destroy it. Thank you for having responded to my call."*

July 25, 1997 *"Dear children! Today I invite you to respond to my call to prayer. I desire, dear children, that during this time you find a corner for personal prayer. I desire to lead you towards prayer with the heart. Only in this way will you comprehend that your life is empty without prayer. You will discover the meaning of your life when you discover God in prayer. That is why, little children, open the door of your heart, and you will comprehend that prayer is a joy without which you cannot live. Thank you for having responded to my call."*

August 25, 1997 *"Dear children! God gives me this time as a gift to you, so that I may instruct and lead you on the path of salvation. Dear children, now you do not comprehend this grace, but soon a time will come when you will lament for these messages. That is why, little children, live all of the words which I have given you through this time of grace, and renew prayer until prayer becomes a joy for you. Especially, I call all those who have consecrated themselves to my Immaculate Heart to become an example to others. I call all priests and religious brothers and sisters to pray the rosary and to teach others to pray. The rosary, little children, is especially dear to me. Through the rosary open your heart to me, and I am able to help you. Thank you for having responded to my call."*

170

September 25, 1997 *"Dear children! Today I call you to comprehend that without love you cannot comprehend that God needs to be in the first place in your life. That is why, little children, I call you all to love, not with a human love but with God's love. In this way, your life will be more beautiful and without distraction. You will comprehend that God gives Himself to you in the simplest way out of love. Little children, so that you may comprehend my words which I give you out of love, pray, pray, pray, and you will be able to accept others with love and forgive all who have done evil to you. Respond with prayer; prayer is a fruit of love towards God the Creator. Thank you for having responded to my call."*

October 25, 1997 *"Dear children! Also today I am with you, and I call all of you to renew yourselves by living my messages. Little children, may prayer be life for you, and may you be an example to others. Little children, I desire for you to become carriers of peace and of God's joy to today's world, that lacks peace. That is why, little children, pray, pray, pray! I am with you, and I bless you with my motherly peace. Thank you for having responded to my call."*

November 25, 1997 *"Dear children! Today I invite you to comprehend your Christian vocation. Little children, I led and am leading you through this time of grace, that you may become conscious of your Christian vocation. Holy martyrs died witnessing that they were a Christian and loved God over everything. Little children, today also I invite you to rejoice and be joyful Christians, responsible and conscious that God called you in a special way to be joyfully extended hands toward those who do not believe, and that through the example of your life, they may receive faith and love for God. Therefore, pray, pray, pray that your heart may open and be sensitive for the Word of God. Thank you for having responded to my call."*

December 25, 1997 *"Dear children! Also today I rejoice with you, and I call you to good things. I desire that each of you reflect and carry peace in your heart and say, 'I want to put God in the first place in my life.' In this way, little children, each of you will become holy. Little children, tell everyone that I want good things for you, and He will respond with such and, little children, good will come to dwell in the heart of each man. Little children, tonight I bring to you the good of my Son, who gave His life to save you. That is why, little children, rejoice and extend your hands to Jesus, who is only good. Thank you for having responded to my call."*

1998

January 25, 1998 *"Dear children! Today again I call all of you to prayer. Only with prayer, dear children, will your heart change, become better, and be more sensitive to the Word of God. Little children, do not permit Satan to pull you apart and to do with you what he wants. I call you to be responsible and determined and to consecrate each day to God in prayer. May Holy Mass, little children, not be a habit for you, but life. By living Holy Mass each day, you will feel the need for holiness, and you will grow in holiness. I am close to you and intercede before God for each of you, so that He may give you strength to change your heart. Thank you for having responded to my call."*

February 25, 1998 *"Dear children! Also today I am with you, and I again call all of you to come closer to me through your prayers. In a special way, I call you to renunciation in this time of grace. Little children, meditate on and live, through your little sacrifices, the passion and death of Jesus for each of you. Only if you come closer to Jesus will you comprehend the immeasurable love He has for each of you. Through prayer and your renunciation you will become more open to the gift of faith and love towards the Church and the people who are around you. I love you and bless you. Thank you for having responded to my call."*

March 25, 1998 *"Dear children! Also today I call you to fasting and renunciation. Little children, renounce that which hinders you from being closer to Jesus. In a special way I call you to pray, because only through prayer will you be able to overcome your will and discover the will of God even in the smallest things. By your daily life, little children, you will become an example and witness that you live for Jesus or against Him and His will. Little children, I desire that you become apostles of love. By loving, little children, it will be recognized that you are mine. Thank you for having responded to my call."*

April 25, 1998 *"Dear children! Today I call you, through prayer, to open yourselves to God as a flower opens itself to the rays of the morning sun. Little children, do not be afraid. I am with you, and I intercede before God for each of you so that your heart receives the gift of conversion. Only in this way, little children, will you comprehend the importance of grace in these times, and God will become nearer to you. Thank you for having responded to my call."*

172

May 25, 1998 *"Dear children! Today I call you, through prayer and sacrifice, to prepare yourselves for the coming of the Holy Spirit. Little children, this is a time of grace, and so again I call you to decide for God the Creator. Allow Him to transform and change you. May your heart be prepared to listen to, and live, everything which the Holy Spirit has in His plan for each of you. Little children, allow the Holy Spirit to lead you on the way of truth and salvation towards eternal life. Thank you for having responded to my call."*

June 25, 1998 *"Dear children! Today I desire to thank you for living my messages. I bless you all with my motherly blessing, and I bring you all before my Son Jesus. Thank you for having responded to my call."*

July 25, 1998 *"Dear children! Today little children, I invite you, through prayer, to be with Jesus, so that through a personal experience of prayer you may be able to discover the beauty of God's creatures. You cannot speak or witness about prayer if you do not pray. That is why, little children, in the silence of your heart remain with Jesus, so that He may change and transform you with His love. This, little children, is a time of grace for you. Make good use of it for your personal conversion, because when you have God, you have everything. Thank you for having responded to my call."*

August 25, 1998 *"Dear children! Today I invite you to come still closer to me through prayer. Little children, I am your Mother, I love you, and I desire that each of you be saved and thus be with me in Heaven. That is why, little children, pray, pray, pray until your life becomes prayer. Thank you for having responded to my call."*

September 25, 1998 *"Dear children! Today I call you to become my witnesses by living the faith of your fathers. Little children, you seek signs and messages and do not see that, with every morning sunrise, God calls you to convert and to return to the way of truth and salvation. You speak much, little children, but you work little on your conversion. That is why, convert and start to live my messages, not with your words but with your life. In this way, little children, you will have the strength to decide for the true conversion of the heart. Thank you for having responded to my call."*

173

October 25, 1998 *"Dear children! Today I call you to come closer to my Immaculate Heart. I call you to renew in your families the fervor of the first days when I called you to fasting, prayer, and conversion. Little children, you accepted my messages with open hearts, although you did not know what prayer was. Today I call you to open yourselves completely to me so that I may transform you and lead you to the heart of my Son Jesus, so that He can fill you with His love. Only in this way, little children, will you find true peace - the peace that only God gives you. Thank you for having responded to my call."*

November 25, 1998 *"Dear children! Today I call you to prepare yourselves for the coming of Jesus. In a special way, prepare your hearts. May holy confession be the first act of conversion for you, and then, dear children, decide for holiness. May your conversion and decision for holiness begin today and not tomorrow. Little children, I call you all to the way of salvation, and I desire to show you the way to Heaven. That is why, little children, be mine and decide with me for holiness. Little children, accept prayer with seriousness and pray, pray, pray. Thank you for having responded to my call."*

December 25, 1998 *"Dear children! In this Christmas joy I desire to bless you. In a special way, little children, I give you the blessing of little Jesus. May He fill you with His peace. Today, little children, you do not have peace, and yet you yearn for it. That is why, with my Son Jesus, on this day I call you to pray, pray, pray, because without prayer you do not have joy or peace or a future. Yearn for peace and seek it, for God is true peace. Thank you for having responded to my call."*

174

1999

January 25, 1999 *"Dear children! I again invite you to prayer. You have no excuse to work more because nature still lies in deep sleep. Open yourselves in prayer. Renew prayer in your families. Put Holy Scripture in a visible place in your families, read it, reflect on it, and learn how God loves His people. His love shows itself also in present times because He sends me to call you to the path of salvation. Thank you for having responded to my call."*

February 25, 1999 *"Dear children! Also today I am with you in a special way contemplating and living the passion of Jesus in my heart. Little children, open your hearts and give me everything that is in them: joys, sorrows and each, even the smallest, pain, that I may offer them to Jesus so that with His immeasurable love, He may burn and transform your sorrows into the joy of His resurrection. That is why, I now call you in a special way, little children, for your hearts to open to prayer, so that through prayer you may become friends of Jesus. Thank you for having responded to my call."*

March 25, 1999 *"Dear children! I call you to prayer with the heart. In a special way, little children, I call you to pray for conversion of sinners, for those who pierce my heart and the heart of my Son Jesus with the sword of hatred and daily blasphemies. Let us pray, little children, for all those who do not desire to come to know the love of God, even though they are in the Church. Let us pray that they convert, so that the Church may resurrect in love. Only with love and prayer, little children, can you live this time which is given to you for conversion. Place God in the first place; then the risen Jesus will become your friend. Thank you for having responded to my call."*

April 25, 1999 *"Dear children! Also today I call you to prayer. Little children, be joyful carriers of peace and love in this peaceless world. By fasting and prayer, witness that you are mine and that you live my messages. Pray and seek! I am praying and interceding for you before God that you convert, that your life and behavior always be Christian. Thank you for having responded to my call."*

May 25, 1999 *"Dear children! Also today I call you to convert and to more firmly believe in God. Children, you seek peace and pray in different ways, but you have not yet given your hearts to God for Him to fill them with His love. So, I am with you to teach you and to bring you closer to the love of God. If you love God above all else, it will be easy for you to pray and to open your hearts to Him. Thank you for having responded to my call."*

June 25, 1999 *"Dear children! Today I thank you for living and witnessing my messages with your life. Little children, be strong and pray so that prayer may give you strength and joy. Only in this way will each of you be mine, and I will lead you on the way of salvation. Little children, pray, and with your life witness my presence here. May each day be a joyful witness for you of God's love. Thank you for having responded to my call."*

July 25, 1999 *"Dear children! Also today I rejoice with you, and I call you all to prayer with the heart. I call all of you, little children, to give thanks to God here with me for the graces which He gives to you through me. I desire for you to comprehend that I want to realize here, not only a place of prayer, but also a meeting of hearts. I desire for my Jesus' and your heart to become one heart of love and peace. That is why, little children, pray and rejoice over everything that God does here, despite the fact that Satan provokes quarrels and unrest. I am with you, and I lead you all on the way of love. Thank you for having responded to my call."*

August 25, 1999 *"Dear children! Also today I call you to give glory to God the Creator in the colors of nature. He speaks to you also through the smallest flower about His beauty and the depth of love with which He has created you. Little children, may prayer flow from your hearts like fresh water from a spring. May the wheat fields speak to you about the mercy of God towards every creature. That is why, renew prayer of thanksgiving for everything He gives you. Thank you for having responded to my call."*

September 25, 1999 *"Dear children! Today again I call you to become carriers of my peace. In a special way, now when it is being said that God is far away, He has truly never been nearer to you. I call you to renew prayer in your families by reading the Sacred Scripture and to experience joy in meeting with God, who infinitely loves His creatures. Thank you for having responded to my call."*

October 25, 1999 *"Dear children! Do not forget: this is a time of grace; that is why, pray, pray, pray! Thank you for having responded to my call."*

176

November 25, 1999 *"Dear children! Also today I call you to prayer. In this time of grace, may the cross be a sign-post of love and unity for you through which true peace comes. That is why, little children, pray especially at this time that little Jesus, the Creator of peace, may be born in your hearts. Only through prayer will you become my apostles of peace in this world without peace. That is why, pray until prayer becomes a joy for you. Thank you for having responded to my call."*

December 25, 1999 *"Dear children! This is the time of grace. Little children, today in a special way with little Jesus, whom I hold in my embrace, I am giving you the possibility to decide for peace. Through your 'yes' for peace and your decision for God, a new possibility for peace is opened. Only in this way, little children, will this century will be for you a time of peace and well-being. Therefore, put little newborn Jesus in the first place in your life, and He will lead you on the way of salvation. Thank you for having responded to my call."*

2000

January 25, 2000 *"Dear children! I call you, little children, to pray without ceasing. If you pray, you are closer to God, and He will lead you on the way of peace and salvation. That is why I call you today to give peace to others. Only in God is there true peace. Open your hearts and become those who give a gift of peace, and others will discover peace in you, and through you, and in this way you will witness God's peace and love which He gives you. Thank you for having responded to my call."*

February 25, 2000 *"Dear children! Wake up from the sleep of unbelief and sin, because this is a time of grace which God gives you. Use this time and seek the grace of healing of your heart from God, so that you may see God and man with the heart. Pray in a special way for those who have not come to know God's love, and witness with your life so that they also can come to know God and His immeasurable love. Thank you for having responded to my call."*

March 25, 2000 *"Dear children! Pray and make good use of this time, because this is a time of grace. I am with you, and I intercede for each one of you before God, for your heart to open to God and to God's love. Little children, pray without ceasing, until prayer becomes a joy for you. Thank you for having responded to my call."*

April 25, 2000 *"Dear children! Also today I call you to conversion. You are concerned too much about material things and little about spiritual ones. Open your hearts and start again to work more on your personal conversion. Decide every day to dedicate time to God and to prayer until prayer becomes a joyful meeting with God for you. Only in this way will your life have meaning, and with joy you will contemplate eternal life. Thank you for having responded to my call."*

May 25, 2000 *"Dear children! I rejoice with you, and in this time of grace I call you to spiritual renewal. Pray, little children, that the Holy Spirit may come to dwell in you in fullness, so that you may be able to witness in joy to all those who are far from faith. Especially, little children, pray for the gifts of the Holy Spirit so that in the spirit of love, every day and in each situation, you may be closer to your fellow-man and that in wisdom and love you may overcome every difficulty. I am with you, and I intercede for each of you before Jesus. Thank you for having responded to my call."*

June 25, 2000 *"Dear children! Today I call you to prayer. The one who prays is not afraid of the future. Little children, do not forget that I am with you, and I love you all. Thank you for having responded to my call."*

July 25, 2000 *"Dear children! Do not forget that you are here on earth on the way to eternity and that your home is in Heaven. That is why, little children, be open to God's love and leave egoism and sin behind. May your joy be only in discovering God in daily prayer. That is why, make good use of this time and pray, pray, pray; for God is near to you in prayer and through prayer. Thank you for having responded to my call."*

August 25, 2000 *"Dear children! I desire to share my joy with you. In my Immaculate Heart I feel that there are many of those who have drawn closer to me and are, in a special way, carrying the victory of my Immaculate Heart in their hearts by praying and converting. I desire to thank you and to inspire you to work even more for God and His kingdom with love and the power of the Holy Spirit. I am with you, and I bless you with my motherly blessing. Thank you for having responded to my call."*

September 25, 2000 *"Dear children! Today I call you to open yourselves to prayer. May prayer become joy for you. Renew prayer in your families and form prayer groups. In this way, you will experience joy in prayer and togetherness. All those who pray and are members of prayer groups are open to God's will in their hearts and joyfully witness God's love. I am with you, I carry all of you in my heart, and I bless you with my motherly blessing. Thank you for having responded to my call."*

October 25, 2000 *"Dear children! Today I desire to open my motherly heart to you and to call you all to pray for my intentions. I desire to renew prayer with you and to call you to fast, which I desire to offer to my Son Jesus for the coming of a new time – a time of spring. In this Jubilee Year many hearts have opened to me, and the Church is being renewed in the Spirit. I rejoice with you, and I thank God for this gift; and you, little children, I call to pray, pray, pray – until prayer becomes a joy for you. Thank you for having responded to my call."*

November 25, 2000 *"Dear children! Today when Heaven is near to you in a special way, I call you to prayer so that through prayer you place God in first place. Little children, today I am near you, and I bless each of you with my motherly blessing so that you have the strength and love for all the people you meet in your earthly life and that you can give God's love. I rejoice with you, and I desire to tell you that your brother Slavko has been born into Heaven and intercedes for you. Thank you for having responded to my call."*

December 25, 2000 *"Dear children! Today when God granted to me that I can be with you, with little Jesus in my arms, I rejoice with you and I give thanks to God for everything He has done in this Jubilee Year. I thank God especially for all the vocations of those who said 'yes' to God completely. I bless you all with my blessing and the blessing of the newborn Jesus. I pray for all of you for joy to be born in your hearts so that in joy you too carry the joy I have today. In this Child I bring to you the Savior of your hearts and the One who calls you to holiness of life. Thank you for having responded to my call."*

2001

January 25, 2001 *"Dear children! Today I call you to renew prayer and fasting with even greater enthusiasm until prayer becomes a joy for you. Little children, the one who prays is not afraid of the future, and the one who fasts is not afraid of evil. Once again, I repeat to you: only through prayer and fasting can wars also be stopped – wars of your unbelief and fear for the future. I am with you and am teaching you, little children: your peace and hope are in God. That is why draw closer to God and put Him in first place in your life. Thank you for having responded to my call."*

February 25, 2001 *"Dear children! This is a time of grace. That is why pray, pray, pray until you comprehend God's love for each of you. Thank you for having responded to my call."*

March 25, 2001 *"Dear children! Also today I call you to open yourselves to prayer. Little children, you live in a time in which God gives great graces, but you do not know how to make good use of them. You are concerned about everything else, but least for the soul and spiritual life. Awaken from the tired sleep of your soul and say 'yes' to God with all your strength. Decide for conversion and holiness. I am with you, little children, and I call you to perfection of your soul and of everything you do. Thank you for having responded to my call."*

April 25, 2001 *"Dear children! Also today, I call you to prayer. Little children, prayer works miracles. When you are tired and sick and you do not know the meaning of your life, take the rosary and pray; pray until prayer becomes for you a joyful meeting with your Savior. I am with you, little children, and I intercede and pray for you. Thank you for having responded to my call."*

May 25, 2001 *"Dear children! At this time of grace, I call you to prayer. Little children, you work much but without God's blessing. Bless and seek the wisdom of the Holy Spirit to lead you at this time so that you may comprehend and live in the grace of this time. Convert, little children, and kneel in the silence of your hearts. Put God in the center of your being so that, in that way, you can witness in joy to the beauty that God continually gives in your life. Thank you for having responded to my call."*

181

June 25, 2001 *"Dear children! I am with you, and I bless you all with my motherly blessing. Especially today when God gives you abundant graces, pray and seek God through me. God gives you great graces; that is why, little children, make good use of this time of grace and come closer to my heart so that I can lead you to my Son Jesus. Thank you for having responded to my call."*

July 25, 2001 *"Dear children! In this time of grace, I call you to come even closer to God through your personal prayer. Make good use of the time of rest and give your soul and your eyes rest in God. Find peace in nature, and you will discover God the Creator, Whom you will be able to give thanks to for all creatures; then you will find joy in your heart. Thank you for having responded to my call."*

August 25, 2001 *"Dear children! Today I call all of you to decide for holiness. May holiness be in first place in your work and in your speech and always in your thoughts and in each situation, little children. In this way, you will also put it into practice; little by little, step by step, prayer and a decision for holiness will enter into your family. Be real with yourselves, and do not bind yourselves to material things but to God. And do not forget, little children, that your life is as passing as a flower. Thank you for having responded to my call."*

September 25, 2001 *"Dear children! Also today I call you to prayer, especially today when Satan wants war and hatred. I call you anew, little children; pray and fast that God may give you peace. Witness peace to every heart and be carriers of peace in this world without peace. I am with you and intercede before God for each of you. And you do not need to fear, because the one who prays is not afraid of evil and has no hatred in his heart. Thank you for having responded to my call."*

October 25, 2001 *"Dear children! Also today I call you to pray from your whole heart and to love each other. Little children, you are chosen to witness peace and joy. If there is no peace, pray, and you will receive it. Through you and your prayer, little children, peace will begin to flow through the world. That is why, little children, pray, pray, pray, because prayer works miracles in human hearts and in the world. I am with you, and I thank God for each of you who has accepted and lives prayer with seriousness. Thank you for having responded to my call."*

November 25, 2001 *"Dear children! In this time of grace, I call you anew to prayer. Little children, pray and prepare your hearts for the coming of the King of Peace, that with His blessing He may give peace to the whole world. Peacelessness has begun to reign in hearts, and hatred reigns in the world. That is why you who live my messages must be the light and extended hands to this faithless world so that all may come to know the God of Love. Do not forget, little children, I am with you and bless you all. Thank you for having responded to my call."*

December 25, 2001 *"Dear children! I call you today and encourage you to prayer for peace. Especially today I call you, carrying the newborn Jesus in my arms for you, to unite with Him through prayer and to become a sign to this peaceless world. Encourage each other, little children, to prayer and love. May your faith be an encouragement to others to believe and to love more. I bless you all and call you to be closer to my heart and to the heart of little Jesus. Thank you for having responded to my call."*

2002

January 25, 2002 *"Dear children! At this time while you are still looking back to the past year, I call you, little children, to look deeply into your heart and to decide to be closer to God and to prayer. Little children, you are still attached to earthly things and little to the spiritual life. May my call today also be an encouragement to you to decide for God and for daily conversion. You cannot be converted, little children, if you do not abandon sins and do not decide for love towards God and neighbor. Thank you for having responded to my call."*

February 25, 2002 *"Dear children! In this time of grace, I call you to become friends of Jesus. Pray for peace in your hearts and work for your personal conversion. Little children, only in this way will you be able to become witnesses of peace and of the love of Jesus in the world. Open yourselves to prayer so that prayer becomes a need for you. Be converted, little children, and work so that as many souls as possible may come to know Jesus and His love. I am close to you, and I bless you all. Thank you for having responded to my call."*

March 25, 2002 *"Dear children! Today I call you to unite with Jesus in prayer. Open your hearts to Him and give Him everything that is in them: joys, sorrows, and illnesses. May this be a time of grace for you. Pray, little children, and may every moment belong to Jesus. I am with you, and I intercede for you. Thank you for having responded to my call."*

April 25, 2002 *"Dear children! Rejoice with me in this time of spring when all nature is awakening and your hearts long for change. Open yourselves, little children, and pray. Do not forget that I am with you, and I desire to take you all to my Son so that He may give you the gift of sincere love towards God and everything that is from Him. Open yourselves to prayer and seek a conversion of your hearts from God; everything else He sees and provides. Thank you for having responded to my call."*

May 25, 2002 *"Dear children! Today I call you to put prayer in first place in your life. Pray, and may prayer, little children, be a joy for you. I am with you and intercede for all of you, and you, little children, be joyful carriers of my messages. May your life with me be joy. Thank you for having responded to my call."*

June 25, 2002 *"Dear children! Today I pray for you and with you that the Holy Spirit may help you and increase your faith, so that you may accept even more the messages that I am giving you here in this holy place. Little children, comprehend that this is a time of grace for each of you; and with me, little children, you are secure. I desire to lead you all on the way of holiness. Live my messages and put into life every word that I am giving you. May they be precious to you because they come from Heaven. Thank you for having responded to my call."*

July 25, 2002 *"Dear children! Today I rejoice with your patron saint and call you to be open to God's will, so that in you and through you, faith may grow in the people you meet in your everyday life. Little children, pray until prayer becomes a joy for you. Ask your holy protectors to help you grow in love towards God. Thank you for having responded to my call."*

August 25, 2002 *"Dear children! Also today I am with you in prayer so that God gives you an even stronger faith. Little children, your faith is small, and you are not even aware how much; despite this, you are not ready to seek the gift of faith from God. That is why I am with you, little children, to help you comprehend my messages and put them into life. Pray, pray, pray, and only in faith and through prayer will your soul find peace and the world find joy to be with God. Thank you for having responded to my call."*

September 25, 2002 *"Dear children! Also in this peaceless time, I call you to prayer. Little children, pray for peace so that in the world every person will feel love towards peace. Only when the soul finds peace in God, does it feel content, and love will begin to flow in the world. And in a special way, little children, you are called to live and witness peace – peace in your hearts and families – and, through you, peace will also begin to flow in the world. Thank you for having responded to my call."*

October 25, 2002 *"Dear children! Also today I call you to prayer. Little children, believe that by simple prayer miracles can be worked. Through your prayer you open your heart to God, and He works miracles in your life. By looking at the fruits, your heart fills with joy and gratitude to God for everything He does in your life and, through you, also to others. Pray and believe little children; God gives you graces and you do not see them. Pray, and you will see them. May your day be filled with prayer and thanksgiving for everything that God gives you. Thank you for having responded to my call."*

185

November 25, 2002 *"Dear children! I call you also today to conversion. Open your heart to God, little children, through Holy Confession, and prepare your soul so that little Jesus can be born anew in your heart. Permit Him to transform you and lead you on the way of peace and joy. Little children, decide for prayer. Especially now, in this time of grace, may your heart yearn for prayer. I am close to you and intercede before God for all of you. Thank you for having responded to my call."*

December 25, 2002 *"Dear children! This is a time of great graces, but also a time of great trials for all those who desire to follow the way of peace. Because of that, little children, again I call you to pray, pray, pray, not with words but with the heart. Live my messages and be converted. Be conscious of this gift that God has permitted me to be with you, especially today when in my arms I have little Jesus - the King of Peace. I desire to give you peace, and that you carry it in your hearts and give it to others until God's peace begins to rule the world. Thank you for having responded to my call."*

2003

January 25, 2003 *"Dear children! With this message I call you anew to pray for peace. Particularly now when peace is in crisis, you be those who pray and bear witness to peace. Little children, be peace in this peaceless world. Thank you for having responded to my call."*

February 25, 2003 *"Dear children! Also today I call you to pray and fast for peace. As I have already said and now repeat to you, little children, only with prayer and fasting can wars also be stopped. Peace is a precious gift from God. Seek, pray, and you will receive it. Speak about peace, and carry peace in your hearts. Nurture it like a flower which is in need of water, tenderness, and light. Be those who carry peace to others. I am with you and intercede for all of you. Thank you for having responded to my call."*

March 25, 2003 *"Dear children! Also today I call you to pray for peace. Pray with the heart, little children, and do not lose hope because God loves His creatures. He desires to save you, one by one, through my coming here. I call you to the way of holiness. Pray, and in prayer you are open to God's will; in this way, in everything you do, you realize God's plan in you and through you. Thank you for having responded to my call."*

April 25, 2003 *"Dear children! I call you also today to open yourselves to prayer. In the foregone time of Lent you have realized how small you are and how small your faith is. Little children, decide also today for God, that in you and through you He may change the hearts of people and also your hearts. Be joyful carriers of the risen Jesus in this peaceless world, which yearns for God and for everything that is from God. I am with you, little children, and I love you with a special love. Thank you for having responded to my call."*

May 25, 2003 *"Dear children! Also today I call you to prayer. Renew your personal prayer, and in a special way pray to the Holy Spirit to help you to pray with the heart. I intercede for all of you, little children, and call all of you to conversion. If you convert, all those around you will also be renewed, and prayer will be a joy for them. Thank you for having responded to my call."*

June 25, 2003 *"Dear children! Also today I call you with great joy to live my messages. I am with you, and I thank you for putting into practice what I am saying to you. I call you to renew my messages even more, with new enthusiasm and joy. May prayer be your daily practice. Thank you for having responded to my call."*

July 25, 2003 *"Dear children! Also today I call you to prayer. Little children, pray until prayer becomes a joy for you. Only in this way will each of you discover peace in the heart, and your soul will be content. You will feel the need to witness to others the love that you feel in your heart and life. I am with you and intercede before God for all of you. Thank you for having responded to my call."*

August 25, 2003 *"Dear children! Also today I call you to give thanks to God in your heart for all the graces which He gives you, also through the signs and colors that are in nature. God wants to draw you closer to Himself and moves you to give Him glory and thanks. Therefore, little children, I call you anew to pray, pray, pray, and do not forget that I am with you. I intercede before God for each of you until your joy in Him is complete. Thank you for having responded to my call."*

September 25, 2003 *"Dear children! Also today I call you to come closer to my heart. Only in this way will you comprehend the gift of my presence here among you. I desire, little children, to lead you to the heart of my Son Jesus; but you resist and do not desire to open your hearts to prayer. Again, little children, I call you not to be deaf but to comprehend my call, which is salvation for you. Thank you for having responded to my call."*

October 25, 2003 *"Dear children! I call you anew to consecrate yourselves to my heart and the heart of my Son Jesus. I desire, little children, to lead you all on the way of conversion and holiness. Only in this way, through you, can we lead more souls on the way of salvation. Do not delay, little children, but say with all your heart, 'I want to help Jesus and Mary so that more brothers and sisters may come to know the way of holiness.' In this way, you will feel the contentment of being friends of Jesus. Thank you for having responded to my call."*

November 25, 2003 *"Dear children! I call you so that this time will be for you an even greater incentive to prayer. In this time, little children, pray that Jesus be born in all hearts, especially in those who do not know Him. Be love, joy and peace in this peaceless world. I am with you and intercede before God for each of you. Thank you for having responded to my call."*

December 25, 2003 *"Dear children! Also today I bless you all with my Son Jesus in my arms, and I carry Him, who is the King of Peace, to you, so that He grant you His peace. I am with you, and I love you all, little children. Thank you for having responded to my call."*

2004

January 25, 2004 *"Dear children! Also today I call you to pray. Pray, little children, in a special way for all those who have not come to know God's love. Pray that their hearts may open and draw closer to my heart and the Heart of my Son Jesus, so that we can transform them into people of peace and love. Thank you for having responded to my call."*

February 25, 2004 *"Dear children! Also today, as never up to now, I call you to open your hearts to my messages. Little children, be those who draw souls to God and not those who distance them. I am with you and love you all with a special love. This is a time of penance and conversion. From the bottom of my heart, I call you to be mine with all your heart, and then you will see that your God is great, because He will give you an abundance of blessings and peace. Thank you for having responded to my call."*

March 25, 2004 *"Dear children! Also today I call you to open yourselves to prayer. Especially now, in this time of grace, open your hearts, little children, and express your love to the Crucified. Only in this way will you discover peace, and prayer will begin to flow from your heart into the world. Be an example, little children, and an incentive for the good. I am close to you, and I love you all. Thank you for having responded to my call."*

April 25, 2004 *"Dear children! Also today I call you to live my messages even more strongly in humility and love so that the Holy Spirit may fill you with His grace and strength. Only in this way will you be witnesses of peace and forgiveness. Thank you for having responded to my call."*

May 25, 2004 *"Dear children! Also today I urge you to consecrate yourselves to my Heart and to the Heart of my Son Jesus. Only in this way will you be mine more each day, and you will inspire each other all the more to holiness. In this way joy will rule your hearts, and you will be carriers of peace and love. Thank you for having responded to my call."*

June 25, 2004 *"Dear children! Also today joy is in my heart. I desire to thank you for making my plan realizable. Each of you is important; therefore, little children, pray and rejoice with me for every heart that has converted and become an instrument of peace in the world. Prayer groups are powerful, and through them I can see, little children, that the Holy Spirit is at work in the world. Thank you for having responded to my call."*

July 25, 2004 *"Dear children! I call you anew: be open to my messages. I desire, little children, to draw you all closer to my Son Jesus; therefore, you pray and fast. Especially I call you to pray for my intentions, so that I can present you to my Son Jesus for Him to transform and open your hearts to love. When you will have love in the heart, peace will rule in you. Thank you for having responded to my call."*

August 25, 2004 *"Dear children! I call you all to conversion of heart. Decide, as in the first days of my coming here, for a complete change of your life. In this way, little children, you will have the strength to kneel and to open your hearts before God. God will hear your prayers and answer them. Before God, I intercede for each of you. Thank you for having responded to my call."*

September 25, 2004 *"Dear children! Also today I call you to be love where there is hatred and food where there is hunger. Open your hearts, little children, and let your hands be extended and generous so that, through you, every creature may thank God the Creator. Pray, little children, and open your heart to God's love, but you cannot if you do not pray. Therefore, pray, pray, pray. Thank you for having responded to my call."*

October 25, 2004 *"Dear children! This is a time of grace for the family, and, therefore, I call you to renew prayer. May Jesus be in the heart of your family. In prayer, learn to love everything that is holy. Imitate the lives of saints so that they may be an incentive and teachers on the way of holiness. May every family become a witness of love in this world without prayer and peace. Thank you for having responded to my call."*

November 25, 2004 *"Dear children! At this time I call you all to pray for my intentions. Especially, little children, pray for those who have not yet come to know the love of God and do not seek God the Savior. You, little children, be my extended hands and by your example draw them closer to my Heart and the Heart of my Son. God will reward you with graces and every blessing. Thank you for having responded to my call."*

December 25, 2004 *"Dear children! With great joy, also today I carry my Son Jesus in my arms to you; He blesses you and calls you to peace. Pray, little children, and be courageous witnesses of Good News in every situation. Only in this way will God bless you and give you everything you ask of Him in faith. I am with you as long as the Almighty permits me. I intercede for each of you with great love. Thank you for having responded to my call."*

191

2005

January 25, 2005 *"Dear children! In this time of grace again I call you to prayer. Pray, little children, for unity of Christians, that all may be of one heart. Unity will really be among you inasmuch as you will pray and forgive. Do not forget: love will conquer only if you pray, and your heart will open. Thank you for having responded to my call."*

February 25, 2005 *"Dear children! Today I call you to be my extended hands in this world that puts God in the last place. You, little children, put God in the first place in your life. God will bless you and give you strength to bear witness to Him, the God of love and peace. I am with you and intercede for all of you. Little children, do not forget that I love you with a tender love. Thank you for having responded to my call."*

March 25, 2005 *"Dear children! Today I call you to love. Little children, love each other with God's love. At every moment, in joy and in sorrow, may love prevail and, in this way, love will begin to reign in your hearts. The risen Jesus will be with you, and you will be his witnesses. I will rejoice with you and protect you with my motherly mantle. Especially, little children, I will watch your daily conversion with love. Thank you for having responded to my call."*

April 25, 2005 *"Dear children! Also today I call you to renew prayer in your families. By prayer and the reading of Sacred Scripture, may the Holy Spirit, who will renew you, enter into your families. In this way, you will become teachers of the Faith in your family. By prayer and your love, the world will set out on a better way, and love will begin to rule in the world. Thank you for having responded to my call."*

May 25, 2005 *"Dear children! I call you anew to live my messages in humility. Especially witness them now when we are approaching the anniversary of my apparitions. Little children, be a sign to those who are far from God and His love. I am with you and bless you all with my motherly blessing. Thank you for having responded to my call."*

June 25, 2005 *"Dear children! Today I thank you for every sacrifice that you have offered for my intentions. I call you, little children, to be my apostles of peace and love in your families and in the world. Pray that the Holy Spirit may enlighten and lead you on the way of holiness. I am with you and bless you all with my motherly blessing. Thank you for having responded to my call."*

July 25, 2005 *"Dear children! Also today I call you to fill your day with short and ardent prayers. When you pray, your heart is open, and God loves you with a special love and gives you special graces. Therefore, make good use of this time of grace and devote it to God more than ever up to now. Do novenas of fasting and renunciation so that Satan be far from you and grace be around you. I am near you and intercede before God for each of you. Thank you for having responded to my call."*

August 25, 2005 *"Dear children! Also today I call you to live my messages. God gave you a gift of this time as a time of grace. Therefore, little children, make good use of every moment and pray, pray, pray. I bless you all and intercede before the Most High for each of you. Thank you for having responded to my call."*

September 25, 2005 *"Dear children! In love I call you: convert, even though you are far from my heart. Do not forget that I am your mother, and I feel pain for each one who is far from my heart; but I do not leave you alone. I believe you can leave the way of sin and decide for holiness. Thank you for having responded to my call."*

October 25, 2005 *"Little children, believe, pray and love, and God will be near you. He will give you the gift of all the graces you seek from Him. I am a gift to you, because, from day to day, God permits me to be with you and to love each of you with immeasurable love. Therefore, little children, in prayer and humility, open your hearts and be witnesses of my presence. Thank you for having responded to my call."*

November 25, 2005 *"Dear children! Also today I call you to pray, pray, pray until prayer becomes life for you. Little children, at this time, in a special way, I pray before God to give you the gift of faith. Only in faith will you discover the joy of the gift of life that God has given you. Your heart will be joyful in thinking of eternity. I am with you and love you with a tender love. Thank you for having responded to my call."*

December 25, 2005 *"Dear children! Also today in my arms I bring you little Jesus, the King of Peace, to bless you with His peace. Little children, in a special way today I call you to be my carriers of peace in this peaceless world. God will bless you. Little children, do not forget that I am your mother. I bless you all with a special blessing, with little Jesus in my arms. Thank you for having responded to my call."*

2006

January 25, 2006 *"Dear children! Also today I call you to be carriers of the Gospel in your families. Do not forget, little children, to read Sacred Scripture. Put it in a visible place and witness with your life that you believe and live the Word of God. I am close to you with my love and intercede before my Son for each of you. Thank you for having responded to my call."*

February 25, 2006 *"Dear children! In this Lenten time of grace, I call you to open your hearts to the gifts that God desires to give you. Do not be closed, but with prayer and renunciation say 'yes' to God, and He will give to you in abundance. Just as in springtime the earth receives the seed and yields a hundredfold, so also your heavenly Father will give to you in abundance. I am with you and love you, little children, with a tender love. Thank you for having responded to my call."*

March 25, 2006 *"Courage, little children! I decided to lead you on the way of holiness. Renounce sin and set out on the way of salvation, the way which my Son has chosen. Through each of your tribulations and sufferings God will find the way of joy for you. Therefore, little children, pray. We are close to you with our love. Thank you for having responded to my call."*

April 25, 2006 *"Dear children! Also today I call you to have more trust in me and my Son. He has conquered by His death and resurrection and, through me, calls you to be a part of His joy. You do not see God, little children, but if you pray you will feel His nearness. I am with you and intercede before God for each of you. Thank you for having responded to my call."*

May 25, 2006 *"Dear children! Also today I call you to put into practice and to live my messages that I am giving you. Decide for holiness, little children, and think of heaven. Only in this way will you have peace in your heart that no one will be able to destroy. Peace is a gift, which God gives you in prayer. Little children, seek and work with all your strength for peace to win in your hearts and in the world. Thank you for having responded to my call."*

June 25, 2006 *"Dear children! With great joy in my heart I thank you for all the prayers that, in these days, you offered for my intentions. Know, little children, that you will not regret it, neither you nor your children. God will reward you with great graces, and you will merit eternal life. I am near you and thank all those who, through these years, have accepted my messages, have poured them into their life, and have decided for holiness and peace. Thank you for having responded to my call."*

July 25, 2006 *"Dear children! At this time do not only think of rest for your body, but, little children, seek time also for the soul. In silence may the Holy Spirit speak to you and permit Him to convert and change you. I am with you, and before God I intercede for each of you. Thank you for having responded to my call."*

August 25, 2006 *"Dear children! Also today I call you to pray, pray, pray. Only in prayer will you be near to me and my Son, and you will see how short this life is. In your heart a desire for Heaven will be born. Joy will begin to rule in your heart, and prayer will begin to flow like a river. In your words there will only be thanksgiving to God for having created you, and the desire for holiness will become a reality for you. Thank you for having responded to my call."*

September 25, 2006 *"Dear children! Also today I am with you and call all of you to complete conversion. Decide for God, little children, and you will find in God the peace your heart seeks. Imitate the lives of saints, and may they be an example for you, and I will inspire you as long as the Almighty permits me to be with you. Thank you for having responded to my call."*

October 25, 2006 *"Dear children! Today the Lord permitted me to tell you again that you live in a time of grace. You are not conscious, little children, that God is giving you a great opportunity to convert and to live in peace and love. You are so blind and attached to earthly things and think of earthly life. God sent me to lead you toward eternal life. I, little children, am not tired, although I see that your hearts are heavy and tired for everything that is a grace and a gift. Thank you for having responded to my call."*

November 25, 2006 *"Dear children! Also today I call you to pray, pray, pray. Little children, when you pray, you are close to God, and He gives you the desire for eternity. This is a time when you can speak more about God and do more for God. Therefore, little children, do not resist but permit Him to lead you, to change you, and to enter into your life. Do not forget that you are travelers on the way toward eternity. Therefore, little children, permit God to lead you as a shepherd leads his flock. Thank you for having responded to my call."*

December 25, 2006 *"Dear children! Also today I bring you the newborn Jesus in my arms. He who is the King of Heaven and earth is your peace. Little children, no one can give you peace as He who is the King of Peace. Therefore, adore Him in your hearts, choose Him, and you will have joy in Him. He will bless you with His blessing of peace. Thank you for having responded to my call."*

2007

January 25, 2007 *"Dear children! Put Sacred Scripture in a visible place in your family and read it. In this way, you will come to know prayer with the heart, and your thoughts will be on God. Do not forget that you are passing like a flower in a field, which is visible from afar but disappears in a moment. Little children, leave a sign of goodness and love wherever you pass, and God will bless you with an abundance of His blessings. Thank you for having responded to my call."*

February 25, 2007 *"Dear children! Open your heart to God's mercy in this Lenten time. The heavenly Father desires to deliver each of you from the slavery of sin. Therefore, little children, make good use of this time, and through meeting with God in confession, leave sin and decide for holiness. Do this out of love for Jesus, who redeemed you all with His blood, so that you may be happy and in peace. Do not forget, little children that your freedom is your weakness; therefore, follow my messages with seriousness. Thank you for having responded to my call."*

March 25, 2007 *"Dear children! I desire to thank you from my heart for your Lenten renunciations. I desire to inspire you to continue to live fasting with an open heart. By fasting and renunciation, little children, you will be stronger in faith. In God you will find true peace through daily prayer. I am with you, and I am not tired. I desire to take you all with me to Heaven; therefore, decide daily for holiness. Thank you for having responded to my call."*

April 25, 2007 *"Dear children! Also today I again call you to conversion. Open your hearts. This is a time of grace while I am with you; make good use of it. Say, 'This is the time for my soul'. I am with you and love you with immeasurable love. Thank you for having responded to my call."*

May 25, 2007 *"Dear children! Pray with me to the Holy Spirit for Him to lead you in the search of God's will on the way to your holiness. And you, who are far from prayer, convert and, in the silence of your heart, seek salvation for your soul and nurture it with prayer. I bless you all individually with my motherly blessing. Thank you for having responded to my call."*

197

June 25, 2007 *"Dear children! Also today, with great joy in my heart, I call you to conversion. Little children, do not forget that you are all important in this great plan, which God leads through Medjugorje. God desires to convert the entire world and to call it to salvation and to the way towards Himself, who is the beginning and the end of every being. In a special way, little children, from the depth of my heart, I call you all to open yourselves to this great grace that God gives you through my presence here. I desire to thank each of you for the sacrifices and prayers. I am with you, and I bless you all. Thank you for having responded to my call."*

July 25, 2007 *"Dear children! Today, on the day of the Patron of your Parish, I call you to imitate the lives of the Saints. May they be, for you, an example and encouragement to a life of holiness. May prayer for you be like the air you breathe in and not a burden. Little children, God will reveal His love to you, and you will experience the joy that you are my beloved. God will bless you and give you an abundance of grace. Thank you for having responded to my call."*

August 25, 2007 *"Dear children! Also today I call you to conversion. May your life, little children, be a reflection of God's goodness and not of hatred and unfaithfulness. Pray, little children, that prayer may become life for you. In this way, in your life you will discover the peace and joy which God gives to those who have an open heart to His love. And you who are far from God's mercy, convert so that God may not become deaf to your prayers and that it may not be too late for you. Therefore, in this time of grace, convert and put God in the first place in your life. Thank you for having responded to my call."*

September 25, 2007 *"Dear children! Also today I call all of you for your hearts to blaze with more ardent love for the Crucified, and do not forget that, out of love for you, He gave His life so that you may be saved. Little children, meditate and pray that your heart may be open to God's love. Thank you for having responded to my call."*

October 25, 2007 *"Dear children! God sent me among you out of love that I may lead you towards the way of salvation. Many of you opened your hearts and accepted my messages, but many have become lost on this way and have never come to know the God of love with the fullness of heart. Therefore, I call you to be love and light where there is darkness and sin. I am with you and bless you all. Thank you for having responded to my call."*

198

November 25, 2007 *"Dear children! Today, when you celebrate Christ, the King of all that is created, I desire for Him to be the King of your lives. Only through giving, little children, can you comprehend the gift of Jesus' sacrifice on the Cross for each of you. Little children, give time to God that He may transform you and fill you with His grace, so that you may be a grace for others. For you, little children, I am a gift of grace and love, which comes from God for this peaceless world. Thank you for having responded to my call."*

December 25, 2007 *"Dear children! With great joy I bring you the King of Peace for Him to give you His blessing. Adore Him and give time to the Creator for whom your heart yearns. Do not forget that you are passers-by on this earth and that things can give you small joys, while through my Son, eternal life is given to you. That is why I am with you, to lead you towards what your heart yearns for. Thank you for having responded to my call."*

2008

January 25, 2008 *"Dear children! With the time of Lent, you are approaching a time of grace. Your heart is like ploughed soil, and it is ready to receive the fruit which will grow into what is good. You, little children, are free to choose good or evil. Therefore, I call you to pray and fast. Plant joy, and the fruit of joy will grow in your hearts for your good, and others will see it and receive it through your life. Renounce sin and choose eternal life. I am with you and intercede for you before my Son. Thank you for having responded to my call."*

February 25, 2008 *"Dear children! In this time of grace, I call you anew to prayer and renunciation. May your day be interwoven with little ardent prayers for all those who have not come to know God's love. Thank you for having responded to my call."*

March 25, 2008 *"Dear children! I call you to work on your personal conversion. You are still far from meeting with God in your heart. Therefore, spend all the more time in prayer and Adoration of Jesus in the Most Blessed Sacrament of the Altar, for Him to change you and to put into your hearts a living faith and a desire for eternal life. Everything is passing, little children; only God is not passing. I am with you, and I encourage you with love. Thank you for having responded to my call."*

April 25, 2008 *"Dear children! Also today I call all of you to grow in God's love as a flower which feels the warm rays of spring. In this way, also you, little children, grow in God's love and carry it to all those who are far from God. Seek God's will and do good to those whom God has put on your way, and be light and joy. Thank you for having responded to my call."*

May 25, 2008 *"Dear children! In this time of grace, when God has permitted me to be with you, little children, I call you anew to conversion. Work on the salvation of the world in a special way while I am with you. God is merciful and gives special graces; therefore, seek them through prayer. I am with you and do not leave you alone. Thank you for having responded to my call."*

June 25, 2008 *"Dear children! Also today, with great joy in my heart, I call you to follow me and to listen to my messages. Be joyful carriers of peace and love in this peaceless world. I am with you, and I bless you all with my Son Jesus, the King of Peace. Thank you for having responded to my call."*

July 25, 2008 *"Dear children! At this time when you are thinking of physical rest, I call you to conversion. Pray and work so that your heart yearns for God the Creator, who is the true rest of your soul and your body. May He reveal His face to you and may He give you His peace. I am with you and intercede before God for each of you. Thank you for having responded to my call."*

August 25, 2008 *"Dear children! Also today I call you to personal conversion. You be those who will convert and, with your life, will witness, love, forgive, and bring the joy of the Risen One into this world, where my Son died and where people do not feel a need to seek Him and to discover Him in their lives. You adore Him, and may your hope be hope to those hearts who do not have Jesus. Thank you for having responded to my call."*

September 25, 2008 *"Dear children! May your life anew be a decision for peace. Be joyful carriers of peace and do not forget that you live in a time of grace, in which God gives you great graces through my presence. Do not close yourselves, little children, but make good use of this time and seek the gift of peace and love for your life so that you may become witnesses to others. I bless you with my motherly blessing. Thank you for having responded to my call."*

October 25, 2008 *"Dear children! In a special way I call you all to pray for my intentions so that, through your prayers, you may stop Satan's plan over this world, which is further from God every day, and which puts itself in the place of God and is destroying everything that is beautiful and good in the souls of each of you. Therefore, little children, arm yourselves with prayer and fasting so that you may be conscious of how much God loves you and may carry out God's will. Thank you for having responded to my call."*

November 25, 2008 *"Dear children! Also today I call you, in this time of grace, to pray for little Jesus to be born in your heart. May He, who is peace itself, give peace to the entire world through you. Therefore, little children, pray without ceasing for this turbulent world without hope, so that you may become witnesses of peace for all. May hope begin to flow through your hearts as a river of grace. Thank you for having responded to my call."*

December 25, 2008 *"Dear children! You are running, working, gathering — but without blessing. You are not praying! Today I call you to stop in front of the manger and to meditate on Jesus, Whom I give to you today also, to bless you and to help you to comprehend that, without Him, you have no future. Therefore, little children, surrender your lives into the hands of Jesus, for Him to lead you and to protect you from every evil. Thank you for having responded to my call."*

2009

January 25, 2009 *"Dear children! Also today I call you to prayer. May prayer be for you like the seed that you will put in my heart, which I will give over to my Son Jesus for you, for the salvation of your souls. I desire, little children, for each of you to fall in love with eternal life, which is your future, and for all worldly things to be a help for you to draw you closer to God the Creator. I am with you for this long because you are on the wrong path. Only with my help, little children, will you open your eyes. There are many of those who, by living my messages, comprehend that they are on the way of holiness towards eternity. Thank you for having responded to my call."*

February 25, 2009 *"Dear children! In this time of renunciation, prayer, and penance, I call you anew to go and confess your sins so that grace may open your hearts, and permit it to change you. Convert, little children; open yourselves to God and to His plan for each of you. Thank you for having responded to my call."*

March 25, 2009 *"Dear children! In this time of spring, when everything is awakening from the winter sleep, you also awaken your souls with prayer so that they may be ready to receive the light of the risen Jesus. Little children, may He draw you closer to His Heart so that you may become open to eternal life. I pray for you and intercede before the Most High for your sincere conversion. Thank you for having responded to my call."*

April 25, 2009 *"Dear children! Today I call you all to pray for peace and to witness it in your families so that peace may become the highest treasure on this peaceless earth. I am your Queen of Peace and your mother. I desire to lead you on the way of peace, which comes only from God. Therefore, pray, pray, pray. Thank you for having responded to my call."*

May 25, 2009 *"Dear children! In this time, I call you all to pray for the coming of the Holy Spirit upon every baptized creature, so that the Holy Spirit may renew you all and lead you on the way of witnessing your faith — you and all those who are far from God and His love. I am with you and intercede for you before the Most High. Thank you for having responded to my call."*

June 25, 2009 *"Dear children! Rejoice with me, convert in joy, and give thanks to God for the gift of my presence among you. Pray that, in your hearts, God may be in the center of your life and with your life witness, little children, so that every creature may feel God's love. Be my extended hands for every creature, so that it may draw closer to the God of love. I bless you with my motherly blessing. Thank you for having responded to my call."*

July 25, 2009 *"Dear children! May this time be a time of prayer for you. Thank you for having responded to my call."*

August 25, 2009 *"Dear children! Today I call you anew to conversion. Little children, you are not holy enough, and you do not radiate holiness to others; therefore, pray, pray, pray, and work on your personal conversion, so that you may be a sign of God's love to others. I am with you and am leading you towards eternity, for which every heart must yearn. Thank you for having responded to my call."*

September 25, 2009 *"Dear children, with joy, persistently work on your conversion. Offer all your joys and sorrows to my Immaculate Heart so that I may lead you all to my most beloved Son, so that you may find joy in His Heart. I am with you to instruct you and to lead you towards eternity. Thank you for having responded to my call."*

October 25, 2009 *"Dear children! Also today I bring you my blessing. I bless you all and I call you to grow on this way, which God has begun through me for your salvation. Pray, fast, and joyfully witness your faith, little children, and may your heart always be filled with prayer. Thank you for having responded to my call."*

November 25, 2009 *"Dear children! In this time of grace I call you all to renew prayer in your families. Prepare yourselves with joy for the coming of Jesus. Little children, may your hearts be pure and pleasing, so that love and warmth may flow through you into every heart that is far from His love. Little children, be my extended hands, hands of love for all those who have become lost, who have no more faith and hope. Thank you for having responded to my call."*

December 25, 2009 *"Dear children! On this joyful day, I bring all of you before my Son, the King of Peace, that He may give you His peace and blessing. Little children, in love share that peace and blessing with others. Thank you for having responded to my call."*

2010

January 25, 2010 *"Dear children! May this time be a time of personal prayer for you, so that the seed of faith may grow in your hearts; and may it grow into a joyful witness to others. I am with you, and I desire to inspire you all; grow and rejoice in the Lord who has created you. Thank you for having responded to my call."*

February 25, 2010 *"Dear children! In this time of grace, when nature also prepares to give the most beautiful colors of the year, I call you, little children, to open your hearts to God the Creator for Him to transform and mold you in His image, so that all the good which has fallen asleep in your hearts may awaken to a new life and a longing towards eternity. Thank you for having responded to my call."*

March 25 2010 *"Dear children! Also today I desire to call you all to be strong in prayer and in the moments when trials attack you. Live your Christian vocation in joy and humility and witness to everyone. I am with you, and I carry you all before my Son Jesus, and He will be your strength and support. Thank you for having responded to my call."*

April 25, 2010 *"Dear children! At this time, when in a special way you are praying and seeking my intercession, I call you, little children, to pray so that through your prayers I can help you to have all the more hearts opened to my messages. Pray for my intentions. I am with you, and I intercede before my Son for each of you. Thank you for having responded to my call."*

May 25, 2010 *"Dear children! God gave you the grace to live and to defend all the good that is in you and around you, and to inspire others to be better and holier; but Satan, too, does not sleep, and through modernism diverts you and leads you to his way. Therefore, little children, in the love for my Immaculate Heart, love God above everything and live His commandments. In this way, your life will have meaning, and peace will rule on earth. Thank you for having responded to my call."*

June 25, 2010 *"Dear children! Joyfully I call you all to live my messages with joy; only in this way, little children, will you be able to be closer to my Son. I desire to lead you all only to Him, and in Him you will find true peace and the joy of your heart. I bless you all and love you with immeasurable love. Thank you for having responded to my call."*

July 25, 2010 *"Dear children! Again I call you to follow me with joy. I desire to lead all of you to my Son, your Savior. You are not aware that without Him you do not have joy and peace, or a future or eternal life. Therefore, little children, make good use of this time of joyful prayer and surrender. Thank you for having responded to my call."*

August 25, 2010 *"Dear children! With great joy, also today I desire to call you anew to pray, pray, pray. May this time be a time of personal prayer for you. During the day, find a place where you will pray joyfully in a recollected way. I love you and bless you all. Thank you for having responded to my call."*

September 25, 2010 *"Dear children! Today I am with you and bless you all with my motherly blessing of peace, and I urge you to live your life of faith even more, because you are still weak and are not humble. I urge you, little children, to speak less and to work more on your personal conversion so that your witness may be fruitful. And may your life be unceasing prayer. Thank you for having responded to my call."*

October 25, 2010 *"Dear children! May this time be a time of prayer for you. My call, little children, desires to be for you a call to decide to follow the way of conversion; therefore, pray and seek the intercession of all the saints. May they be for you an example, an incentive, and a joy towards eternal life. Thank you for having responded to my call."*

November 25, 2010 *"Dear children! I look at you and I see in your heart death without hope, restlessness, and hunger. There is no prayer or trust in God; that is why the Most High permits me to bring you hope and joy. Open yourselves. Open your hearts to God's mercy, and He will give you everything you need and will fill your hearts with peace, because He is peace and your hope. Thank you for having responded to my call."*

December 25, 2010 *"Dear children! Today I and my Son desire to give you an abundance of joy and peace so that each of you may be a joyful carrier and witness of peace and joy in the places where you live. Little children, be a blessing and be peace. Thank you for having responded to my call."*

2011

January 25, 2011 *"Dear children! Also today I am with you, and I am looking at you and blessing you, and I am not losing hope that this world will change for the good and that peace will reign in the hearts of men. Joy will begin to reign in the world because you have opened yourselves to my call and to God's love. The Holy Spirit is changing a multitude of those who have said 'yes'. Therefore, I desire to say to you, 'thank you for having responded to my call.'"*

February 25, 2011 *"Dear children! Nature is awakening, and on the trees the first buds are seen, which will bring most beautiful flowers and fruit. I desire that you also, little children, work on your conversion and that you be those who witness with their life, so that your example may be a sign and an incentive for conversion to others. I am with you, and before my Son Jesus I intercede for your conversion. Thank you for having responded to my call."*

March 25, 2011 *"Dear children! In a special way today I desire to call you to conversion. As of today, may new life begin in your heart. Children, I desire to see your 'yes', and may your life be a joyful living of God's will at every moment of your life. In a special way today, I bless you with my motherly blessing of peace, love, and unity in my heart and in the heart of my Son Jesus. Thank you for having responded to my call."*

April 25, 2011 *"Dear children! As nature gives the most beautiful colors of the year, I also call you to witness with your life and to help others to draw closer to my Immaculate Heart, so that the flame of love for the Most High may sprout in their hearts. I am with you, and I unceasingly pray for you that your life may be a reflection of Heaven here on earth. Thank you for having responded to my call."*

May 25, 2011 *"Dear children! My prayer today is for all of you who seek the grace of conversion. You knock on the door of my heart, but without hope and prayer, in sin, and without the Sacrament of Reconciliation with God. Leave sin and decide, little children, for holiness. Only in this way can I help you, hear your prayers, and seek intercession before the Most High. Thank you for having responded to my call."*

207

June 25, 2011 *"Dear children! Give thanks with me to the Most High for my presence with you. My heart is joyful watching the love and joy in the living of my messages. Many of you have responded, but I wait for, and seek, all the hearts that have fallen asleep to awaken from the sleep of unbelief. Little children, draw even closer to my Immaculate Heart so that I can lead all of you toward eternity. Thank you for having responded to my call."*

July 25, 2011 *"Dear children! May this time be for you a time of prayer and silence. Rest your body and spirit; may they be in God's love. Permit me, little children, to lead you; open your hearts to the Holy Spirit so that all the good that is in you may blossom and bear fruit one hundred fold. Begin and end the day with prayer with the heart. Thank you for having responded to my call."*

August 25, 2011 *"Dear children! Today I call you to pray and fast for my intentions, because Satan wants to destroy my plan. Here I began with this parish and invited the entire world. Many have responded, but there is an enormous number of those who do not want to hear or accept my call. Therefore, you who have said 'yes', be strong and resolute. Thank you for having responded to my call."*

Message of September 25, 2011 *"Dear children! I call you, for this time to be for all of you, a time of witnessing. You, who live in the love of God and have experienced His gifts, witness them with your words and life that they may be for the joy and encouragement to others in faith. I am with you and incessantly intercede before God for all of you that your faith may always be alive and joyful, and in the love of God. Thank you for having responded to my call."*

October 25, 2011 *"Dear children! I am looking at you, and in your hearts I do not see joy. Today I desire to give you the joy of the Risen One, that He may lead you and embrace you with His love and tenderness. I love you, and I am praying for your conversion without ceasing before my Son Jesus. Thank you for having responded to my call."*

November 25, 2011 *"Dear children! Today I desire to give you hope and joy. Everything that is around you, little children, leads you towards worldly things, but I desire to lead you towards a time of grace, so that through this time you may be all the closer to my Son, so that He can lead you towards His love and eternal life, for which every heart yearns. You, little children, pray, and may this time for you be one of grace for your soul. Thank you for having responded to my call."*

December 25, 2011 *"Dear children! Also today in my arms I am carrying my Son Jesus to you, for Him to give you His peace. Pray, little children, and witness so that in every heart, not human but God's peace may prevail, which no one can destroy. It is that peace in the heart which God gives to those whom He loves. By your baptism you are all, in a special way, called and loved; therefore, witness and pray that you may be my extended hands to this world, which yearns for God and peace. Thank you for having responded to my call."*

2012

January 25, 2012 *"Dear children! With joy also today I call you to open your hearts and to listen to my call. Again I desire to draw you closer to my Immaculate Heart, where you will find refuge and peace. Open yourselves to prayer, until it becomes a joy for you. Through prayer, the Most High will give you an abundance of grace, and you will become my extended hands in this restless world which longs for peace. Little children, with your lives witness faith and pray that faith may grow day by day in your hearts. I am with you. Thank you for having responded to my call."*

February 25, 2012 *"Dear children! At this time, in a special way I call you, 'pray with the heart'. Little children, you speak much and pray little. Read and meditate on Sacred Scripture, and may the words written in it be life for you. I encourage and love you, so that in God you may find your peace and the joy of living. Thank you for having responded to my call."*

March 25, 2012 *"Dear children! Also today, with joy, I desire to give you my motherly blessing and to call you to prayer. May prayer become a need for you to grow more in holiness every day. Work more on your conversion, because you are far away, little children. Thank you for having responded to my call."*

April 25, 2012 *"Dear children! Also today I am calling you to prayer, and may your heart, little children, open towards God as a flower opens towards the warmth of the sun. I am with you, and I intercede for all of you. Thank you for having responded to my call."*

May 25, 2012 *"Dear children! Also today I call you to conversion and to holiness. God desires to give you joy and peace through prayer but you, little children, are still far away - attached to the earth and to earthly things. Therefore, I call you anew to open your heart and your sight towards God and the things of God - and joy and peace will come to reign in your hearts. Thank you for having responded to my call."*

June 25, 2012 *"Dear children! With great hope in the heart, also today I call you to prayer. If you pray, little children, you are with me, and you are seeking the will of my Son and are living it. Be open and live prayer and, at every moment, may it be for you the savor and joy of your soul. I am with you, and I intercede for all of you before my Son Jesus. Thank you for having responded to my call."*

July 25, 2012 *"Dear children! Today I call you to the 'good'. Be carriers of peace and goodness in this world. Pray that God may give you the strength so that hope and pride may always reign in your heart and life because you are God's children and carriers of His hope to this world that is without joy in the heart, and is without a future, because it does not have its heart open to God, who is your salvation. Thank you for having responded to my call."*

August 25, 2012 *"Dear children! Also today with a hopeful heart, I am praying for you, and am thanking the Most High for every one of you who lives my messages in his heart. Give thanks to God's love that I can love and lead each of you through my Immaculate Heart also toward conversion. Open your hearts, and decide for holiness, and hope will give birth to joy in your hearts. Thank you for having responded to my call."*

September 25, 2012 *"Dear children! When in nature you look at the richness of the colors which the Most High gives to you, open your heart and pray with gratitude for all the good that you have and say: 'I am here created for eternity', and yearn for heavenly things because God loves you with immeasurable love. This is why He also gave me to you to tell you: 'Only in God is your peace and hope, dear children.' Thank you for having responded to my call."*

October 25, 2012 *"Dear children! Today I call you to pray for my intentions. Renew fasting and prayer because Satan is cunning and attracts many hearts to sin and perdition. I call you, little children, to holiness and to live in grace. Adore my Son so that He may fill you with His peace and love for which you yearn. Thank you for having responded to my call."*

November 25, 2012 *"Dear children! In this time of grace, I call all of you to renew prayer. Open yourselves to Holy Confession so that each of you may accept my call with the whole heart. I am with you and I protect you from the ruin of sin, but you must open yourselves to the way of conversion and holiness that your heart may burn out of love for God. Give Him time and He will give Himself to you and thus, in the will of God you will discover the love and the joy of living. Thank you for having responded to my call."*

December 25, 2012 Our Lady came with little Jesus in her arms and she did not give a message, but little Jesus began to speak and said: *"I am your peace, live my commandments."* With a sign of the cross, Our Lady and little Jesus blessed us together.

2013

January 25, 2013 *"Dear children! Also today I call you to prayer. May your prayer be as strong as a living stone, until with your lives you become witnesses. Witness the beauty of your faith. I am with you and intercede before my Son for each of you. Thank you for having responded to my call."*

February 25, 2013 *"Dear children! Also today I call you to prayer. Sin is pulling you towards worldly things and I have come to lead you towards holiness and the things of God, but you are struggling and spending your energies in the battle with the good and the evil that are in you. Therefore, little children, pray, pray, pray until prayer becomes a joy for you and your life will become a simple walk towards God. Thank you for having responded to my call."*

March 25, 2013 *"Dear children! In this time of grace I call you to take the cross of my beloved Son Jesus in your hands and to meditate on His passion and death. May your suffering be united in His suffering and love will win, because He who is love gave Himself out of love to save each of you. Pray, pray, pray until love and peace begin to reign in your hearts. Thank you for having responded to my call."*

April 25, 2013 *"Dear children! Pray, pray, keep praying until your heart opens in faith as a flower opens to the warm rays of the sun. This is a time of grace which God gives you through my presence but you are far from my heart, therefore, I call you to personal conversion and to family prayer. May Sacred Scripture always be an incentive for you. I bless you all with my motherly blessing. Thank you for having responded to my call."*

May 25, 2013 *"Dear children! Today I call you to be strong and resolute in faith and prayer, until your prayers are so strong so as to open the Heart of my beloved Son Jesus. Pray little children, pray without ceasing until your heart opens to God's love. I am with you and I intercede for all of you and I pray for your conversion. Thank you for having responded to my call."*

June 25, 2013 *"Dear children! With joy in the heart I love you all and call you to draw closer to my Immaculate Heart so I can draw you still closer to my Son Jesus, and that He can give you His peace and love, which are nourishment for each one of you. Open yourselves, little children, to prayer — open yourselves to my love. I am your mother and cannot leave you alone in wandering and sin. You are called, little children, to be my children, my beloved children, so I can present you all to my Son. Thank you for having responded to my call."*

July 25, 2013 *"Dear children! With joy in my heart I call all of you to live your faith and to witness it with your heart and by your example in every way. Decide, little children, to be far from sin and temptation and may there be joy and love for holiness in your hearts. I love you, little children, and accompany you with my intercession before the Most High. Thank you for having responded to my call."*

August 25, 2013 *"Dear children! Also today, the Most High is giving me the grace to be with you and to lead you towards conversion. Every day I am sowing and am calling you to conversion, that you may be prayer, peace, love - the grain that by dying will give birth a hundredfold. I do not desire for you, dear children, to have to repent for everything that you could have done but did not want to. Therefore, little children, again, with enthusiasm say: 'I want to be a sign to others.' Thank you for having responded to my call."*

September 25, 2013 *"Dear children! Also today I call you to prayer. May your relationship with prayer be a daily one. Prayer works miracles in you and through you, therefore, little children, may prayer be a joy for you. Then your relationship with life will be deeper and more open and you will comprehend that life is a gift for each of you. Thank you for having responded to my call."*

October 25, 2013 *"Dear children! Today I call you to open yourselves to prayer. Prayer works miracles in you and through you. Therefore, little children, in the simplicity of heart seek of the Most High to give you the strength to be God's children and for Satan not to shake you like the wind shakes the branches. Little children, decide for God anew and seek only His will, and then you will find joy and peace in Him. Thank you for having responded to my call."*

November 25, 2013 *"Dear children! Today I call all of you to prayer. Open the doors of your heart profoundly to prayer, little children, to prayer with the heart; and then the Most High will be able to act upon your freedom and conversion will begin. Your faith will become firm so that you will be able to say with all your heart: 'My God, my all.' You will comprehend, little children, that here on earth everything is passing. Thank you for having responded to my call."*

December 25, 2013 *"Dear children! I am carrying to you the King of Peace that He may give you His peace. You, little children, pray, pray, pray. The fruit of prayer will be seen on the faces of the people who have decided for God and His Kingdom. I, with my Son Jesus, bless you all with a blessing of peace. Thank you for having responded to my call."*

2014

January 25, 2014 *"Dear children! Pray, pray, pray for the radiance of your prayer to have an influence on those whom you meet. Put the Sacred Scripture in a visible place in your families and read it, so that the words of peace may begin to flow in your hearts. I am praying with you and for you, little children, that from day to day you may become still more open to God's will. Thank you for having responded to my call."*

February 25, 2014 *"Dear children! You see, hear and feel that in the hearts of many people there is no God. They do not want Him, because they are far from prayer and do not have peace. You, little children, pray - live God's commandments. You be prayer, you who from the very beginning said 'yes' to my call. Witness God and my presence and do not forget, little children: I am with you and I love you. From day to day I present you all to my Son Jesus. Thank you for having responded to my call."*

March 25, 2014 *"Dear children! I am calling you anew: begin the battle against sin as in the first days, go to confession and decide for holiness. The love of God will begin to flow through you into the world, peace will begin to rule in your hearts and God's blessing will fill you. I am with you and intercede for all of you before my Son Jesus. Thank you for having responded to my call."*

April 25, 2014 *"Dear children! Open your hearts to the grace which God is giving you through me, as a flower that opens to the warm rays of the sun. Be prayer and love for all those who are far from God and His love. I am with you and I intercede for all of you before my Son Jesus, and I love you with immeasurable love. Thank you for having responded to my call."*

May 25, 2014 *"Dear children! Pray and be aware that without God you are dust. Therefore, turn your thoughts and heart to God and to prayer. Trust in His love. In God's spirit, little children, you are all called to be witnesses. You are precious and I call you, little children, to holiness, to eternal life. Therefore, be aware that this life is passing. I love you and call you to a new life of conversion. Thank you for having responded to my call."*

June 25, 2014 *"Dear children! The Most High is giving me the grace that I can still be with you and to lead you in prayer towards the way of peace. Your heart and soul thirst for peace and love, for God and His joy. Therefore, little children, pray, pray, pray and in prayer you will discover the wisdom of living. I bless you all and intercede for each of you before my Son Jesus. Thank you for having responded to my call."*

July 25, 2014 *"Dear children! You are not aware of the graces that you are living at this time in which the Most High is giving you signs for you to open and convert. Return to God and to prayer, and may prayer begin to reign in your hearts, families and communities, so that the Holy Spirit may lead and inspire you to every day be more open to God's will and to His plan for each of you. I am with you and with the saints and angels intercede for you. Thank you for having responded to my call."*

August 25, 2014 *"Dear children! Pray for my intentions, because Satan wants to destroy my plan which I have here and to steal your peace. Therefore, little children, pray, pray, pray that God can act through each of you. May your hearts be open to God's will. I love you and bless you with my motherly blessing. Thank you for having responded to my call."*

September 25, 2014 *"Dear children! Also today I call you to also be like the stars, which by their light give light and beauty to others so they may rejoice. Little children, also you be the radiance, beauty, joy and peace – and especially prayer – for all those who are far from my love and the love of my Son Jesus. Little children, witness your faith and prayer in joy, in the joy of faith that is in your hearts; and pray for peace, which is a precious gift from God. Thank you for having responded to my call."*

October 25, 2014 *"Dear children! Pray in this time of grace and seek the intercession of all the saints who are already in the light. From day to day may they be an example and encouragement to you on the way of your conversion. Little children, be aware that your life is short and passing. Therefore, yearn for eternity and keep preparing your hearts in prayer. I am with you and intercede before my Son for each of you, especially for those who have consecrated themselves to me and to my Son. Thank you for having responded to my call."*

November 25, 2014 *"Dear children! In a special way, today I am calling you to prayer. Pray, little children, so that you may comprehend who you are and where you need to go. Be carriers of the good news and be people of hope. Be love for all those who are without love. Little children, you will be everything and will achieve everything only if you pray and are open to God's will – to God who desires to lead you towards eternal life. I am with you and intercede for you from day to day before my Son Jesus. Thank you for having responded to my call."*

December 25, 2014 *"Dear children! Also today, in my arms I am carrying my Son Jesus to you and I am asking from Him peace for you and peace among you. Pray to and adore my Son for His peace and joy to enter into your hearts. I am praying for you to be all the more open to prayer. Thank you for having responded to my call."*

2015

January 25, 2015 *"Dear children! Also today I call you: live your vocation in prayer. Now, as never before, Satan wants to suffocate man and his soul by his contagious wind of hatred and unrest. In many hearts there is no joy because there is no God or prayer. Hatred and war are growing from day to day. I am calling you, little children, begin anew, with enthusiasm, the walk of holiness and love; since I have come among you because of this. Together let us be love and forgiveness for all those who know and want to love only with a human love and not with that immeasurable love of God to which God calls you. Little children, may hope in a better tomorrow always be in your heart. Thank you for having responded to my call."*

February 25, 2015 *"Dear children! In this time of grace I call all of you: pray more and speak less. In prayer seek the will of God and live it according to the commandments to which God calls you. I am with you and am praying with you. Thank you for having responded to my call."*

March 25, 2015 *"Dear children! Also today the Most High permits me to be with you and to lead you on the way of conversion. Many hearts have shut themselves to grace and have become deaf to my call. You, little children, pray and fight against temptation and all the evil plans which the devil offers you through modernism. Be strong in prayer and with the cross in your hands pray that evil may not use you and may not conquer in you. I am with you and pray for you. Thank you for having responded to my call."*

April 25, 2015 *"Dear children! I am with you also today to lead you to salvation. Your soul is restless because your spirit is weak and tired from all worldly things. You, little children, pray to the Holy Spirit that He may transform you and fill you with His strength of faith and hope, so that you may be firm in this battle against evil. I am with you and intercede for you before my Son Jesus. Thank you for having responded to my call."*

May 25, 2015 *"Dear children! Also today I am with you and with joy I call all of you: pray and believe in the power of prayer. Open your hearts, little children, so that God may fill you with His love and you will be a joy to others. Your witness will be powerful and everything you do will be interwoven with God's tenderness. I am with you*

219

and I pray for you and your conversion until you put God in the first place. Thank you for having responded to my call."

June 25, 2015 *"Dear children! Also today the Most High gives me the grace to be able to love you and to call you to conversion. Little children, may God be your tomorrow and not war and lack of peace; not sorrow but joy and peace must begin to reign in the heart of every person - but without God you will never find peace. Therefore, little children, return to God and to prayer so that your heart may sing with joy. I am with you and I love you with immeasurable love. Thank you for having responded to my call."*

July 25, 2015 *"Dear children! With joy I am with you also today and I call all of you, little children, pray, pray, pray so as to comprehend the love which I have for you. My love is stronger than evil, little children, therefore draw closer to God so as to feel my joy in God. Without God, little children, you do not have a future, you do not have hope or salvation; therefore leave evil and choose good. I am with you and, with you, I intercede before God for all of your needs. Thank you for having responded to my call."*

August 25, 2015 *"Dear children! Also today I am calling you to be prayer. May prayer be for you the wings for an encounter with God. The world is in a moment of trial, because it forgot and abandoned God. Therefore you, little children, be those who seek and love God above all. I am with you and I am leading you to my Son, but you must say your 'yes' in the freedom of children of God. I intercede for you and I love you, little children, with an endless love. Thank you for having responded to my call."*

September 25, 2015 *"Dear children! Also today I am praying to the Holy Spirit to fill your hearts with a strong faith. Prayer and faith will fill your heart with love and joy and you will be a sign for those who are far from God. Little children, encourage each other to prayer with the heart, so that prayer may fulfill your life; and each day, you, little children, will be, above all, witnesses of serving God in adoration and of your neighbor in need. I am with you and intercede for all of you. Thank you for having responded to my call."*

October 25, 2015 *"Dear children! Also today, my prayer is for all of you, especially for all those who have become hard of heart to my call. You are living in the days of grace and are not conscious of the gifts which God is giving to you through my presence.*

Little children, decide also today for holiness and take the example of the saints of this time and you will see that holiness is a reality for all of you. Rejoice in the love, little children, that in the eyes of God you are unrepeatable and irreplaceable, because you are God's joy in this world. Witness peace, prayer and love. Thank you for having responded to my call."

November 25, 2015 *"Dear children! Today I am calling all of you: pray for my intentions. Peace is in danger, therefore, little children, pray and be carriers of peace and hope in this restless world where Satan is attacking and tempting in every way. Little children, be firm in prayer and courageous in faith. I am with you and intercede before my Son Jesus for all of you. Thank you for having responded to my call."*

December 25, 2015 *"Dear children! Also today I am carrying my Son Jesus to you and from this embrace I am giving you His peace and a longing for Heaven. I am praying with you for peace and am calling you to be peace. I am blessing all of you with my motherly blessing of peace. Thank you for having responded to my call."*

2016

January 25, 2016 *"Dear children! Also today I am calling all of you to prayer. You cannot live without prayer, because prayer is a chain which brings you closer to God. Therefore, little children, in humility of heart return to God and to His commandments so that with all of your heart you are able to say: as it is in Heaven so may it be on earth. You, little children, are free to in freedom decide for God or against Him. See where Satan wants to pull you into sin and slavery. Therefore, little children, return to my heart so that I can lead you to my Son Jesus who is the Way, the Truth and the Life. Thank you for having responded to my call."*

February 25, 2016 *"Dear children! In this time of grace, I am calling all of you to conversion. Little children, you love little and pray even less. You are lost and do not know what your goal is. Take the cross, look at Jesus and follow Him. He gives Himself to you to the death on the cross, because He loves you. Little children, I am calling you: return to prayer with the heart so as to find hope and the meaning of your existence, in prayer. I am with you and am praying for you. Thank you for having responded to my call."*

March 25, 2016 *"Dear children! Today I am carrying my love to you. God permitted me to love you and, out of love, to call you to conversion. You, little children, are poor in love and you still have not comprehended that my Son Jesus, out of love, gave His life to save you and to give you eternal life. Therefore, pray, little children, pray so that in prayer you may comprehend God's love. Thank you for having responded to my call."*

April 25, 2016 *"Dear children! My Immaculate Heart bleeds as I look at you in sin and sinful habits. I am calling you: return to God and to prayer that it may be good for you on earth. God is calling you through me for your hearts to be hope and joy for all those who are far away. May my call be for you a balm for the soul and heart so that you may glorify God, the Creator, who loves you and is calling you to eternity. Little children, life is short; you, make good use of this time and do what is good. Thank you for having responded to my call."*

May 25, 2016 *"Dear children! My presence is a gift from God for all of you and an encouragement for conversion. Satan is strong and wants to put disorder and unrest in your hearts and thoughts. Therefore, you, little children, pray so that the Holy Spirit may lead you on the real way of joy and peace. I am with you and intercede before my Son for you. Thank you for having responded to my call."*

June 25, 2016 *"Dear children! Give thanks to God with me for the gift of my being with you. Pray, little children, and live God's commandments that it may be good for you on earth. Today, on this day of grace, I desire to give you my motherly blessing of peace and of my love. I intercede for you with my Son and call you to persevere in prayer so that, with you, I can realize my plans. Thank you for having responded to my call."*

July 25, 2016 *"Dear children! I am looking at you and I see you lost; and you do not have prayer or joy in your heart. Return to prayer, little children, and put God in the first place and not man. Do not lose the hope which I am carrying to you. May this time, little children, every day, be a greater seeking of God in the silence of your heart; and pray, pray, pray until prayer becomes joy for you. Thank you for having responded to my call."*

August 25, 2016 *"Dear children! Today I desire to share Heavenly joy with you. You, little children, open the door of your heart so that hope, peace and love, which only God gives, may grow in your heart. Little children, you are too bound to the earth and earthly things, that is why, Satan is rolling you like the wind rolls the waves of the sea. Therefore, may the chain of your life be prayer with the heart and Adoration of my Son Jesus. Give over your future to Him so that, in Him, you may be joy and an example with your lives to others. Thank you for having responded to my call."*

September 25, 2016 *"Dear children! Today, I am calling you to prayer. May prayer be life to you. Only in this way will your heart be filled with peace and joy. God will be near you and you will feel Him in your heart as a friend. You will speak with Him as with someone whom you know and, little children, you will have a need to witness, because Jesus will be in your heart and you, united in Him. I am with you and love all of you with my motherly love. Thank you for having responded to my call."*

October 25, 2016 *"Dear children! Today I am calling you: pray for peace. Leave selfishness and live the messages which I am giving you. Without them, you cannot change your life. By living prayer, you will have peace. By living in peace, you will feel the need to witness, because you will discover God whom you now feel to be far away. Therefore, little children, pray, pray, pray and permit God to enter into your hearts. Return to fasting and confession so as to overcome the evil in you and around you. Thank you for having responded to my call."*

November 25, 2016 *"Dear children! Also today, I am calling you to return to prayer. In this time of grace, God has permitted me to lead you towards holiness and a simple life - that in little things you discover God the Creator; that you fall in love with Him; and that your life be a thanksgiving to the Most High for everything He is giving you. Little children, in love, may your life be a gift for others and God will bless you; but you, witness without interest - out of love for God. I am with you and intercede before my Son for all of you. Thank you for having responded to my call."*

December 25, 2016 *"Dear children! With great joy, today I am carrying my Son Jesus to you, for Him to give you His peace. Open your hearts, little children, and be joyful that you can receive it. Heaven is with you and is fighting for peace in your hearts, in the families and in the world; and you, little children, help with your prayers for it to be so. I bless you with my Son Jesus and call you not to lose hope; and for your gaze and heart to always be directed towards Heaven and eternity. In this way, you will be open to God and to His plans. Thank you for having responded to my call."*

2017

January 25, 2017 *"Dear children! Today I am calling you to pray for peace: peace in human hearts, peace in the families and peace in the world. Satan is strong and wants to turn all of you against God, and to return you to everything that is human, and to destroy in the heart all feelings towards God and the things of God. You, little children, pray and fight against materialism, modernism and egoism, which the world offers to you. Little children, you decide for holiness and I, with my Son Jesus, intercede for you. Thank you for having responded to my call."*

February 25, 2017 *"Dear children! Today I am calling you to profoundly live your faith and to implore the Most High to strengthen it, so that winds and storms cannot break it. May the roots of your faith be prayer and hope in eternal life. Already now, little children, work on yourselves in this time of grace, wherein God is giving you the grace - through renunciation and the call to conversion - to be people of clear and persevering faith and hope. Thank you for having responded to my call."*

March 25, 2017 *"Dear children! In this time of grace, I am calling all of you to open your hearts to God's mercy, to begin a new life through prayer, penance and a decision for holiness. This time of spring moves you to a new life, to a renewal, in your thoughts and hearts. Therefore, little children, I am with you to help you to say 'yes' to God and to God's commandments with resoluteness. You are not alone; I am with you through the grace which the Most High gives me for you and your descendants. Thank you for having responded to my call."*

Messages Collected by Various Authors 1981-1987

Fr. Svetozar Kraljevic (1983)

Our Lady tells the visionaries:

"I know that many will not believe you, and that many who have an impassioned faith will cool off. You remain firm, and motivate people to instant prayer, penance, and conversion. At the end, you will be happier."

"In God differences do not exist among his people; religion need not separate people. Every person must be respected, despite his or her particular profession of faith."

"God presides over all religions, as a king controls his subjects, through his priests and ministers. The sole mediator of salvation is Jesus Christ."

Do differences exist among the believers of different churches? (A question asked in reference to a certain Protestant community.)

"It is not equally efficacious to belong to or pray in any church or community, because the Holy Spirit grants his power differently among the churches and ministers. All believers do not pray the same way. It is intentional that all apparitions are under the auspices of the Catholic Church."

To the visionaries:

"When you will suffer difficulties and need something, come to me."

"I cannot cure. God alone cures. Pray! I will pray with you. Believe firmly. Fast; do penance. I will help you as long as it is in my power to do it. God comes to help everyone. I am not God. I need your sacrifices and your prayers to help me."

"Faith cannot be alive without prayer."

"The Mass is the greatest prayer of God. You will never be able to understand its greatness. That is why you must be perfect and humble at Mass, and you should prepare yourselves there."

For a priest who questions, "Is it preferable to pray to you or to pray to Jesus?"
"I beseech you, pray to Jesus! I am His Mother, and I intercede for you with Him. But all prayers go to Jesus. I will help, I will pray, but everything does not depend solely on me, but also on your strength and the strength of those who pray."

With respect to the souls in Purgatory:
"These persons wait for your prayers and your sacrifices."

"The most beautiful prayer is the Creed."

"The most important thing is to believe."

"All prayers are good, if they are said with faith."

"My Son wants to win all souls to Him, but the devil strives to obtain something. The devil makes a great effort to infiltrate among you at all costs."

Conversation with Fr. Bonifacio and Fr. Petar Ljubicic:
"It does not suffice to pray. You must change your life, your heart. Love the others; have love for others. Love what you do and always think about Jesus, and you will understand what is good and what is bad."

Fr. Janko Bubalo (1981)
Vicka, "At the very beginning, the Gospa tells us,
'You may leave, but let little Jakov stay with me.'
And Vicka adds, "Jakov is an extraordinary boy, and the Gospa knew it."

To Mirjana:
"My Son struggles for each of you, but Satan fights Him also. He prowls around you, sets traps for you. He tries to divide you, you the visionaries, to plant discord among you, to confuse you so you will detest yourselves, and will abandon yourselves to him."

Vicka adds, "Our Lady has said it to us on several occasions."

Frigerio Botta (1984)

"The world can only be saved through peace. But it will only have peace in its meeting with God."

"The world lives amidst very strong tensions. It is on the edge of catastrophe."

"I have come here because there are many believers. I want to remain with you in order to convert many and to bring peace to everyone. Begin by loving your enemies. Do not judge, do not slander, and do not despise, but give only love. Bless your adversaries and pray for them. I know well that you are not capable of doing it; I advise you to pray each day at least five minutes to the Sacred Heart, so that you can receive the gift of Divine Love, with which you will be able to love your enemies."

"It is necessary to convert oneself to God in order to obtain peace. Tell the whole world; tell it without delay, that I ardently wish conversion. Be converted; do not wait. I will ask my Son that He not chastise the world. Convert yourselves, renounce everything, and be ready for everything."

"Do not go in search of extraordinary ways; take rather the Gospel and read it. There everything will be clear."

"You only learn to pray through praying."

"Offer your time to God and let yourself be guided by the Holy Spirit. Then your work will go well, and you will have free time. Those who abandon themselves to God do not have a place in their hearts for fear. The difficulties which you will face will contribute to your growth and to the glory of the Lord. For that, reject fear."

"Prayer always leads to peace and serenity."

"No one is dispensed from fasting, except those who are gravely ill. Prayer and works of charity cannot replace fasting. I recommend to you in a special way to attend Holy Mass every day."

"Mass represents the highest form of prayer. You must be humble and respectful during Holy Mass and prepare yourself for it with care."

"May the Holy Father announce with courage, peace, and love to the world. May He not consider Himself the Father of Catholics, but of all mankind."

Andre Castella (1984-85)

Reported by Mirjana:

"Tell the faithful that I need their prayers and prayers from all the people. It is necessary to pray as much as possible and do penance, because very few people have been converted up until now. There are many Christians who live like pagans. There are always so few, true believers."

To the priest who asked what they should do:

"Carry out well your responsibility, and do what the Church asks you to do."

One day the Gospa reproached Jakov for his behavior at school towards his friends.

"You must love them all."

"I love them all. But they are so annoying to me."

"Then accept it as a sacrifice and offer it."

A group of seminarians from Zagreb and Djakovo, attended an apparition.

Marija: "The Gospa looked at each one of us, and told us with a smile: *'Tell them that with prayer one obtains everything.'"*

Our Lady received a young nun with open arms, while she kept her hands joined before the others. Questioned by Mirjana, Our Lady said,

"I will take with me very soon all those to whom I extended my arms."

To a nun who asked about her brother, who had died in an accident,

"I understand the question. He died in the state of grace. He needs Masses and prayers."

Asked by the visionaries why she had chosen them, Our Lady replied,

"I do not choose the best. Are you angry with my choice, my angels?"

Mirjana reports to a religious, a close friend, this word from the Gospa,

"The hour has come when the demon is authorized to act with all his force and power. The present hour is the hour of Satan."

"Many pretend to see Jesus and the Mother of God and to understand their words, but they are, in fact, lying. It is a very grave sin, and it is necessary to pray very much for them."

"I am anxious for people to know what is happening in Medjugorje. Speak about it so that all will be converted."

To the visionaries who ask regarding the apparitions and their purpose,
"Is it, after all, that I bore you? Everything passes exactly according to God's plan. Have patience; persevere in prayer and in penance. Everything happens in its own time."

Regarding a Catholic priest, confused because of the cure of an Orthodox child,
"Tell this priest, tell everyone, that it is you who are divided on earth. The Muslims and the Orthodox, for the same reason as Catholics, are equal before my Son and me. You are all my children. Certainly, all religions are not equal, but all men are equal before God, as St. Paul says. It does not suffice to belong to the Catholic Church to be saved, but it is necessary to respect the commandments of God in following one's conscience. Those who are not Catholics are no less creatures made in the image of God, and are destined to rejoin someday the House of the Father. Salvation is available to everyone, without exception. Only those who refuse God deliberately are condemned. To him, who has been given little, little will be asked for. To whomever has been given much (to Catholics), very much will be required. It is God alone, in His infinite justice, who determines the degree of responsibility and pronounces judgment."

Fr. Robert Faricy (1985)
On the subject of Christ,
"I am His Mother, and I intercede for you, near to Him."

George Totto (1985)
"Let the faithful meditate each day on the life of Jesus while praying the Rosary."

"Every prayer which comes from the heart is agreeable to God."

"You do not celebrate the Eucharist as you should. If you would know what grace and what gifts you receive, you would prepare yourselves for it each day for an hour at least. You should go to confession once a month. You should consecrate three days to reconciliation each month: the first Friday of the month, followed by Saturday, and Sunday."

The parish at Medjugorje had established an hour of adoration before the Most Blessed Sacrament the first Friday of the month. On the Saturday which followed, an hour of devotion before the cross, with prayers for sinners, was established. And on Sunday, the Holy Mass was followed by a meal of reconciliation.

Yves-Maria Blais (1986)

"I do not have the right to impose on anyone what they should do. You have reason and a will. You should, after having prayed, reflect and decide."

"Receive the peace of my Son. Live it and spread it."

"Permit Jesus to perform great works in you. The lock of the door of your heart is rusted. Permit Him to open it. May it be open through your prayer, your fasting, your conversion."

"Pray slowly and meditate while saying the prayers of the rosary. Take a quarter of an hour to recite five Our Father's, Hail Mary's, and Glory Be's."

"I love you so much. And if you love me, you will be able to feel it. I bless you in the name of the Most Holy Trinity and in my name. Remain in peace."

"You will find everything in the Gospels."

"Let the word of God begin to speak in your heart."

"Begin to love your enemies. Do not judge or slander. Do not scorn. Do not curse. Only give your adversaries love. Bless them and pray for them. I know that you are not capable of doing it, but I advise you to pray each day at least five minutes to the Sacred Heart, so that He can give you Divine love, with which you will be able to love even your enemies."

"You can direct your prayers not only to those who are already in Heaven, but also to those who are in Purgatory, because with their prayer, they can help you to reach eternal happiness."

"One must follow the authority of the Church with certainty. Yet, before she expresses an opinion, it is necessary to advance spiritually, because she will not be able to express a judgment in a vacuum, but in a confirmation which presupposes growth of the child. First comes birth, followed by Baptism, then Confirmation. The Church comes to confirm him who is born of God. We must walk and advance in the spiritual life, affected by these messages."

Dr. Mark Miravalle (1986)

Before December, 1983:

"So many believers never pray. Have the people pray! Faith cannot be alive without prayer."

"I am not able to cure you. God alone can cure you. Pray! I will pray with you. Believe firmly, fast, do penance. God comes to help each one. I am not God. I need your prayers and your sacrifices to help me."

"You do not need a sign; you yourselves must be a sign."

"Peace is necessary for prayer. Peace should be present before prayer, and while one is praying. Prayer should, of course, lead to peace and reflection."

"Why ask so many questions? The answer is found in the Gospels."

Between June and December, 1984:

"Dear children, the love of God has not spread over all the earth. That is why, pray!"

"Dear children, I wish that the whole world become my children, but they do not want to. I want to give them all things. That is why, pray!"

"Dear children, I love you so much. When you love me, you will be able to feel it. I bless you in the name of the Most Holy Trinity and in my name. Go in peace."

Boa Nova

"These are my last apparitions to mankind. With the events which are preparing themselves, and which are near, the power which Satan still holds will be withdrawn from him. The present century has been under his power. Now that he is conscious of losing the battle, he is becoming more aggressive. He attacks the family, separates husband and wife. He creates divisions among the priests, and even gives himself to physical attacks. Protect yourselves, above all, through prayer, through blessed sacred objects, through community prayer."

(1987)
"Love your Serbian, Orthodox and Muslim brothers, and the atheists who persecute you."

Concerning information from Bishop Franic:
"All your prayers touch me very much, especially your daily Rosary."

Fr. Tomislav Vlasic and Fr. Slavko Barbaric
The exact dates of these messages are not known, but span Sep 1983 - Sep 1986.

"I've already said many times, that peace in the world is in a state of crisis. Become again brothers to one another. Pray and fast more in order to be saved."

"Pray, fast, and let God act."

"If you want to be very happy, lead a simple, humble life, pray very much, and do not sink into problems. Let God resolve them."

"Peace should follow your prayer."

"Often prayer said in a loud voice keeps Jesus at a distance, because men want to conquer with their own strength. Then there is no more place for God. Prayers said in a loud voice are good, but they must come from peace in the heart."

"Even joy and songs can hinder the rise of the groups, if the people deliver themselves only to emotion."

"When I tell you, pray, pray, do not understand it only as an increase in quantity. What I want is to carry you to a profound continuous desire of God."

"The most important thing is to believe, that is, to open one's self to God; pray and fast."

Response from Our Lady to two questions from Fr. Tomislav Vlasic:
"Have you come to purify the new renewal movements, which are multiplying?"
"It is exactly so."

"How could Jesus pray all night without getting tired? What was His method?"
"He had a great desire for God and for the salvation of souls. Prayer is a dialogue with God, a meeting with the Gospel."

"What do you say about Oriental meditations? (Zen, Transcendental meditation),"
"Why do you call them 'meditations', when it deals with human works? The true meditation is a meeting with Jesus. When you discover joy, interior peace, you must know there is only one God and only one Mediator, Jesus Christ."

"Your days will not be the same according to whether you pray, or you do not pray."

Responses to questions asked by the visionaries at the request of Fr. Tomislav Vlasic:
"What do you tell the priests and religious?"
"Be strong in faith and protect the faith of your people."

"What do you advise us for Advent?"
"Do what the Church tells you."

"Do you want to give a sign for priests?"
"Have them take the Gospel, and they will understand everything. Go to the heart. Words are not sufficient. Go to the heart."

In autumn 1983 Our Lady said,
"I would be happy for people, families, to pray a minimum of half-an-hour in the morning and in the evening."
"The people shook their heads at this," stated Fr. Tomislav.

In the spring of 1984, Our Lady said,

"I know that in the parish and in all the parishes, you can pray four hours a day, but you do not understand it yet because you live only for your work. One does not live from work alone, but also from prayer."

"When I objected to Her, 'If one asks so much, people will go away,' She replied, *"Not even you understand. That makes hardly a sixth of your day."*

"You do not think of wars, of evil, of chastisements. If you think about evil, you are on the road where one meets it. Your role is to accept Divine peace, to live it, and spread it."

(1985) To Ivan's prayer group,
"Even the little things, entrust them to me. Consecrate them to my mission."

To the question, "How does one behave before Satan?"
"Fervent prayer, humility, reciprocal love will prevent Satan from approaching you."

To a question conveyed through Fr. Tomislav Vlasic at the beginning of Lent, 1985, "What do you most wish for the fast?" Our Lady responds insisting on something else:
"Honesty, love, humility, and sincerity will lead you to me."

"What should one do in the midst of so many discussions and publications on Medjugorje?"
"See! Now I am there, in each family, in each home. I am everywhere because I love. Do the same. The world lives from love."

After having repeated a song three times:
"Excuse me for making you repeat, but I wish you to sing with the heart. You must really do everything with the heart."

"One has to be already prepared. If there are some sins, one must pull them out; otherwise, one will not be able to enter into prayer. If one has concerns, he should submit them to God."

That same evening She said:

"Take off your jackets. Here it is warm. Remember what Jesus said, 'Have faith.' You must abandon yourselves to God. You must not preoccupy yourselves during prayer. During prayer you must not be preoccupied with your sins. Sins must remain behind. Many come to pray but do not enter into prayer. When you have entered into prayer, then you are able to pray for God's plans, because when God is there, he inspires your plans. Do not ask for the blessing, just as you have done the last time. You asked for it, and you did not obtain it."

(Because it is not a magic thing, she crowns what God has inspired in you in prayer, observes Fr. Tomislav Vlasic.)

"Prayer must be enjoyment in God; blossoming in God, be full of peace, be full of joy."

"Many Christians do not ever enter into prayer. They arrive at the beginning, but they remain there." (If you enter into prayer after you have been relieved of all your concerns, remorse, analysis), *"Then you will be able to ask God to inspire your plans from within. You will feel what God wants,"* (inside of you, yourself and your group), *"and then ask for the blessing."*

"Your work will not go well without prayer in the morning. Pray then in the morning, and pray in the evening. Understand that your work cannot be done well without prayer."

"Come early to church. Sometimes it is better not to come to Mass than to come in a hurry and to return home in a hurry."

"These apparitions are the last for humanity."

Against temptations of analysis, which are temptations from the devil,
"With respect to sin, it suffices to give it serious consideration, and soon, move ahead and correct the sin."

"Your humility must be proud (high minded). Your pride should be humble. If you have received a gift from God, you must be proud, but do not say that it is yours. Say, rather, that it is God's."

To Mirjana in 1984 (Probably Aug-Sep),
"Every adult is capable of knowing God. The sin of the world lies in this: It does not look for God."

To Marija, during her one week retreat in September, and in response to her question, "Have you anything concrete for me?"
"Yes. I give you my love so that you can give it to others."

Our Lady said with sadness:
"Those who say, 'I do not believe in God', how difficult it will be for them when they will approach the Throne of God and hear the voice, 'Enter into Hell'."

To a group that was praying for a person in crisis,
"You cannot do anything. I can change her. You must only love her. Do not create any barriers in her life, because as long as there are barriers, the river foams and rises. Leave her free, like the river. Do not build any more bridges, because as long as one builds bridges, the river is restricted and does not flow freely. Leave her free to flow like the river flows."

A month later the group, frustrated in its prayer, asks, "But how is it that this girl (in crisis) does not change?" Answer, after a long moment of prayer,
"Let her run like the river. Do not create any barriers. Do not build any bridges. Consider well and see how many barriers you have already created, how many bridges you have built. Be attentive not to close her. This young girl is at the point of opening up. She has confidence in you. Be patient still. Understand that you can do nothing. You must only love and leave everything to me."

To Marija, for her prayer group,
"Dear children, seek to make your hearts happy through the means of prayer. Dear children, be the joy for all mankind; be the hope of mankind. You will only be able to obtain it through the means of prayer. Pray, pray!"

"Many have begun to pray for healing here at Medjugorje, but, when they have returned to their homes, they abandon prayer, forget, and also lose many graces."

To Vicka:
"Do you want to offer yourself also for the salvation of the world? I need your sacrifices."

Mirjana's 2nd of the Month Messages

October 2, 2004 *"Dear children, today watching you with a heart full of love, I want to tell you that what you persistently seek, what you long for, my little children, is before you. It is sufficient with a clean heart to put my Son in the first place, and then you will see. Listen to me, and let me lead you on this motherly way."*

November 2, 2004 *"Dear children, I need you. I call you and ask for your help. Make peace with yourselves, with God, and with your neighbors. Then help me. Convert unbelievers. Wipe the tears from my face."*

December 2, 2004 *"Dear children, I come to you as a mother, who, above all, loves her children. My children, I want to teach you to love! I pray for this! I pray that in each of your neighbors you recognize my Son, because the path to my Son, who is true peace and love, leads you through love towards your neighbors. My children, pray and fast that your hearts be open for this, my intention."*

January 2, 2005 *"Dear children, my motherly heart begs you to accept prayer, because it is your salvation! Pray, pray, pray, my children."*

March 2, 2005 *"Dear children, do as I do! Come, give your love and give everyone an example of my Son!"*

April 2, 2005 Mirjana, "I would not call this a message. Our Lady blessed everyone and all the things that were to be blessed, with her motherly blessing, but she again stressed that the most important blessing is from the priest."

- Our Lady said: *"At this point I'm asking you to renew the Church!"*
- Mirjana asked: "Is this possible? Can we do it?"
- Our Lady replied, *"My children, I will be with you. My Apostles, I'll be with you and help you. Renew first yourself and your family, and then everything will be easier."*
- Then Mirjana said, "Then, Mother, just be with us."

May 2, 2005 *"Dear children, I am with you so that I can take you all to my Son. I wish to lead you all to salvation. Follow me, because in just this way you will find true peace and happiness. My little children, come with me!"*

July 2, 2005 *"Dear Children, as your mother, I rejoice with you, for as a mother I invited you. I am bringing My Son to you, My Son, Your God. Cleanse your hearts and bow your head before your only God. Let my motherly heart leap with joy. Thank you."*

August 2, 2005 *"Dear children, I came to you with open arms, so that I could take you all into my arms, under my mantle. I cannot do this while your hearts are filled with false light and false idols. Cleanse them, and let my angels sing in them. Then I will take you under my mantle and give you my Son, true peace, and happiness. Do not wait, my children. Thank you!"*

September 2, 2005 *"Dear children, I, as a mother come to and am showing you how much your God, your Father loves you. And you? Where are you, my children? What takes the first place in your hearts? Why do you not put my Son in first place? My children, allow God's blessings to fall upon you. Let God's peace overcome you, peace that my Son gives, only He."*

October 2, 2005 *"Dear children, I come to you as a mother. I bring you my Son, peace, and love. Cleanse your hearts, and take my Son with you. Give others this true peace and happiness."*

December 2, 2005 *"Dear children, let it be at this holy time that love and the grace of my Son descend upon you. Only a pure heart, filled with prayer and compassion, can feel the love of my Son. Pray for those who do not have the grace to feel the love of my Son. My children, help me! Thank you."*

January 2, 2006 *"Dear children, My Son was born! Your Savior is here with you! What prevents your hearts from accepting Him? What is it that is false within your hearts? Cleanse them with fasting and prayer. Recognize and accept my Son. Only He can give you true peace and true love. The path to eternal life is He, my Son. Thank you."*

March 2, 2006 "She greeted us sadly with, *'Praised be Jesus.'* She blessed all articles that we brought to be blessed and all those present. She talked to me about the situation in the world, with emphasis on those who did not know the love of God. Three times she repeated, *'God is love!'* I asked her some questions about the sick and the like, and Our Lady responded."

April 2, 2006 *"Dear Children, I am coming to you because, with my own example, I wish to show you the importance of prayer for those who have not come to know the love of God. You ask yourself if you are following me? My children, do you not recognize the signs of the times? Do you not speak of them? Come follow me. As a mother I call you. Thank you for having responded."*

May 2, 2006 *"Dear Children, I am coming to you as a mother. I am coming with an open heart full of love for you. My children, cleanse your hearts from everything that prevents you from receiving me, from recognizing the love of my Son. Through you, my heart desires to win, desires to triumph. Open your hearts. I will lead you to this. Thank you."*

June 2, 2006 Mirjana, *"Our Lady blessed all present and all religious articles that we brought for blessing. With a serious expression on her face, she emphasized once again the priestly blessing. With pain and love she said: 'Remember my children; that is my Son blessing you. Do not accept this so lightly.' After that Our Lady talked about some things that are supposed to happen, and She said, 'There is no path without my Son. Do not think that you will have peace and joy if He is not in first place.' Our Lady was not sad or joyful; I would say that she was more concerned with a look of care on her face."*

July 2, 2006 *"Dear Children, God created you with free will to comprehend and to choose life or death. I as a mother, with motherly love, desire to help you to comprehend and to choose life. My children, do not deceive yourselves with false peace and false joy. Permit me, my children, to show you the true way, the way that leads to life, my Son. Thank you."*

August 2, 2006 *"Dear Children! In these peaceless times I am coming to you to show you the way to peace. I love you with an immeasurable love and I desire for you to love each other and to see in everyone my Son, the immeasurable love. The way to peace leads solely and only through love. Give your hand to me, your mother, and permit me to lead you. I am the Queen of Peace. Thank you."*

September 2, 2006 Our Lady said the following: *"You know that we have been gathering for me to help you to come to know the love of God."*

Our Lady then spoke about the future and said:

"I am gathering you under my motherly mantle to help you to come to know God's love and His greatness. My children, God is great. Great are His works. Do not deceive yourselves that you can do anything without Him, not even to take a step. My children, instead set out and witness His love. I am with you. Thank you."

October 2, 2006 *"Dear Children! I am coming to you in this your time to direct the call to eternity to you. This is the call of love. I call you to love because only through love will you come to know the love of God. Many think that they have faith in God and that they know His laws. They try to live according to them; but they do not do what is the most important; they do not love Him. My children, pray and fast. This is the way which will help you to open yourselves and to love. Only through the love of God is eternity gained. I am with you. I will lead you with the motherly love. Thank you for having responded."*

Our Lady added at the end:

"My children, priests' hands are the blessed hands of my Son. Respect them."

November 2, 2006 *Dear Children! My coming to you, my children, is God's love. God is sending me to warn you and to show you the right way. Do not shut your eyes before the truth, my children. Your time is a short time. Do not permit delusions to begin to rule over you. The way on which I desire to lead you is the way of peace and love. This is the way which leads to my Son, your God. Give me your hearts that I may put my Son in them and make my apostles of you, apostles of peace and love. Thank you."*

Afterwards, in conclusion, Our Lady said for us not to forget our shepherds in our prayers.

December 2, 2006 *"Dear Children! In this joyful time of expectation of my Son, I desire that all the days of your earthly life may be a joyful expectation of my Son. I am calling you to holiness. I call you to be my apostles of holiness so that, through you, the Good News may illuminate all those whom you will meet. Fast and pray, and I will be with you. Thank you."*

January 2, 2007 *"Dear Children! In this holy time full of God's graces and His love which sends me to you, I implore you not to have a heart of stone. May fasting and prayer be your weapon for drawing closer to and coming to know Jesus, my Son. Follow me and my luminous example. I will help you. I am with you. Thank you."*

Mirjana added: *The expression on Our Lady's face during the entire time was one of pain and sorrow. She spoke to me of things I cannot yet speak of. She blessed us and the religious articles. The expression on her face was especially serious when she was emphasizing the priestly blessing and asked for prayer and fasting for them.*

March 2, 2007 The apparition lasted three to four minutes. Our Lady was resolute. She said:

"Today I will speak to you about what you have forgotten"

"Dear Children! My name is love. That I am among you for so much of your time is love, because the Great Love sends me. I am asking the same of you. I am asking for love in your families. I am asking that you recognize love in your brother. Only in this way, through love, will you see the face of the Greatest Love. May fasting and prayer be your guiding star. Open your hearts to love, namely salvation. Thank you."

April 2, 2007 *"Dear children, do not be hard hearted towards the mercy of God, which has been pouring out upon you for so long a time. In this special time of prayer, permit me to transform your hearts so that you may help me to have my Son resurrect in all hearts and that my heart may triumph. Thank you!"*

243

Mirjana, "Our Lady added, '*Your shepherds need your prayers.*' Our Lady blessed all of us, and all religious articles, and once again emphasized that She gives her motherly blessing. But the greatest blessing is the blessing from the priests."

May 2, 2007 *"Dear children, today I come to you with a motherly desire that you give me your hearts. My children, do so with complete confidence and without fear. I will put in your hearts my Son and His mercy. Then you, my children, with different eyes see the world around you. You will see your neighbor. You will feel his pain and suffering. You will not turn your head from those who suffer, because my Son is turning their heads. Children, do not hesitate."*

Mirjana, "Our Lady blessed everyone and all religious articles."

June 2, 2007 *"Dear children! Also in this difficult time God's love sends me to you. My children, do not be afraid; I am with you. With complete trust give me your hearts, that I may help you to recognize the signs of the time in which you live. I will help you to come to know the love of my Son. I will triumph through you. Thank you."*

Mirjana, "Our Lady blessed all of us, and all religious articles brought for blessing. Once again She reminded us to pray for priests, and that a priest's blessing is a blessing from Her Son Jesus."

July 2, 2007 *"Dear children! In the great love of God, I come to you today to lead you on the way of humility and meekness. The first station on that way, my children, is confession. Reject your arrogance and kneel down before my Son. Comprehend, my children, that you have nothing, and you can do nothing. The only thing that you have and that you possess is sin. Be cleansed and accept meekness and humility. My Son could have won with strength, but He chose meekness, humility, and love. Follow my Son and give me your hands so that together we may climb the mountain and win. Thank you."*

Mirjana, "Again Our Lady spoke about the importance of priests and their blessing. Our Lady referred to this as a spiritual climb."

August 2, 2007 *"Dear children, today I look in your hearts, and looking at them my heart trembles with pain. My children! I desire from you unconditional, pure love for God. You will know that you are on the right path when with your body you are on the earth, and with your soul you are always with God. Through this unconditional and pure love you will see my Son in every person. You will feel in union with God. As a Mother I will be happy because I will have your holy and unified hearts. My children, I will have your salvation. Thank you."*

At the beginning of the apparition Our Lady showed Mirjana what is waiting for us if there is not holiness in our hearts and our brotherly union in Christ. It was not nice. She asked us to pray for our shepherds because she said that without them there is no unity.

September 2, 2007 *"Dear children, in this time of God's signs, do not be afraid because I am with you. The great love of God sends me to lead you to salvation. Give me your simple hearts, purified by fasting and prayer. Only in the simplicity of your hearts is your salvation. I will be with you and lead you. Thank you."*

Mirjana, "Our Lady blessed everyone and all of the religious articles."

October 2, 2007 *"Dear children, I call you to accompany me in my mission of God with an open heart and complete trust. The path on which I lead you towards God is difficult, but persevere, and in the end we will all rejoice in God. Therefore, my children, do not stop praying for the gift of faith. Only faith in God's Word will be the light in this darkness which desires to envelop us. Do not be afraid; I am with you. Thank you."*

Mirjana described that at the end of the apparition, she saw an intense strong light as Heaven was opening, and Our Lady was entering into Heaven through that light.

November 2, 2007 *"Dear children, today I call you to open your hearts to the Holy Spirit and permit Him to transform you. My children, God is the immeasurable good, and, therefore, as a mother, I implore you to pray, pray, pray, fast, and hope that it is possible to achieve good, because from that good love is born. The Holy Spirit will strengthen that love in you, and you will be able to call God your Father. Through this*

245

exalted love, you will truly come to love all people and, through God, you will regard them as brothers and sisters. Thank you."

Mirjana, "While Our Lady was blessing, She said: *'On the way on which I lead you to my Son, those who represent Him walk beside me.'"*

December 2, 2007 Mirjana:"She blessed all of us, and all religious articles. Our Lady was very sad. All the time her eyes were filled with tears."

"Dear children, today, while I am looking at your hearts, my heart is filled with pain and trepidation. My children, stop for a moment and look into your hearts. Is my Son, your God truly in first place? Are His commandments truly the measure of your life? I am warning you again: without faith there is neither closeness of God nor the Word of God, which is the light of salvation and the light of common sense."
Mirjana added, "I painfully asked Our Lady not to leave us, and not to take her hands away from us. She painfully smiled at my request and left. This time Our Lady did not say, 'Thank you.'"

January 2, 2008 *"Dear children, with all the strength of my heart, I love you and give myself to you. As a mother fights for her children, I pray and fight for you. I ask you not to be afraid to open yourselves so as to be able to love with the heart and give yourselves to others. The more that you do this with the heart, the more you will receive, and the better you will understand my Son and His gift to you. Through the love of my Son and me, may you all be recognized. Thank you."*

Mirjana, "Our Lady blessed all those present and religious articles brought for blessing. She asked for prayer and fasting for our shepherds."

February 2, 2008 *"Dear children, I am with you. As a mother I am gathering you because I want to erase from your hearts that which I see now. Accept the love of my Son and erase from your hearts fear, pain, suffering, and disappointment. I have chosen you in a special way to be a light of the love of my Son. Thank you."*

March 2, 2008 *"Dear children, please especially during this Lenten season respond to God's goodness, because He has chosen you, and me He has sent to be among you. Cleanse yourselves of sin, and in Jesus, my Son, recognize the peaceful sacrifice for the* *sins of the whole world. Let Him be the purpose of your lives. May your lives be in service of the Divine love of my Son. Thank you, my children."*

Mirjana, "Our Lady blessed us all and all our religious articles, and again, She asked us to pray for our Shepherds."

April 2, 2008 *"Dear children, again today as I am with you in the great love of God, I desire to ask you, 'Are you also with me? Are your hearts open for me? Do you permit me with my love to purify and prepare them for my Son?' My children, you have been chosen because, in your time, the great grace of God has descended on earth. Do not hesitate to accept it. Thank you."*

Mirjana, "Our Lady blessed everyone present and all the religious articles. As she was leaving, behind her in the blueness was a most beautiful warm light."

May 2, 2008 *"Dear children, by God's will I am here with you in this place. I desire that you open your hearts to me and to accept me as a mother. With my love I will teach you simplicity of life and richness of mercy, and I will lead you to my Son. The way to Him can be difficult and painful, but do not be afraid, I will be with you. My hands will hold you to the very end, to eternal happiness; therefore, do not be afraid to open yourselves to me. Thank you. Pray for priests. My Son gave them to you as a gift."*

June 2, 2008 *"Dear children, I am with you by the grace of God, to make you great, great in faith and love, all of you. You whose hearts have been made hard as a stone by sin and guilt, and you devout souls, I desire to illuminate with a new light. Pray that my prayer may meet open hearts, that I may be able to illuminate them with the strength of faith and open the ways of love and hope. Be persevering. I will be with you."*

Mirjana, "Our Lady blessed all those present, and all religious articles brought for blessing. As Our Lady said this, She was looking at those present to whom this referred to, with a painful expression and tears in her eyes."

July 2, 2008 *"Dear children, with motherly love I desire to encourage you to love your neighbor. Let my Son be the source of that love. He who could have done everything by force, chose love and gave an example to you. Also today, through me, God expresses to you immeasurable goodness, and you, my children, are obliged to respond to it. Behave with the same goodness and generosity towards the souls whom you meet. May your love convert them. In that way my Son and His love will rise in you. Thank you."*
Our Lady added, *"Your shepherds should be in your hearts and your prayers."*

August 2, 2008 *"Dear children, in my coming to you, here among you, the greatness of God is reflected, and the way with God to eternal happiness is opened. Do not feel weak, alone, or abandoned. With faith, prayer, and love climb to the hill of salvation. May the Mass, the most exalted and most powerful act of your prayer, be the center of your spiritual life. Trust and love, my children. Those whom my Son chose and called will help you in this as well. To you and to them especially, I give my motherly blessing. Thank you."*
Mirjana, "Our Lady blessed all people present, and all religious articles brought for blessing."

September 2, 2008 *"Dear children, today with my motherly heart I call you gathered around me to love your neighbor. My children, stop. Look in the eyes of your brother and see Jesus, my Son. If you see joy, rejoice with him. If there is pain in the eyes of your brother, with your tenderness and goodness, cast it away, because without love you are lost. Only love is effective; it works miracles. Love will give you unity in my Son and victory in my heart. Therefore, my children, love."*

Mirjana, "Our Lady blessed all those who were present, and all of the religious articles. Once again she called us to pray for our shepherds."

October 2, 2008 *"Dear children, again I call you to faith. My motherly heart desires for your heart to be open so that it can say to your heart, 'Believe.' My children, only faith will give you strength in life's trials. It will renew your soul and open the way of hope. I am with you. I gather you around me because I desire to help you, so that you can help your neighbors to discover faith, which is the only joy and happiness of life. Thank you."*

Mirjana, "Our Lady blessed all those present, and all religious articles. Once again she called us to pray for priests, especially at this time."

November 2, 2008 *"Dear children, today I call you to a complete union with God. Your body is on earth, but I ask that your souls, as often as possible, be near to God. You will achieve this through prayer, prayer with an open heart. In that way you will thank God for the immeasurable goodness which He gives to you through me and, with a sincere heart, you will accept the obligation to treat the souls whom you meet with equal goodness. Thank you, my children."*

Our Lady added, *"With the heart I pray to God to give strength and love to your shepherds to help you in this and to lead you."*

December 2, 2008 *"Dear children, in this holy time of joyful expectation, God has chosen you little ones to realize His great intentions. My children, be humble. Through your humility, God, with His wisdom, will make of your souls a chosen home. You will illuminate it with good works and thus, with an open heart, you will welcome the birth of my Son in all of His generous love. Thank you, dear children."*

January 2, 2009 *"Dear children, while great heavenly grace is being lavished upon you, your hearts remain hard and without response. My children, why do you not give me your hearts completely? I only desire to put in them peace and salvation, my Son. With my Son your souls will be directed to noble goals, and you will never get lost. Even in greatest darkness you will find the way. My children, decide for a new life with the name of my Son on your lips. Thank you."*

February 2, 2009 *"Dear children, with a motherly heart today I want to remind you, namely, of God's infinite love and the patience which ensues from it. Your Father sends me and waits. He is waiting for your open hearts, ready for His works. He is waiting for your hearts, united in Christian love and mercy in the spirit of my Son. Do not waste time, children, because you are not the masters of time. Thank you."*

March 2, 2009 *"Dear children, here I am among you. I am looking into your wounded and restless hearts. You have become lost, my children. Your wounds from sin are becoming greater and greater and are distancing you all the more from the real truth. You are seeking hope and consolation in the wrong places, while I am offering you sincere devotion, which is nurtured by love, sacrifice, and truth. I am giving you my Son."*

Mirjana, "Our Lady blessed everyone present, and all the religious articles that were brought to be blessed, and She was sad!"

April 2, 2009 *"Dear children, God's love is in my words. My children, that is the love which desires to turn you to righteousness and truth. That is the love which desires to save you from delusion. And you, my children? Your hearts remain closed; they are hard and do not respond to my calls. They are insincere. With motherly love I am praying for you because I desire for all of you to resurrect in my Son. Thank you."*

May 2, 2009 Mirjana, Our Lady was very sad. She only gave a message and blessed us.

"Dear children! Already for a long time I am giving you my motherly heart and offering my Son to you. You are rejecting me. You are permitting sin to overcome you more and more. You are permitting it to master you and to take away your power of discernment. My poor children, look around you and look at the signs of the times. Do you think that you can do without God's blessing? Do not allow darkness to envelop you. From the depth of your hearts cry out for my Son. His Name disperses even the greatest darkness. I will be with you; just call on me, 'Here we are Mother; lead us.' Thank you."

June 2, 2009 *"Dear children! my love seeks your complete and unconditional love, which will not leave you the same as you are; instead it will change you and teach you to trust in my Son. My children, with my love I am saving you and making you true witnesses of the goodness of my Son. Therefore, my children, do not be afraid to witness love in the name of my Son. Thank you."*

While Our Lady was leaving, Mirjana saw a cross, and in the middle of the cross a heart, with a crown of thorns around the heart. Our Lady was not sad.

July 2, 2009 *"Dear children, I am calling you because I need you. I need hearts ready for immeasurable love, hearts that are not burdened by vanity, hearts that are ready to love as my Son loved, that are ready to sacrifice themselves as my Son sacrificed Himself. I need you. In order to come with me, forgive yourselves, forgive others, and adore my Son. Adore Him also for those who have not come to know Him, those who do not love Him. Therefore, I need you. Therefore, I call you. Thank you."*

October 2, 2009 *"Dear children, as I look at you, my heart writhes with pain. Where are you going, my children? Have you sunk so deeply into sin that you do not know how to stop yourselves? You justify yourselves with sin and live according to it. Kneel down beneath the Cross and look at my Son. He conquered sin and died so that you, my children, may live. Permit me to help you not to die but to live with my Son forever. Thank you!"*

December 2, 2009 *"Dear children, at this time of preparation and joyful expectation I, as a mother, desire to point you to what is the most important for your soul. Can my Son be born in it? Is it cleansed by love from lies, arrogance, hatred and malice? Above all else, does your soul love God as your Father, and does it love your fellow brother in Christ? I am pointing you to the way which will raise your soul to a complete union with my Son. I desire for my Son to be born in you. What a joy that would be for me as mother. Thank you."*

January 2, 2010 *"Dear children, today I am calling you with complete trust and love to set out with me because I desire to acquaint you with my Son. Do not be afraid. My children, I am here with you; I am next to you. I am showing you the way to forgive yourselves, to forgive others, and, with sincere repentance of heart, to kneel before the Father. Make everything die in you that hinders you from loving and saving, that you may be with Him and in Him. Decide for a new beginning, a beginning of sincere love of God Himself. Thank you."*

February 2, 2010 *"Dear children, with motherly love today I call you today to be a lighthouse to all souls who wander in the darkness of ignorance of God's love so that you may shine all the brighter and draw all the more souls. Do not permit the untruths which come out of your mouth to silence your conscience. Be perfect. I am leading you with my motherly hand, a hand of love. Thank you."*

April 2, 2010 *"Dear children, today I bless you in a special way, and I pray for you to return to the right way to my Son, your Savior, your Redeemer, to Him who gave you eternal life. Reflect on everything human, on everything that does not permit you to set out after my Son, on what is temporary, imperfect and limited, and then think of my Son, of His Divine infiniteness. By your surrender and prayer ennoble your body and perfect your soul. Be ready, my children. Thank you."*

May 2, 2010 *"Dear children, today, through me, the good Father calls you with your soul filled with love to set out on a spiritual visitation. Dear children, be filled with grace, sincerely repent for your sins, and yearn for the good. Yearn also in the name of those who have not come to know the perfection of the good. You will be more pleasing to God. Thank you."*

June 2, 2010 *"Dear Children, today I call you with prayer and fasting to clear the path in which my Son will enter into your hearts. Accept me as a mother and a messenger of God's love and His desire for your salvation. Free yourself of everything from the past which burdens you, that gives you a sense of guilt, that which previously led you astray in error and darkness. Accept the light. Be born anew in the righteousness of my Son. Thank you."*

July 2, 2010 *"Dear children, my motherly call, which I direct to you today, is a call of truth and life. My Son, who is life, loves you and knows you in truth. To come to know and to love yourself, you must come to know my Son; to come to know and to love others, you must see my Son in them. Therefore, my children, pray, pray, that you may comprehend and surrender with a spirit that is free, be completely transformed, and, in this way, may have the Kingdom of Heaven in your heart on earth. Thank you!"*

August 2, 2010 *"Dear children, today I call you to begin to build with me the Kingdom of Heaven in your hearts so that you may forget what is personal and, led by the example of my Son, think what is of God. What does He desire of you? Do not permit Satan to open the paths of earthly happiness, the paths without my Son. My children, they are false and last a short while. My Son exists. I offer you eternal happiness and peace and unity with my Son, with God. I offer you the Kingdom of God. Thank you."*

September 2, 2010 *"Dear children, I am beside you because I desire to help you to overcome trials, which this time of purification puts before you. My children, one of those is not to forgive, and not to ask for forgiveness. Every sin offends love and distances you from it, and love is my Son. Therefore, my children, if you desire to walk with me towards the peace of God's love, you must learn to forgive and to ask for forgiveness. Thank you."*

October 2, 2010 *"Dear children, today I call you to a humble devotion. Your hearts need to be just. May your crosses be your means in the battle against the sins of the present time. May your weapon be patience and boundless love, a love that knows how to wait and which will make you capable of recognizing God's signs, so that your life, by humble love, may show the truth to all those who seek it in the darkness of lies. My children, my apostles, help me to open the paths to my Son. Once again I call you to pray for your shepherds. Alongside them I will triumph. Thank you."*

November 2, 2010 *"Dear children, with motherly perseverance and love I am bringing you the light of life to destroy the darkness of death in you. Do not reject me, my children. Stop and look within yourselves and see how sinful you are. Be aware of your sins and pray for forgiveness. My children, you do not desire to accept that you are weak and little, but you can be strong and great by doing God's will. Give me your cleansed hearts so that I may illuminate them with the light of life, my Son. Thank you."*

December 2, 2010 *"Dear children, today I am praying here with you that you may gather the strength to open your hearts and thus to become aware of the mighty love of the suffering God. Through His love, goodness, and meekness, I am also with you. I invite you for this special time of preparation to be a time of prayer, penance, and conversion. My children, you need God. You cannot go forward without my Son. When you comprehend and accept this, what was promised to you will be realized. Through the Holy Spirit the Kingdom of Heaven will be born in your hearts. I am leading you to this. Thank you."*

January 2, 2011 *"Dear children, today I call you to unity in Jesus, my Son. My motherly heart prays that you may comprehend that you are God's family. Through the spiritual freedom of will, which the Heavenly Father has given you, you are called to become cognizant (to come to the knowledge) of the truth, the good, or the evil. May prayer and fasting open your hearts and help you to discover the Heavenly Father through my Son. In discovering the Father, your life will be directed to carrying out God's will and the realization of God's family in the way that my Son desires. I will not leave you alone on this path. Thank you."*

February 2, 2011 *"Dear children, you are gathering around me, you are seeking your way, you are seeking, you are seeking the truth but are forgetting what is the most important: you are forgetting to pray properly. Your lips pronounce countless words, but your spirit does not feel anything. Wandering in darkness, you even imagine God Himself according to yourselves and not such as He really is in His love. Dear children,* *proper prayer comes from the depth of your heart, from your suffering, from your joy, from your seeking the forgiveness of sins. This is the way to come to know the right God, and by that, also yourselves, because you are created according to Him. Prayer will bring you to the fulfillment of my desire, of my mission here with you, to the unity in God's family. Thank you."*

Mirjana, "Our Lady blessed everyone present, thanked them, and called us to pray for priests."

March 2, 2011 *"Dear children, my motherly heart suffers tremendously as I look at my children who persistently put what is human before what is of God, at my children, who, despite everything that surrounds them and despite all the signs that are sent to them, think that they can walk without my Son. They cannot! They are walking to eternal perdition. That is why I am gathering you, who are ready to open your heart to me, you who are ready to be apostles of my love, to help me, so that by living God's love you may be an example to those who do not know it. May fasting and prayer give you strength in that, and I bless you with motherly blessing in the name of the Father and of the Son and of the Holy Spirit. Thank you."*

Mirjana, "Our Lady was very sad."

April 2, 2011 *"Dear children, with motherly love I desire to open the heart of each of you and to teach you personal unity with the Father. To accept this, you must comprehend that you are important to God and that He is calling you individually. You must comprehend that your prayer is a conversation of a child with the Father, that love is the way by which you must set out love for God and for your neighbor. That is, my children, the love that has no boundaries. That is the love that emanates from truth and continues to the end. Follow me, my children, so that also others, in recognizing the truth and love in you, may follow you. Thank you."* Mirjana, "Once again Our Lady called us to pray for our shepherds (priests) and said, 'They have a special place in my heart. They represent my Son.'"

May 2, 2011 *"Dear children, God the Father is sending me to show you the way of salvation, because He, my children, desires to save you and not to condemn you. That is why I, as a mother, am gathering you around me, because with my motherly love I desire to help you to be free of the dirtiness of the past and to begin to live anew and differently. I am calling you to resurrect in my Son. Along with confession of sins,* *renounce everything that has distanced you from my Son and that has made your life empty and unsuccessful. Say 'yes' to the Father with the heart and set out on the way of salvation to which He is calling you through the Holy Spirit. Thank you. I am especially praying for the shepherds (priests) for God to help them to be alongside you with a fullness of heart."*

June 2, 2011 *"Dear children, as I call you to prayer for those who have not come to know the love of God, if you were to look into your hearts you would comprehend that I am speaking about many of you. With an open heart, sincerely ask yourselves if you want the living God or whether you want to eliminate Him and live as you want. Look around you, my children, and see where the world is going, the world that thinks of doing everything without the Father, and which wanders in the darkness of temptation. I am offering to you the light of the Truth and the Holy Spirit. According to God's plan I am with you to help you to have my Son, His Cross and Resurrection, triumph in your hearts. As a mother, I desire and pray for your unity with my Son and His works. I am with you; you decide. Thank you."*

July 2, 2011 *"Dear children, today I call you to a difficult and painful step for your unity with my Son. I call you to complete admission and confession of sins, to purification. An impure heart cannot be in my Son and with my Son. An impure heart cannot give the fruit of love and unity. An impure heart cannot do correct and just things; it is not an example of the beauty of God's love to those who surround it and to those who have not come to know that love. You, my children, are gathering around me full of enthusiasm, desires, and expectations, and I implore the Good Father, through the Holy Spirit, to put my Son's faith into your purified hearts. My children, obey me, and set out with me."*

Mirjana, "As Our Lady was leaving, to her left She showed darkness and to her right a Cross in golden light."

August 2, 2011 *"Dear children, today I call you to be born anew in prayer and through the Holy Spirit to become a new people with my Son, a people who knows that if they have lost God, they have lost themselves; a people who knows that, with God, despite all sufferings and trials, they are secure and saved. I call you to gather into God's family and to be strengthened with the Father's strength. As individuals, my children, you cannot stop the evil that wants to begin to rule in this world and to destroy*

255

it. But, according to God's will, all together, with my Son, you can change everything and heal the world. I call you to pray with all your heart for your shepherds, because my Son chose them. Thank you."

September 2, 2011 *"Dear children, with all my heart and soul full of faith and love in the Heavenly Father, I gave my Son to you and am giving Him to you anew. My Son has brought you, the people of the entire world, to know the only true God and His love. He has led you on the way of truth and made you brothers and sisters. Therefore, my children, do not wander, do not close your heart before that truth, hope, and love. Everything around you is passing, and everything is falling apart; only the glory of God remains. Therefore, renounce everything that distances you from the Lord. Adore Him alone, because He is the only true God. I am with you, and I will remain with you. I am especially praying for the shepherds that they may be worthy representatives of my Son and may lead you with love on the way of truth. Thank you."*

October 2, 2011 *"Dear children, also today my motherly heart calls you to prayer, to your personal relationship with God the Father, to the joy of prayer in Him. God the Father is not far away from you, and He is not unknown to you. He revealed Himself to you through my Son and gave you Life that is my Son. Therefore, my children, do not give in to temptations that want to separate you from God the Father. Pray! Do not attempt to have families and societies without Him. Pray! Pray that your hearts may be flooded with the goodness which comes only from my Son, Who is sincere goodness. Only hearts filled with goodness can comprehend and accept God the Father. I will continue to lead you. In a special way I implore you not to judge your shepherds. My children, are you forgetting that God the Father called them? Pray! Thank you."*

November 2, 2011 *"Dear children, the Father has not left you to yourselves. Immeasurable is His love, the love that is bringing me to you, to help you to come to know Him, so that, through my Son, all of you can call Him 'Father' with the fullness of heart, that you can be one people in God's family. However, my children, do not forget that you are not in this world only for yourselves, and that I am not calling you here only for your sake. Those who follow my Son think of the brother in Christ as of their very selves, and they do not know selfishness. That is why I desire that you be the light of my Son, that to all those who have not come to know the Father, to all those who wander in the darkness of sin, despair, pain, and loneliness, you may illuminate the way, and that with your life, you may show them the love of God. I am with you. If*

256

you open your hearts, I will lead you. Again I am calling you to pray for your shepherds. Thank you."

December 2, 2011 *"Dear children, as a mother I am with you so that with my love, prayer, and example I may help you to become a seed of the future, a seed that will grow into a firm tree and spread its branches throughout the world. For you to become a seed of the future, a seed of love, implore the Father to forgive you your omissions up to now. My children, only a pure heart, unburdened by sin, can open itself, and only honest eyes can see the way by which I desire to lead you. When you become aware of this, you will become aware of the love of God; it will be given (as a gift) to you. Then you will give it (as a gift) to others as a seed of love. Thank you."*

January 2, 2012 *"Dear children, with motherly concern I look in your hearts and see in them pain and suffering. I see a wounded past and an incessant search. I see my children who desire to be happy but do not know how. Open yourselves to the Father. That is the way to happiness, the way by which I desire to lead you. God the Father never leaves His children alone, especially not in pain and despair. When you comprehend and accept this, you will be happy. Your search will end. You will love, and you will not be afraid. Your life will be hope and truth, which is my Son. Thank you. I implore you, pray for those whom my Son has chosen. Do not judge, because you will all be judged."*

February 2, 2012 *"Dear children, I am with you for so much time, and already for so long I have been pointing you to God's presence and His infinite love, which I desire for all of you to come to know. And you, my children? You continue to be deaf and blind as you look at the world around you and do not want to see where it is going without my Son. You are renouncing Him, and He is the source of all graces. You listen to me while I am speaking to you, but your hearts are closed, and you are not hearing me. You are not praying to the Holy Spirit to illuminate you. My children, pride has come to rule. I am pointing out humility to you. My children, remember that only a humble soul shines with purity and beauty, because it has come to know the love of God. Only a humble soul goes to heaven, because my Son is in it. Thank you. Again I implore you to pray for those whom my Son has chosen; those are your shepherds."*

March 2, 2012 *"Dear children, through the immeasurable love of God I am coming among you, and I am persistently calling you into the arms of my Son. With a motherly heart I am imploring you, my children, but I am also repeatedly warning you, that concern for those who have not come to know my Son be in first place for you. Do not think that by looking at yourself and your life, they are not overcome by a desire to come to know Him. Pray to the Holy Spirit for my Son to be impressed within you. Pray that you can be apostles of the divine light in this time of darkness and hopelessness. This is a time of your trial. With a rosary in hand and love in the heart set out with me. I am leading you towards Easter in my Son. Pray for those whom my Son has chosen that they can always live through Him and in Him, the High Priest. Thank you."*

April 2, 2012 *"Dear children, as the Queen of Peace, I desire to give peace to you, my children, true peace which comes through the heart of my Divine Son. As a mother I pray that wisdom, humility, and goodness may come to reign in your hearts, that peace may reign, that my Son may reign. When my Son will be the ruler in your hearts, you will be able to help others to come to know Him. When heavenly peace comes to rule over you, those who are seeking it in the wrong places, thus causing pain to my motherly heart, will recognize it. My children, great will be my joy when I see that you are accepting my words and that you desire to follow me. Do not be afraid; you are not alone. Give me your hands, and I will lead you. Do not forget your shepherds. Pray that in their thoughts they may always be with my Son, who called them to witness Him. Thank you."*

May 02, 2012 *"Dear children, with motherly love I implore you to give me your hands; permit me to lead you. I, as a mother, desire to save you from restlessness, despair, and eternal exile. My Son, by His death on the Cross, showed how much He loves you; He sacrificed Himself for your sake and the sake of your sins. Do not keep rejecting His sacrifice and do not keep renewing His sufferings with your sins. Do not keep shutting the doors of Heaven to yourselves. My children, do not waste time. Nothing is more important than unity in my Son. I will help you because the Heavenly Father is sending me so that together we can show the way of grace and salvation to all those who do not know Him. Do not be hard hearted. Have confidence in me and adore my Son. My children, you cannot be without the shepherds. May they be in your prayers every day. Thank you."*

June 02, 2012 *"Dear children, I am continuously among you because, with my endless love I desire to show you the door of Heaven. I desire to tell you how it is opened: through goodness, mercy, love and peace, through my Son. Therefore, my children, do not waste time on vanities. Only knowledge of the love of my Son can save you. Through that salvific love and the Holy Spirit He chose me and I, together with Him, am choosing you to be apostles of His love and will. My children, great is the responsibility upon you. I desire that by your example you help sinners regain their sight, enrich their poor souls, and bring them back into my embrace. Therefore, pray, pray, fast, and confess regularly. If receiving my Son in the Eucharist is the center of your life, then do not be afraid; you can do everything. I am with you. Every day I pray for the shepherds, and I expect the same of you, because, my children, without their guidance and strengthening through their blessing, you cannot do it. Thank you."*

July 02, 2012 *"My children, again in a motherly way, I implore you to stop for a moment and to reflect on yourselves and on the transience of this, your earthly life. Then reflect on eternity and the eternal beatitude. What do you want? Which way do you want to set out on? The Father's love sends me to be a mediatrix for you, to show you with motherly love the way which leads to the purity of soul, a soul unburdened by sin, a soul that will come to know eternity. I am praying that the light of the love of my Son may illuminate you, so that you may triumph over weaknesses and come out of misery. You are my children, and I desire for all of you to be on the way of salvation. Therefore, my children, gather around me that I may have you come to know the love of my Son and thus open the door of eternal beatitude. Pray as I do for your shepherds. Again I caution you: do not judge them, because my Son chose them. Thank you."*

August 02, 2012 *"Dear children, I am with you and I am not giving up. I desire to have you come to know my Son. I desire for my children to be with me in eternal life. I desire for you to feel the joy of peace and to have eternal salvation. I am praying that you may overcome human weaknesses. I am imploring my Son to give you pure hearts. My dear children, only pure hearts know how to carry a cross, and know how to sacrifice for all those sinners who have offended the Heavenly Father and who, even today, offend Him, although they have not come to know Him. I am praying that you may come to know the light of true faith, which comes only from prayer of pure hearts. It is then that all those who are near you will feel the love of my Son. Pray for those whom my Son has chosen to lead you on the way to salvation. May your mouth refrain from every judgment. Thank you."*

September 02, 2012 *"Dear children, as my eyes are looking at you, my soul is seeking those souls with whom it desires to be one; the souls who have understood the importance of prayer for those of my children who have not come to know the love of the Heavenly Father. I am calling you because I need you. Accept the mission, and do not be afraid. I will strengthen you. I will fill you with my graces. With my love I will protect you from the evil spirit. I will be with you. With my presence I will console you in difficult moments. Thank you for your open hearts. Pray for priests. Pray that the unity between my Son and them may be all the stronger so that they may be one. Thank you."*

October 02, 2012 *"Dear children, I am calling you and am coming among you because I need you. I need apostles with a pure heart. I am praying, and you should also pray, that the Holy Spirit may enable and lead you, that He may illuminate you and fill you with love and humility. Pray that He may fill you with grace and mercy. Only then will you understand me, my children. Only then will you understand my pain because of those who have not come to know the love of God. Then you will be able to help me. You will be my light-bearers of God's love. You will illuminate the way for those who have been given eyes but do not want to see. I desire for all of my children to see my Son. I desire for all of my children to experience His Kingdom. Again I call you and implore you to pray for those whom my Son has called. Thank you."*

November 02, 2012 *"Dear children, as a mother I implore you to persevere as my apostles. I am praying to my Son to give you Divine wisdom and strength. I am praying that you may discern everything around you according to God's truth and to strongly resist everything that wants to distance you from my Son. I am praying that you may witness the love of the Heavenly Father according to my Son. My children, great grace has been given to you to be witnesses of God's love. Do not take the given responsibility lightly. Do not sadden my motherly heart. As a mother I desire to rely on my children, on my apostles. Through fasting and prayer you are opening the way for me to pray to my Son for Him to be beside you and for His name to be holy through you. Pray for the shepherds because none of this would be possible without them. Thank you."*

December 02, 2012 *"Dear children, with motherly love and motherly patience anew I call you to live according to my Son, to spread His peace and His love, so that, as my apostles, you may accept God's truth with all your heart and pray for the Holy Spirit to guide you. Then you will be able to faithfully serve my Son, and show His love to others with your life. According to the love of my Son and my love, as a mother, I strive to bring all of my strayed children into my motherly embrace and to show them the way of faith. My children, help me in my motherly battle and pray with me that sinners may become aware of their sins and repent sincerely. Pray also for those whom my Son has chosen and consecrated in His name. Thank you."*

January 02, 2013 *"Dear children, with much love and patience I strive to make your hearts like unto mine. I strive, by my example, to teach you humility, wisdom and love because I need you; I cannot do without you my children. According to God's will I am choosing you, by His strength I am strengthening you. Therefore, my children, do not be afraid to open your hearts to me. I will give them to my Son and in return, He will give you the gift of Divine peace. You will carry it to all those whom you meet, you will witness God's love with your life and you will give the gift of my Son through yourselves. Through reconciliation, fasting and prayer, I will lead you. Immeasurable is my love. Do not be afraid. My children, pray for the shepherds. May your lips be shut to every judgment, because do not forget that my Son has chosen them and only He has the right to judge. Thank you."*

February 02, 2013 *"Dear children, love is bringing me to you – the love which I desire to teach you also – real love; the love which my Son showed you when He died on the Cross out of love for you; the love which is always ready to forgive and to ask for forgiveness. How great is your love? My motherly heart is sorrowful as it searches for love in your hearts. You are not ready to submit your will to God's will out of love. You cannot help me to have those who have not come to know God's love to come to know it, because you do not have real love. Consecrate your hearts to me and I will lead you. I will teach you to forgive, to love your enemies and to live according to my Son. Do not be afraid for yourselves. In afflictions my Son does not forget those who love. I will be beside you. I will implore the Heavenly Father for the light of eternal truth and love to illuminate you. Pray for your shepherds so that through your fasting and prayer they can lead you in love. Thank you."*

March 02, 2013 *"Dear children! Anew, in a motherly way, I am calling you not to be of a hard heart. Do not shut your eyes to the warnings which the Heavenly Father sends to you out of love. Do you love Him above all else? Do you repent for having often forgotten that the Heavenly Father, out of His great love, sent his Son to redeem us by the Cross? Do you repent for not yet having accepted the message? My children, do not resist the love of my Son. Do not resist hope and peace. Along with your prayer and fasting, by His cross, my Son will cast away the darkness that wants to surround you and come to rule over you. He will give you the strength for a new life. Living it according to my Son, you will be a blessing and a hope to all those sinners who wander in the darkness of sin. My children, keep vigil. I, as a mother, am keeping vigil with you. I am especially praying and watching over those whom my Son called to be light-bearers and carriers of hope for you - for your shepherds. Thank you."*

April 02 2013 *"Dear children; I am calling you to be one with my Son in spirit. I am calling you, through prayer, and the Holy Mass when my Son unites Himself with you in a special way, to try to be like Him; that, like Him, you may always be ready to carry out God's will and not seek the fulfillment of your own. Because, my children, it is according to God's will that you are and that you exist, and without God's will you are nothing. As a mother I am asking you to speak about the glory of God with your life because, in that way, you will also glorify yourself in accordance to His will. Show humility and love for your neighbor to everyone. Through such humility and love, my Son saved you and opened the way for you to the Heavenly Father. I implore you to keep opening the way to the Heavenly Father for all those who have not come to know Him and have not opened their hearts to His love. By your life, open the way to all those who still wander in search of the truth. My children, be my apostles who have not lived in vain. Do not forget that you will come before the Heavenly Father and tell Him about yourself. Be ready! Again I am warning you, pray for those whom my Son called, whose hands He blessed and whom He gave as a gift to you. Pray, pray, pray for your shepherds. Thank you."*

May 2, 2013 *"Dear children; Anew, I am calling you to love and not to judge. My Son, according to the will of the Heavenly Father, was among you to show you the way of salvation, to save you and not to judge you. If you desire to follow my Son, you will not judge but love like your Heavenly Father loves you. And when it is the most difficult for you, when you are falling under the weight of the cross do not despair, do not judge, instead remember that you are loved and praise the Heavenly Father because of*

262

His love. My children, do not deviate from the way on which I am leading you. Do not recklessly walk into perdition. May prayer and fasting strengthen you so that you can live as the Heavenly Father would desire; that you may be my apostles of faith and love; that your life may bless those whom you meet; that you may be one with the Heavenly Father and my Son. My children, that is the only truth, the truth that leads to your conversion, and then to the conversion of all those whom you meet - those who have not come to know my Son - all those who do not know what it means to love. My children, my Son gave you a gift of the shepherds. Take good care of them. Pray for them. Thank you."

June 02, 2013 *"Dear children, In this restless time, anew I am calling you to set out after my Son - to follow Him. I know of the pain, suffering and difficulties, but in my Son you will find rest; in Him you will find peace and salvation. My children, do not forget that my Son redeemed you by His Cross and enabled you, anew, to be children of God; to be able to, anew, call the Heavenly Father: "Father". To be worthy of the Father, love and forgive, because your Father is love and forgiveness. Pray and fast, because that is the way to your purification, it is the way of coming to know and becoming cognizant of the Heavenly Father. When you become cognizant of the Father, you will comprehend that He is all you need. I, as a mother, desire my children to be in a community of one single people where the Word of God is listened to and carried out.* Therefore, my children, set out after my Son. Be one with Him. Be God's children. Love your shepherds as my Son loved them when He called them to serve you. Thank you."* *Our Lady said this resolutely and with emphasis.

July 02, 2013 *"Dear children, with a motherly love I am imploring you to give me the gift of your hearts, so I can present them to my Son and free you – free you from all the evil enslaving and distancing you all the more from the only Good – my Son – from everything which is leading you on the wrong way and is taking peace away from you. I desire to lead you to the freedom of the promise of my Son, because I desire for God's will to be fulfilled completely here; and that through reconciliation with the Heavenly Father, through fasting and prayer, apostles of God's love may be born – apostles who will freely, and with love, spread the love of God to all my children – apostles who will spread the love of the trust in the Heavenly Father and who will keep opening the gates of Heaven. Dear children, extend the joy of love and support to your shepherds, just as my Son has asked them to extend it to you. Thank you."*

August 02, 2013 *"Dear children, If only you would open your hearts to me with complete trust, you would comprehend everything. You would comprehend with how much love I am calling you; with how much love I desire to change you, to make you happy; with how much love I desire to make you followers of my Son and give you peace in the fullness of my Son. You would comprehend the immeasurable greatness of my motherly love. That is why, my children, pray because through prayer your faith grows and love is born, the love along which even the cross is not unendurable because you do not carry it alone. In union with my Son you glorify the name of the Heavenly Father. Pray, pray for the gift of love, because love is the only truth: it forgives everything, it serves everyone and it sees a brother in everyone. My children, my apostles, great is the trust that the Heavenly Father has given you through me, His handmaid, to help those who do not know Him, that they may reconcile with Him and follow Him. That is why I am teaching you love, because only if you have love will you be able to respond to Him. Again I am calling you to love your shepherds and to pray that, at this difficult time, the name of my Son may be glorified under their guidance. Thank you."*

September 02, 2013 *"Dear children, I love you all. All of you, all of my children, all of you are in my heart. All of you have my motherly love, and I desire to lead all of you to come to know God's joy. This is why I am calling you. I need humble apostles who, with an open heart, will accept the Word of God and help others to comprehend the meaning of their life alongside God's word. To be able to do this my children, through prayer and fasting, you must learn to listen with the heart and to learn to keep submitting yourselves. You must learn to keep rejecting everything that distances you from God's word and to yearn only for that which draws you closer to it. Do not be afraid. I am here. You are not alone. I am imploring the Holy Spirit to renew and strengthen you. I am imploring the Holy Spirit that, as you help others, you too may be healed. I am imploring Him that, through Him, you may be God's children and my apostles."*

Then with great concern Our Lady said, *"For the sake of Jesus, for the sake of my Son, love those whom He has called and long for the blessing only from the hands which He has consecrated. Do not permit evil to come to reign. Anew I repeat — only alongside your shepherds will my heart triumph. Do not permit evil to separate you from your shepherds. Thank you."*

October 02, 2013 *"Dear children, I love you with a motherly love and with a motherly patience I wait for your love and unity. I pray that you may be a community of God's children, of my children. I pray that as a community you may joyfully come back to life in the faith and in the love of my Son. My children, I am gathering you as my apostles and am teaching you how to bring others to come to know the love of my Son; how to bring to them the Good News, which is my Son. Give me your open, purified hearts and I will fill them with the love for my Son. His love will give meaning to your life and I will walk with you. I will be with you until the meeting with the Heavenly Father. My children, it is those who walk towards the Heavenly Father with love and faith who will be saved. Do not be afraid. I am with you. Put your trust in your shepherds as my Son trusted when He chose them, and pray that they may have the strength and the love to lead you. Thank you."*

November 02, 2013 *"Dear children, anew, in a motherly way, I am calling you to love, to continually pray for the gift of love, to love the Heavenly Father above everything. When you love Him you will love yourself and your neighbor. This cannot be separated. The Heavenly Father is in each person. He loves each person and calls each person by name. Therefore, my children, through prayer hearken to the will of the Heavenly Father. Converse with Him. Have a personal relationship with the Father, which will deepen even more your relationship as a community of my children - my apostles. As a mother I desire that, through the love for the Heavenly Father, you may be raised above earthly vanities, and may help others to gradually come to know, and come closer to the Heavenly Father. My children, pray, pray, pray for the gift of love because 'love' is my Son. Pray for your shepherds that they may always have love for you as my Son had, and showed by giving His life for your salvation. Thank you."*

December 02, 2013 *"Dear children, with a motherly love and a motherly patience I am looking at your ceaseless wandering and how lost you are. That is why I am with you. I desire to help you to first find and come to know yourself, so that, then, you would be able to recognize and to admit everything that does not permit you to get to know the love of the Heavenly Father, honestly and wholeheartedly. My children, the Father comes to be known through the cross. Therefore, do not reject the cross. Strive to comprehend and accept it with my help. When you will be able to accept the cross you will also understand the love of the Heavenly Father; you will walk with my Son and with me; you will differ from those who have not come to know the love of the Heavenly Father, those who listen to Him but do not understand Him, those who do not walk*

265

with Him - who have not come to know Him. I desire for you to come to know the truth of my Son and to be my apostles; that, as children of God, you may rise above the human way of thinking and always, and in everything, seek God's way of thinking, anew. My children, pray and fast that you may be able to recognize all of this which I am seeking of you. Pray for your shepherds and long to come to know the love of your Heavenly Father, in union with them. Thank you."

January 02, 2014 "Dear children, for you to be able to be my apostles and to be able to help all those who are in darkness, to come to know the light of the love of my Son, you must have pure and humble hearts. You cannot help for my Son to be born in, and to reign in, the hearts of those who do not know Him, if He does not reign – if He is not the King – in your heart. I am with you. I am walking with you as a mother. I am knocking on your hearts. They cannot open because they are not humble. I am praying, and you my beloved children also pray, that you may be able to open pure and humble hearts to my Son and to receive the gifts which He has promised you. Then you will be led by the love and strength of my Son. Then, you will be my apostles who everywhere around them spread the fruits of God's love. My Son will act from within you and through you, because you will be 'one'. My motherly heart yearns for this – for unity of all of my children – through my Son. With great love I bless, and pray for those who are chosen by my Son – for your shepherds. Thank you." At first Our Lady was sad and then decisive.

February 02, 2014 "Dear children, with motherly love I desire to teach you sincerity, because I desire that, in your actions as my apostles, you be exact, resolute, and above all sincere. I desire that, by the grace of God, you be open for a blessing. I desire that by fasting and prayer you obtain from the Heavenly Father the cognition of what is natural and holy – Divine. Filled with cognition, under the shelter of my Son and myself, you will be my apostles who will know how to spread the Word of God to all those who do not know of it; and you will know how to overcome obstacles that will stand in your way. My children, by means of a blessing, God's grace will descend upon you and you will be able to retain it through fasting, prayer, purification and reconciliation. You will have the efficiency which I seek of you. Pray for your shepherds that the ray of God's grace may illuminate their ways. Thank you."

March 2, 2014 *"Dear children, I am coming to you as a mother and I desire that in me, as in a mother, you may find your abode, consolation and rest. Therefore, my children, apostles of my love, pray. Pray with humble devotion, obedience and complete trust in the Heavenly Father. Trust as I have trusted when it was said to me that I will bring the blessing of the promise. May out of your hearts, from your lips, always come forth 'May your will be done!' Therefore, trust and pray so that I can intercede for you before the Lord, for him to give you the Heavenly Blessing and fill you with the Holy Spirit. Then he will be able to help all those who do not know the Lord – you, apostles of my love, will help them to call him 'Father' with complete trust. Pray for your shepherds and place your trust in their blessed hands. Thank you. "*

April 02, 2014 *"Dear children, with a motherly love I desire to help you with your life of prayer and penance to be a sincere attempt at drawing closer to my Son and His divine light - that you may know how to separate yourselves from sin. Every prayer, every Mass and every fasting is an attempt at drawing closer to my Son, a reminder of His glory and a refuge from sin - it is a way to a renewed union of the good Father and His children. Therefore, my dear children, with hearts open and full of love, cry out the name of the Heavenly Father that He may illuminate you with the Holy Spirit. Through the Holy Spirit you will become a spring of God's love. All those who do not know my Son, all those thirsting for the love and peace of my Son, will drink from this spring. Thank you. Pray for your shepherds. I pray for them and I desire that they may always feel the blessing of my motherly hands and the support of my motherly heart."*

May 02, 2014 *"Dear children, I, your mother, am with you for the sake of your well-being, for the sake of your needs and for the sake of your personal cognition. The Heavenly Father gave you the freedom to decide on your own and to become cognizant on your own. I desire to help you. I desire to be a mother to you, a teacher of the truth – so that in the simplicity of an open heart, you may become cognizant of the immeasurable purity and light which comes from it and shatters darkness, the light which brings hope. I, my children, understand your pain and suffering. Who could understand you better than a mother? And you, my children? Small is the number of those who understand and follow me. Great is the number of those who are lost - of those who have not yet become cognizant of the truth in my Son. Therefore, my apostles, pray and act. Bring the light and do not lose hope. I am with you. In a special way I am with your shepherds. With a motherly heart I love and protect them, because they lead you to Heaven that was promised to you by my Son. Thank you."*

June 02, 2014 *"Dear children, I call you all and accept you as my children. I am praying that you may accept me and love me as a mother. I have united all of you in my heart, I have descended among you and I bless you. I know that you desire consolation and hope from me because I love you and intercede for you. I ask of you to unite with me in my Son and to be my apostles. For you to be able to do so, I am calling you, anew, to love. There is no love without prayer - there is no prayer without forgiveness because love is prayer - forgiveness is love. My children, God created you to love and you love so as to forgive. Every prayer that comes out of love unites you with my Son and the Holy Spirit, and the Holy Spirit illuminates you and makes you my apostles - apostles who will do everything they do in the name of the Lord. They will pray with their works and not just with words, because they love my Son and comprehend the way of truth which leads to eternal life. Pray for your shepherds that they may always lead you with a pure heart on the way of truth and love - the way of my Son. Thank you."*

July 02, 2014 *"Dear children, I, the mother of all of you gathered here and the mother of the entire world, am blessing you with a motherly blessing and call you to set out on the way of humility. That way leads to the coming to know the love of my Son. My Son is almighty, He is in everything. If you, my children, do not become cognizant of this, then darkness/blindness rule in your soul. Only humility can heal you. My children, I always lived humbly, courageously and in hope. I knew, I became cognizant that God is in us and we are in God. I am asking the same of you. I desire for all of you to be with me in eternity, because you are a part of me. I will help you on your way. My love will envelop you like a mantle and make of you apostles of my light - of God's light. With the love that comes forth from humility you will bring light to where darkness/blindness rule. You will be bringing my Son who is the light of the world. I am always alongside your shepherds and I pray that they may always be an example of humility for you. Thank you."*

September 02, 2014 *"Dear children, I, your mother, am coming anew among you out of love which has no end, from endless love of the endless Heavenly Father. And as I am looking into your hearts I see that many of you accept me as a mother and, with sincere and pure hearts, you desire to be my apostles. But, I am also the mother of those of you who do not accept me and who, in the hardness of your hearts, do not desire to come to know the love of my Son. And you do not know how much my heart suffers and how much I pray to my Son for you. I pray to Him to heal your souls because He can do so. I pray to Him to illuminate you with the miracle of the Holy Spirit so that* *you may stop, always anew, betraying, cursing and wounding Him. With all my heart I pray for you to understand that only my Son is the salvation and the light of the world. And you, my children, my dear apostles, always carry my Son in your hearts and thoughts. In this way you are carrying love. All those who do not know Him will recognize Him in your love. I am always beside you. In a special way I am beside your shepherds because my Son has called them to lead you on the way to eternity. Thank you, my apostles, for your sacrifice and love."*

October 02, 2014 *"Dear children, with motherly love I implore you, love one another. May there be in your hearts, as my Son desired from the very beginning, love for the Heavenly Father and for your neighbor in the first place - above everything of this world. My dear children, do you not recognize the signs of the times? Do you not recognize that all of this that is around you, all that is happening, is because there is no love? Comprehend that salvation is in true values. Accept the might of the Heavenly Father, love Him and honor Him. Walk in the footsteps of my Son. You, my children, my dear apostles, you are always gathering around me anew, because you are thirsty. You thirst for peace, love and happiness. Drink out of my hands. My hands are offering to you my Son who is the spring of clear water. He will bring your faith back to life and purify your hearts, because my Son loves pure hearts and pure hearts love my Son. Only pure hearts are humble and have firm faith. I ask for such hearts of you, my children. My Son told me that I am the mother of the entire world. I ask of those of you who accept me as such to help me, with your life, prayer and sacrifice, for all of my children to accept me as a mother - so that I may lead them to the spring of the clear water. Thank you. My dear children, as your shepherds offer you the Body of my Son with their blessed hands, always in your hearts give thanks to my Son for the sacrifice and for the shepherds that He always gives you anew."*

November 02, 2014 *"Dear children, I am with you with the blessing of my Son, with you who love me and who strive to follow me. I also desire to be with you who do not accept me. To all of you I am opening my heart full of love and I am blessing you with my motherly hands. I am a mother who understands you. I lived your life and lived through your sufferings and joys. You who are living in pain understand my pain and suffering because of those of my children who do not permit the light of my Son to illuminate them; those of my children who are living in darkness. This is why I need you - you who have been illuminated by the light and have comprehended the truth. I am calling you to adore my Son so that your soul may grow and reach true spirituality.*

269

My apostles, it is then that you will be able to help me. To help me means to pray for those who have not come to know the love of my Son. In praying for them you are showing to my Son that you love Him and follow Him. My Son promised me that evil will never win, because you, the souls of the just, are here; you who strive to say your prayers with the heart; you who offer your pain and suffering to my Son; you who comprehend that life is only a blink; you who yearn for the Kingdom of Heaven. All of this makes you my apostles and leads you towards the victory of my heart. Therefore, my children, purify your hearts and adore my Son. Thank you."

December 02, 2014 *"Dear children, Remember - for I am telling you - that love will win. I know that many of you are losing hope because around you, you see suffering, pain, jealousy, envy... but, I am your mother. I am in the Kingdom but am also here with you. My Son is sending me anew to help you. Therefore, do not lose hope; instead, follow me - because the victory of my heart is in the name of God. My beloved Son is thinking of you as he has always thought of you. Believe him and live him. He is the life of the world. My children, to live my Son means to live the Gospel. This is not easy. This means love, forgiveness and sacrifice. This purifies and it opens the Kingdom. Sincere prayer, which is not only words but is a prayer which the heart speaks, will help you. Likewise fasting (will help you), because it is still more of love, forgiveness and sacrifice. Therefore, do not lose hope but follow me. I am imploring you anew to pray for your shepherds so that they may always look to my Son who was the first Shepherd of the world and whose family was the entire world."*

January 02, 2015 *"Dear children, I am here among you as a mother who desires to help you to come to know the truth. While I lived your life on earth I had knowledge of the truth, and by this alone, a piece of Heaven on earth. That is why I desire the same for you, my children. The Heavenly Father desires pure hearts filled with the knowledge of the truth. He desires for you to love all those whom you meet, because I also love my Son in all of you. This is the beginning of coming to know the truth. Many false truths are being offered to you. You will overcome them with a heart cleansed by fasting, prayer, penance and the Gospel. This is the only truth and it is the truth which my Son left you. You do not need to examine it much. What is asked of you, as I also have done, is to love and to give. My children, if you love, your heart will be a home for my Son and me, and the words of my Son will be the guiding light in your life. My children, I will make use of you, apostles of love, to help all of my children to come to know the truth. My children, I have always prayed for the Church of my Son, and so I* *also ask the same of you. Pray that your shepherds may come to shine forth with the love of my Son. Thank you."*

February 02, 2015 *"Dear children! I am here, I am among you. I am looking at you, am smiling at you and I love you in the way that only a mother can. Through the Holy Spirit who comes through my purity, I see your hearts and I offer them to my Son. Already for a long time I have been asking of you to be my apostles, to pray for those who have not come to know God's love. I am asking for prayer said out of love, prayer which carries out works and sacrifices. Do not waste time thinking about whether you are worthy to be my apostles. The Heavenly Father will judge everyone; and you, love Him and listen to Him. I know that all of this confuses you, even my very stay among you, but accept it with joy and pray that you may comprehend that you are worthy to work for Heaven. My love is upon you. Pray that my love may win in all hearts, because that is the love which forgives, gives and never stops. Thank you."*

March 02, 2015 *"Dear children! You are my strength. You, my apostles, who with your love, humility and silence of prayer are making it possible for one to come to know my Son. You live in me. You carry me in your heart. You know that you have a mother who loves you and who has come to bring love. I am looking at you in the Heavenly Father - your thoughts, your pains, your sufferings - and I offer them to my Son. Do not be afraid and do not lose hope, because my Son listens to his mother. Since he was born he loves and I desire for all of my children to come to know that love. I desire that all those who left him because of their pain and misunderstanding may return to him and that all those who have never known him may come to know him. That is why you are here, my apostles, and I as a mother am with you. Pray for the firmness of faith, because love and mercy come from firm faith. Through love and mercy you will help all those who are not aware that they are choosing darkness instead of light. Pray for your shepherds because they are the strength of the Church which my Son left to you. Through my Son, they are the shepherds of souls. Thank you."*

April 2, 2015 *"Dear children, I have chosen you, my apostles, because all of you carry something beautiful within you. You can help me to have the love, for the sake of which my Son died and then resurrected, win anew. Therefore, I am calling you, my apostles, to try to see something good in every creature of God, in all of my children, and to try to understand them. My children, you are all brothers and sisters through the same Holy Spirit. You, filled with love for my Son, can speak of what you know to all those who*

271

have not come to know that love. You have come to know the love of my Son, you have comprehended His Resurrection, with joy you cast your gaze towards Him. My motherly desire is for all of my children to be united in love for Jesus. Therefore, I am calling you, my apostles, to live the Eucharist with joy, because in the Eucharist my Son gives Himself to you anew and with His example shows the love and sacrifice towards the neighbor. Thank you."

May 2, 2015 *"Dear children, open your hearts and try to feel how much I love you and how much I desire for you to love my Son. I desire for you to come to know Him all the better, because it is impossible to know Him and not to love Him - because He is love. I, my children, know you. I know your pain and suffering because I lived through them. I laugh with you in your joy and I cry with you in your pain. I will never leave you. I will always speak to you with motherly tenderness. And I, as a mother, need your open hearts to spread the love of my Son with wisdom and simplicity. I need you to be open and sensitive to the good and mercy. I need you to be united with my Son, because I desire for you to be happy and to help me to bring happiness to all of my children. My apostles, I need you to show everyone the truth of God, so that my heart, which suffered and today suffers so much pain, can win in love. Pray for the holiness of your shepherds, so that in the name of my Son they can work miracles, because holiness works miracles. Thank you."*

June 2, 2015 *"Dear children, I desire to work through you, my children, my apostles, so that, in the end, I may gather all my children there where everything is prepared for your happiness. I am praying for you, that through works you can convert others, because the time has come for acts of truth, for my Son. My love will work in you - I will make use of you. Have trust in me, because everything that I desire, I desire for your good, the eternal good created by the Heavenly Father. You, my children, my apostles, are living an earthly life in union with my children who have not come to know the love of my Son, who do not call me 'mother' - but do not be afraid to witness Truth. If you are not afraid and witness courageously, the truth will miraculously win, but remember, strength is in love. My children, love is repentance, forgiveness, prayer, sacrifice and mercy. If you will know how to love, by your works you will convert others, you will enable the light of my Son to penetrate into souls. Thank you. Pray for your shepherds. They belong to my Son. He called them. Pray that they may always have the strength and the courage to shine with the light of my Son."*

272

July 02, 2015 *"Dear children, I am calling you to spread the faith in my Son - your faith. You, my children illuminated by the Holy Spirit, my apostles, transmit it to others - to those who do not believe, who do not know, who do not want to know - but for that you must pray a lot for the gift of love, because love is the mark of true faith - and you will be apostles of my love. Love always, anew, revives the pain and the joy of the Eucharist, it revives the pain of the Passion of my Son, by which He showed you what it means to love immeasurably; it revives the joy for having left you His body and blood to feed you with Himself - and in this way, to be one with you. Looking at you with tenderness, I feel immeasurable love which strengthens me in my desire to bring you to a firm faith. Firm faith will give you joy and happiness on earth and in the end the encounter with my Son. This is His desire. Therefore, live Him, live love, live the light that always illuminates you in the Eucharist. I implore you to pray a lot for your shepherds, to pray so as to have all the more love for them because my Son gave them to you to feed you with His body and to teach you love. Therefore, also you are to love them. But, my children, remember, love means to endure and to give, and never, ever to judge. Thank you."*

August 02, 2015 *"Dear children, I, as a mother who loves her children, see how difficult the time in which you live is. I see your suffering, but you need to know that you are not alone. My Son is with you. He is everywhere. He is invisible, but you can see Him if you live Him. He is the light which illuminates your soul and gives you peace. He is the Church which you need to love and to always pray and fight for - but not only with words, instead with acts of love. My children, bring it about for everyone to come to know my Son, bring it about that He may be loved, because the truth is in my Son born of God - the Son of God. Do not waste time deliberating too much; you will distance yourselves from the truth. With a simple heart accept His word and live it. If you live His word, you will pray. If you live His word, you will love with a merciful love; you will love each other. The more that you will love, the farther away you will be from death. For those who will live the word of my Son and who will love, death will be life. Thank you. Pray to be able to see my Son in your shepherds. Pray to be able to embrace Him in them."*

September 02, 2015 *"Dear children, My dear apostles of love, my carriers of truth, again I am calling you and gathering you around me to help me, to help all of my children who thirst for love and truth—who thirst for my Son. I am a grace from the Heavenly Father, sent to help you to live the word of my Son. Love one another. I lived your earthly life. I know that it is not always easy, but if you will love each other, you will pray with the heart, you will reach spiritual heights and the way to heaven will be opened for you. I, your mother, am waiting for you there because I am there. Be faithful to my Son and teach others faithfulness. I am with you. I will help you. I will teach you faith that you may know how to transmit it to others in the right way. I will teach you truth that you may know how to discern. I will teach you love that you may come to know what real love is. My children, my Son will make it so as to speak through your words and your actions. Thank you."*

October 02, 2015 *"Dear children, I am here among you to encourage you, to fill you with my love and to call you anew to be witnesses of the love of my Son. Many of my children do not have hope, they do not have peace, they do not have love. They are seeking my Son, but do not know how and where to find Him. My Son is opening wide His arms to them, and you are to help them to come to His embrace. My children, that is why you must pray for love. You must pray very, very much to have all the more love, because love conquers death and makes life last. Apostles of my love, my children, with an honest and simple heart unite in prayer regardless of how far you are from each other. Encourage each other in spiritual growth as I am encouraging you. I am watching over you and am with you whenever you think of me. Pray also for your shepherds, for those who renounced everything for the sake of my Son and for your sake. Love them and pray for them. The Heavenly Father is listening to your prayers. Thank you."*

November 02, 2015 *"Dear children, anew I desire to speak to you about love. I have gathered you around me in the name of my Son according to His will. I desire that your faith be firm, flowing forth from love. Because, those of my children who understand the love of my Son and follow it, live in love and hope. They have come to know the love of God. Therefore, my children, pray, pray so as to be able to love all the more and to do works of love. Because, faith alone without love and works of love is not what I am asking of you: my children, this is an illusion of faith. It is a boasting of self. My Son seeks faith and works, love and goodness. I am praying, and I am also asking you to pray, and to live love; because I desire that my Son, when He looks at the hearts of all of my children, can see love and goodness in them and not hatred and*

274

indifference. My children, apostles of my love, do not lose hope, do not lose strength. You can do this. I am encouraging and blessing you. Because all that is of this world, which many of my children, unfortunately, put in the first place, will disappear; and only love and works of love will remain and open the door of the Kingdom of Heaven. I will wait for you at this door. At this door, I desire to welcome and embrace all of my children. Thank you!"

December 02, 2015 *"Dear children, I am always with you because my Son entrusted you to me. And you, my children, you need me, you are seeking me, you are coming to me and you are bringing joy to my motherly heart. I have, and always will have, love for you; for you who suffer and who offer your pains and sufferings to my Son and to me. My love seeks the love of all of my children, and my children seek my love. Through love, Jesus seeks unity between Heaven and earth; between the Heavenly Father and you, my children - His Church. Therefore, it is necessary to pray much, to pray and love the Church to which you belong. Now, the Church is suffering and needs apostles who by loving unity, by witnessing and giving, show the ways of God. The Church needs apostles who by living the Eucharist with the heart do great works; it needs you, my apostles of love. My children, from the very beginning the Church was persecuted and betrayed, but day by day it grew. It is indestructible because my Son gave it a heart - the Eucharist, and the light of His resurrection shone and will continue to shine upon it. Therefore, do not be afraid. Pray for your shepherds that they may have the strength and the love to be bridges of salvation. Thank you."*

January 2, 2016 *"Dear children, as a mother, I am joyful to be among you because I desire to speak anew about the words of my Son and of His love. I hope that you will accept me with the heart, because the words of my Son and His love are the only light and hope in the darkness of today. This is the only truth and you who will accept and live it will have pure and humble hearts. My Son loves those who are pure and humble. Pure and humble hearts bring to life the words of my Son, they live them, they spread them and they make it possible for everyone to hear them. The words of my Son bring back life to those who listen to them. The words of my Son bring back love and hope. Therefore, my beloved apostles, my children, live the words of my Son. Love each other as He loved you. Love each other in His name, in memory of Him. The Church is advancing and growing because of those who listen to the words of my Son; because of those who love; because of those who suffer and endure in silence and in the hope of final*

275

redemption. Therefore, my beloved children, may the words of my Son and His love be the first and the last thought of your day. Thank you."

February 2, 2016 *"Dear children, I have called you and am calling you anew to come to know my Son, to come to know the truth. I am with you and am praying for you to succeed. My children, you must pray much in order to have all the more love and patience; to know how to endure sacrifice and to be poor in spirit. Through the Holy Spirit, my Son is always with you. His Church is born in every heart that comes to know Him. Pray that you can come to know my Son; pray that your soul may be one with Him. That is the prayer and the love which draws others and makes you my apostles. I am looking at you with love, with a motherly love. I know you; I know your pain and sorrows, because I also suffered in silence. My faith gave me love and hope. I repeat, the Resurrection of my Son and my Assumption into Heaven is hope and love for you. Therefore, my children, pray to come to know the truth; to have firm faith which will lead your heart and which will transform your pain and sufferings into love and hope. Thank you."*

March 2, 2016 *"Dear children, My coming to you is a gift from the Heavenly Father for you. Through His love I am coming to help you to find the way to the truth, to find the way to my Son. I am coming to confirm the truth to you. I desire to remind you of the words of my Son. He pronounced words of salvation for the entire world, the words of love for everyone - that love which He proved by His sacrifice. But even today, many of my children do not know Him, they do not want to come to know Him, they are indifferent. Because of their indifference my heart suffers painfully. My Son has always been in the Father. By being born on earth He brought the divine and from me received the human. With Him the word came among us. With Him came the light of the world which penetrates hearts, illuminates them and fills them with love and consolation. My children, all those who love my Son can see Him, because His face can be seen through the souls which are filled with love for Him. Therefore, my children, my apostles, listen to me. Leave vanity and selfishness. Do not live only for what is earthly and material. Love my Son and make it so that others may see His face through your love for Him. I will help you to come to know Him all the more. I will speak to you about Him. Thank you."*

April 2, 2016 *"Dear children, do not have hearts that are hard, closed and filled with fear. Permit my motherly love to illuminate them and fill them with love and hope; so that, as a mother, I may soothe your pains because I know them, I experienced them. Pain elevates and is the greatest prayer. My Son, in a special way, loves those who suffer pains. He sent me to soothe them for you and bring hope. Trust in Him. I know that it is difficult for you because you see more and more darkness around you. My children, it is necessary to break it by prayer and love. The one who prays and loves is not afraid, he has hope and a merciful love, he sees the light and sees my Son. As my apostles, I call you to keep trying to be an example of merciful love and hope. Always pray anew for all the more love because merciful love brings light which breaks every darkness - it brings my Son. Do not be afraid, you are not alone, I am with you. I implore you to pray for your shepherds that at every moment they may have love, that they may work for my Son with love - through Him and in memory of Him. Thank you."*

May 2, 2016 *"Dear children, my motherly heart desires your true conversion and a firm faith so that you may be able to spread love and peace to all those who surround you. But, my children, do not forget: each of you is a unique world before the Heavenly Father. Therefore, permit the continuous working of the Holy Spirit to work on you. Be my spiritually pure children. In spirituality is beauty. Everything that is spiritual is alive and very beautiful. Do not forget that in the Eucharist, which is the heart of faith, my Son is always with you. He comes to you and breaks bread with you; because, my children, for your sake He died, He resurrected and is coming anew. These words of mine are familiar to you because they are the truth, and the truth does not change. It is only that many of my children have forgotten it. My children, my words are neither old nor new, they are eternal. Therefore, I invite you, my children, to observe well the signs of the times, to 'gather the shattered crosses' and to be apostles of the revelation. Thank you."*

June 2, 2016 *"Dear children, as the Mother of the Church, as your mother, I am smiling as I look at you: how you are coming to me, how you are gathering around me, how you are seeking me. My comings among you are proof of how much Heaven loves you. They indicate to you the way to eternal life, to salvation. My apostles, you who strive to have a pure heart and to have my Son in it, you are on the good way. You who are seeking my Son are seeking the good way. He left many signs of His love. He left hope. It is easy to find Him if you are ready for sacrifice and penance - if you have*

277

patience, mercy and love for your neighbors. Many of my children do not see and do not hear because they do not want to. They do not accept my words and my works, yet through me, my Son calls everyone. His Spirit illuminates all of my children in the light of the Heavenly Father, in the unity of Heaven and Earth, in mutual love - because love invokes love and makes works more important than words. Therefore, my apostles, pray for your Church, love it and do works of love. No matter how betrayed or wounded, it is here because it comes from the Heavenly Father. Pray for your shepherds so that in them you may see the greatness of the love of my Son. Thank you."

July 2, 2016 "Dear children, my real, living presence among you should make you happy because this is the great love of my Son. He is sending me among you so that, with a motherly love, I may grant you safety; that you may comprehend that pain and joy, suffering and love, make your soul live intensely; that I may call you anew to glorify the Heart of Jesus, the heart of faith, the Eucharist. From day to day through the centuries, my Son, alive, returns among you - He returns to you, though He has never left you. When one of you, my children, returns to Him, my motherly heart leaps with joy. Therefore, my children, return to the Eucharist, to my Son. The way to my Son is difficult, full of renunciations, but at the end, there is always the light. I understand your pains and sufferings, and with motherly love I wipe your tears. Trust in my Son, because He will do for you what you would not even know how to ask for. You, my children, you should be concerned only for your soul, because it is the only thing on earth that belongs to you. You will bring it, dirty or clean, before the Heavenly Father. Remember, faith in the love of my Son will always be rewarded. I implore you, in a special way, to pray for those whom my Son called to live according to Him and to love their flock. Thank you."

August 2, 2016 "Dear children, I have come to you - among you - for you to give me your concerns so that I may offer them to my Son; that I may intercede for you before Him for your good. I know that each of you has his concerns, his trials. Therefore, I am inviting you in a motherly way: come to the table of my Son. He is breaking bread for you; He is giving Himself to you; He is giving you hope; He is asking for more faith, hope and serenity from you. He is seeking of you to battle within against egoism, judgement and human weaknesses. Therefore, as a mother, I am saying: pray; because prayer gives you strength for the interior battle. My Son, when He was little, often said to me that there will be many who will love me and call me 'mother'. Among you, I feel love. Thank you. For the sake of that love I am imploring my Son that none of you, *my children, will return home the same as he came; that you may take with you all the more hope, mercy and love; that you may be my apostles of love who will witness with their lives that the Heavenly Father is the source of life and not of death. Dear children, anew, in a motherly way I am imploring you, pray for the chosen ones of my Son, for their blessed hands - for your shepherds - that they may preach my Son with all the more love and in this way bring about conversions. Thank you."*

September 2, 2016 *"Dear children, according to the will of my Son and my motherly love, I am coming to you, my children, but especially to those who have not yet come to know the love of my Son. I am coming to you who think of me and who invoke me. To you, I am giving my motherly love and I am carrying the blessing of my Son. Do you have pure and open hearts, and do you see the gifts, the signs of my presence and love? My children, in your earthly life, be led by my example. My life was pain, silence and immeasurable faith and trust in the Heavenly Father. Nothing is by chance: neither pain, nor joy, nor suffering, nor love. All of these are graces which my Son grants to you and which lead you to eternal life. Of you, my Son asks for love and prayer in Him. As a mother I will teach you: to love and to pray in Him means to pray in the silence of your soul and not only reciting with your lips; it is even the least beautiful gesture done in the name of my Son - it is patience, mercy, the acceptance of pain and sacrifice done for the sake of another. My children, my Son is looking at you. Pray that you also may see His face and that it may be revealed to you. My children, I am revealing to you the only and real truth. Pray that you may comprehend it and be able to spread love and hope; that you may be able to be apostles of my love. In a special way, my motherly heart loves the shepherds. Pray for their blessed hands. Thank you."*

October 2, 2016 *"Dear children, the Holy Spirit, according to the Heavenly Father, made me the mother - the mother of Jesus - and by this alone, also your mother. That is why I am coming to hear you, that I may open my motherly arms to you; to give you my heart and to call you to remain with me, because from the top of the cross my Son entrusted you to me. Unfortunately, many of my children have not come to know the love of my Son; many of them do not want to come to know Him. Oh, my children, how much bad is done by those who must see or interpret in order to come to believe. That is why, you, my children, my apostles, in the silence of your heart, listen to the voice of my Son, so that your heart may be His home, that it may not be dark and sad, but that it may be illuminated with the light of my Son. Seek hope with faith, because faith is the life of the soul. Anew I am calling you: pray, pray to live faith in humility,* in spiritual peace, and illuminated by the light. My children, do not strive to comprehend everything immediately, because I also did not comprehend everything immediately; but I loved, and I believed in the divine words which my Son spoke - He who was the first light and the beginning of redemption. Apostles of my love - you who pray, sacrifice yourselves, love and do not judge - you go and spread the truth, the words of my Son, the Gospel, because you are the living Gospel; you are the rays of the light of my Son. My Son and I will be with you to encourage you and to test you. My children, always implore the blessing of those, and only of those whose hands have been blessed by my Son, of your shepherds. Thank you."

November 2, 2016 *"Dear children, to come to you and to make myself known to you is a great joy for my motherly heart. It is a gift from my Son for you and for others who are coming. As a mother, I am calling you: love my Son above everything. In order to love Him with all your heart, you need to come to know Him. You will come to know Him through prayer. Pray with the heart and with your feelings. To pray means to think of His love and sacrifice. To pray means to love, to give, to suffer and to offer. I am calling you, my children, to be apostles of prayer and love. My children, it is a time of vigilance. In this vigil, I am calling you to prayer, love and trust. As my Son will be looking in your hearts, my motherly heart desires for Him to see unconditional trust and love in them. The united love of my apostles will live, will conquer and will expose evil. My children, I was a chalice of the God-man; I was God's instrument. That is why I am calling you, my apostles, to be a chalice of the true and pure love of my Son. I am calling you to be an instrument through which all those who have not come to know the love of God - who have never loved - may comprehend, accept and be saved. Thank you, my children."*

January 2, 2017 *"Dear children, My Son was the source of love and light when he spoke on earth to the people of all peoples. My apostles, follow His light. This is not easy. You must be little. You must make yourselves smaller than others; with the help of faith to be filled with His love. Not a single person on earth can experience a miraculous experience without faith. I am with you. I am making myself known to you by these comings, by these words; I desire to witness to you my love and motherly care. My children, do not waste time posing questions to which you never receive an answer. At the end of your journey on earth, the Heavenly Father will give them to you. Always know that God knows everything; God sees, God loves. My most beloved Son illuminates lives, dispels darkness; and my motherly love which carries me to you is* inexpressible, mysterious but real. I am expressing my feelings to you: love, understanding and motherly benevolence. Of you, my apostles, I am asking for your roses of prayer which need to be acts of love. To my motherly heart these are the dearest prayers. I offer these to my Son who was born for your sake. He looks at you and hears you. We are always close to you. This is the love which calls, unites, converts, encourages and fulfills. Therefore, my apostles, always love one another and above all, love my Son. This is the only way to salvation, to eternal life. This is my dearest prayer which fills my heart with the most beautiful scent of roses. Pray, always pray for your shepherds that they may have the strength to be the light of my Son. Thank you."

February 2, 2017 "Dear children, you who are striving to offer every day of your life to my Son, you who are trying to live with Him, you who are praying and sacrificing - you are hope in this peaceless world. You are rays of the light of my Son, a living gospel, and you are my beloved apostles of love. My Son is with you. He is with those who think of Him - those who pray. But in the same way, He is patiently waiting for those who do not know Him. Therefore, you, apostles of my love, pray with the heart and with your works show the love of my Son. This is the only hope for you, and this is also the only way to eternal life. I, as a mother, I am here with you. Your prayers directed to me are the most beautiful roses of love for me. I cannot but be where I sense the scent of roses. There is hope. Thank you."

March 2, 2017 "Dear children, with motherly love I am coming to help you to have more love and that means more faith. I am coming to help you to live with love the words of my Son, so that the world would be different. Therefore, apostles of my love, I am gathering you around myself. Look at me with the heart, speak to me as to a mother about your pains, sufferings and your joys. Ask me to pray to my Son for you. My Son is merciful and just. My motherly heart would desire for you also to be like that. My motherly heart would desire that you, apostles of my love, speak of my Son and of me to all those around you with your life; so that the world would be different; that simplicity and purity would return; that faith and hope would return. Therefore, my children, pray, pray, pray with the heart, pray with love, pray with good works. Pray that everyone would come to know my Son, so that the world would change, that the world would be saved. With love live the words of my Son. Do not judge, instead love one another so that my heart could triumph. Thank you."

April 2, 2017 *"Dear children, apostles of my love, it is up to you to spread the love of my Son to all those who have not come to know it; you, the little lights of the world, whom I am teaching with motherly love to shine clearly with full brilliance. Prayer will help you, because prayer saves you, prayer saves the world. Therefore, my children, pray with words, feelings, merciful love and sacrifice. My Son has shown you the way - He who became incarnate and made of me the first chalice, with His exalted sacrifice He has shown you how you need to love. Therefore, my children, do not be afraid to speak the truth. Do not be afraid to change yourself and the world by spreading love, by doing everything for my Son to be known and loved by loving others in Him. As a mother, I am always with you. I am imploring my Son to help you for love to reign in your life - love that lives, love that draws, love which gives life. I am teaching you such love - pure love. It is up to you, my apostles, to recognize it, live it and spread it. Pray with feeling for your shepherds so that they can witness my Son with love. Thank you."*

The Annual Apparitions

Mirjana Dragicevic-Soldo

Mirjana Dragicevic-Soldo had daily apparitions from June 24, 1981 to December 25, 1982. On that day, Our Lady told her:

"Mirjana, I chose you, and I told you everything that is necessary. I entrusted you with the knowledge of many abominations, which you must carry with dignity. Think of me, and how much I too shed tears because of this. You must always be brave. You quickly understood my messages, and so you must understand that now I must leave. Be brave!"

Entrusting to her the tenth secret, Our Lady told her that for the rest of her life she would have one yearly apparition, on March 18th.

March 18, 1995

The apparition lasted ten minutes. After it, Mirjana, in tears, withdrew to her room. Here is what she said about her meeting with Our Lady.

"I prayed the Our Father and the Glory Be with our Lady three times. The first one was for unbelievers, especially for those who have not experienced God's love. The second was for the souls in Purgatory, and the third for the intentions of those who were present at the apparition. Our Lady blessed all those present and also all the religious articles. Our Lady was not happy during the apparition as She has been known to be during past apparitions for my birthday. She talked to me about the secrets, but I cannot say anything about that."

In answer to questions why Mirjana cried and if Our Lady gave any message, the visionary answered,

"It is hard for me when Our Lady goes away. The meeting with Our Lady is a fulfillment of everything. I feel completed. But when She leaves, I realize that I'm here, on earth, and that I'm going on without her as if I were forsaken, even though I know I am not. It is really hard, so hard."

"In the message, Our Lady spoke about the love that we need. Her wish is that people love one another because God is love, and if we love God, we will love one another. I understand this message as one of consolation, and that we don't have to fear anything if we have love. And this was Our Lady's message:"

"Dear children! Already for many years as a Mother, I have been teaching you faith and God's love. You have not shown gratitude to the dear Father; nor have you given Him glory. You have become empty, and your heart has become hard and without love toward your neighbors' sufferings. I am teaching you love and showing you that the dear Father loved you, but you have not loved Him. He sacrificed his Son for your salvation, my children. As long as you do not love, you will not know your Father's love. You won't get to know Him, because God is love. Love, and don't be afraid, my children, because there is no fear in love. If your hearts are open to the Father, and if they are full of love toward Him, then why any fear of what is to come? Those who are afraid are the ones who do not love because they are waiting for punishments and because they know how empty and hard they are. Children, I am leading you to love, to the dear Father. I am leading you to eternal life. Eternal life is my Son. Receive Him and you have received love."

March 18, 1996

After the apparition, Mirjana transmitted Our Lady's message,
"Dear children! On this message, which I give you today through my servant, I desire for you to reflect a long time. My children, great is the love of God. Do not close your eyes, do not close your ears, while I repeat to you: 'Great is his love!' Hear my call and my supplication, which I direct to you. Consecrate your heart and make in it the home of the Lord. May He dwell in it forever. My eyes and my heart will be here, even when I will no longer appear. Act in everything as I ask you and lead you to the Lord. Do not reject from yourself the name of God, that you may not be rejected. Accept my messages that you may be accepted. Decide, my children; it is the time of decision. Be of just and innocent heart that I may lead you to your Father, (for this I am here) in his great love. Thank you for being here!"

March 18, 1997

The apparition was at 1:50pm and lasted six minutes. Our Lady did not speak about the secrets, but gave the following message,

"Dear children, as a mother I beseech you, do not go on the way you have been going. That is a way without love toward neighbor and toward my Son. On that way, you will find only hardness and emptiness of heart, and not the peace that everyone is crying out for. Genuine peace will be had only by the one who sees and loves my Son in his neighbor. In whose heart my Son reigns, that one knows what peace is and tranquility. Thank you having responded to my call."

March 18, 1998

The apparition lasted between four and five minutes. Our Lady spoke to her about the secrets, blessed all those present, and gave the following message,

"Dear children! I call you to be my light, in order to enlighten all those who still live in darkness, to fill their hearts with Peace, my Son. Thank you for having responded to my call!"

March 18, 1999

The apparition lasted for six minutes from 10:14am to 10:20am. Our Lady spoke about the secrets. She blessed everyone.

"Dear children, I want you to surrender your hearts to me so that I may take you on the way which leads to the light and to eternal life. I do not want your hearts to wander in today's darkness. I will help you. I will be with you on this way of discovery of the love and the mercy of God. As a mother, I ask you to permit me to do this. Thank you for having responded to my call."

March 18, 2000

The apparition started at 9:55am and lasted about five minutes. Our Lady prayed over everyone and blessed everyone. Mirjana especially recommended the sick. This time Our Lady did not say anything about the secrets.

"Dear children, do not seek peace and happiness in vain, in the wrong places, and in wrong things. Do not permit your hearts to become hard by loving vanity. Invoke the name of my Son. Receive Him in your heart. Only in the name of my Son will you experience true happiness and true peace in your heart. Only in this way will you come to know the love of God and spread it further. I am calling you to be my apostles."

March 18, 2001

The apparition lasted five minutes from 9:45am to 9:50am. Our Lady blessed everyone and gave a message. She was resolute and clear in Her words.

"Dear children, today I call you to love and mercy. Give love to each other as your Father gives it to you. Be merciful (pause) - with your heart. Do good works, not permitting them to wait for you too long. Every mercy that comes from the heart brings you closer to my Son."

March 18, 2002

The apparition lasted from 9:27am to 9:34am, and Our Lady gave the following message,

"Dear children, as a mother, I implore you, open your heart and offer it to me, and fear nothing. I will be with you and will teach you how to put Jesus in first place. I will teach you to love Him and to belong to Him completely. Comprehend, dear children, that without my Son there is no salvation. You should become aware that He is your beginning and your end. Only with this awareness can you be happy and merit eternal life. As your mother, I desire this for you. Thank you for having responded to my call."

March 18, 2003

The apparition lasted from 8:55am to 9:02am, and Our Lady gave the following message,

"Dear children, particularly at this holy time of penance and prayer, I call you to make a choice. God gave you free will to choose life or death. Listen to my messages with the heart that you may become cognizant of what you are to do and how you will find the way to life. My children, without God you can do nothing; do not forget this even for a single moment. For what are you and what will you be on earth, when you will return to it again? Do not anger God, but follow me to life. Thank you for being here."

March 18, 2004

This year several thousand pilgrims gathered to pray the rosary at the Cenacolo Community in Medjugorje. The apparition lasted from 1:58pm to 2:03pm, and Our Lady gave the following message:

"Dear children! Also today, watching you with a heart full of love, I desire to tell you that what you persistently seek, what you long for, my little children, is before you. It is sufficient that, in a cleaned heart, you place my Son in first place, and then you will be able to see. Listen to me and permit me to lead you to this in a motherly way."

March 18, 2005

This year several thousand pilgrims gathered to pray the rosary at the Cenacolo Community in Medjugorje. The apparition lasted from 2:09pm to 2:14pm, and Our Lady gave the following message:

"Dear children! I come to you as the mother who, above all, loves her children. My children, I desire to teach you to love also. I pray for this. I pray that you will recognize my Son in each of your neighbors. The way to my Son, who is true peace and love, passes through the love for all neighbors. My children, pray and fast for your heart to be open for this, my intention."

March 18, 2006

This year several thousand pilgrims gathered to pray the rosary at the Cenacolo Community in Medjugorje. The apparition lasted from 1:59pm to 2:04pm, and Our Lady gave the following message:

"Dear children! In this Lenten time I call you to interior renunciation. The way to this leads you through love, fasting, prayer, and good works. Only with total interior renunciation will you recognize God's love and the signs of the time in which you live. You will be witnesses of these signs and will begin to speak about them. I desire to bring you to this. Thank you for having responded to me."

March 18, 2007

This year several thousand pilgrims gathered to pray the rosary at the Cenacolo Community in Medjugorje. The apparition lasted from 2:07pm to 2:12pm, and Our Lady gave the following message:

"Dear children! I come to you as a Mother with gifts. I come with love and mercy. Dear children, mine is a big heart. In it I desire all of your hearts, purified by fasting and prayer. I desire that through love our hearts may triumph together. I desire that through that triumph you may see the real Truth, the real Way, and the real Life. I desire that you may see my Son. Thank you."

Mirjana, "Our Lady blessed all of us, and all religious articles. Again She emphasized that it is only Her Motherly blessing, and She asked for daily prayers for those whom She said my Son has chosen and blessed." Mirjana clarified that she believed Our Lady was referring to priests.

March 18, 2008

This year several thousand pilgrims gathered to pray the rosary at the Cenacolo Community in Medjugorje. The apparition lasted from 2:01pm to 2:08pm.

Mirjana transmitted the following: "I have never seen Our Lady address us in this manner. She extended her hands towards us, and with her hands extended in this way," She said,

"Dear children, today I extend my hands towards you. Do not be afraid to accept them. They desire to give you love and peace and to help you in salvation. Therefore, my children, receive them. Fill my heart with joy, and I will lead you towards holiness. The way on which I lead you is difficult and full of temptations and falls. I will be with you, and my hands will hold you. Be persevering so that, at the end of the way, we can all together, in joy and love, hold the hands of my Son. Come with me; fear not. Thank you."

March 18, 2009

Several thousand pilgrims gathered in prayer of the rosary at the Blue Cross. The apparition lasted from 1:52pm to 1:58pm.

"Dear children! Today I call you to look into your hearts sincerely and for a long time. What will you see in them? Where is my Son in them, and where is the desire to follow me to Him? My children, may this time of renunciation be a time when you will ask yourself, 'What does my God desire of me personally? What am I to do?' Pray, fast, and have a heart full of mercy. Do not forget your shepherds. Pray that they may not get lost, that they may remain in my Son so as to be good shepherds to their flock."

Our Lady looked at all those present and added, *"Again I say to you, if you knew how much I love you, you would cry with happiness. Thank you."*

March 18, 2010

Several thousand pilgrims gathered in prayer of the rosary at the Blue Cross. The apparition lasted from 1:50pm to 1:54pm.

"Dear children! Today I call you to love with all your heart and with all your soul. Pray for the gift of love, because when the soul loves, it calls my Son to itself. My Son does not refuse those who call Him and who desire to live according to Him. Pray for those who do not comprehend love, who do not understand what it means to love. Pray that God may be their Father and not their Judge. My children, you be my apostles; be my river of love. I need you. Thank you."

March 18, 2011

Several thousand pilgrims gathered in prayer of the rosary at the Blue Cross. The apparition lasted from 1:46pm to 1:50pm.

"Dear children! I am with you in the name of the greatest Love, in the name of dear God, who has come close to you through my Son and has shown you real love. I desire to lead you on the way of God. I desire to teach you real love so that others may see it in you, that you may see it in others, that you may be a brother to them, and that others may see a merciful brother in you. My children, do not be afraid to open your hearts to me. With motherly love, I will show you what I expect of each of you, what I expect of my apostles. Set out with me. Thank you."

March 18, 2012
Several thousand pilgrims gathered in prayer of the rosary at the Blue Cross. The apparition lasted from 2:00pm to 2:05pm.

"Dear children! I am coming among you because I desire to be your mother, your intercessor. I desire to be the bond between you and the Heavenly Father, your mediatrix. I desire to take you by the hand and to walk with you in the battle against the impure spirit. My children, consecrate yourselves to me completely. I will take your lives into my motherly hands, and I will teach you peace and love, and then I will give you over to my Son. I am asking you to pray and fast, because only in this way will you know how to witness my Son in the right way through my motherly heart. Pray for your shepherds that, united in my Son, they may always joyfully proclaim the Word of God. Thank you."

March 18, 2013
Several thousand pilgrims gathered in prayer of the rosary at the Blue Cross. The apparition lasted from 1:52pm to 1:58pm.

"Dear children! I call you to, with complete trust and joy, bless the name of the Lord and, day by day, to give Him thanks from the heart for His great love. My Son, through that love which He showed by the Cross, gave you the possibility to be forgiven for everything; so that you do not have to be ashamed or to hide, and out of fear not to open the door of your heart to my Son. To the contrary, my children, reconcile with the Heavenly Father so that you may be able to come to love yourselves as my Son loves you. When you come to love yourselves, you will also love others; in them you will see my Son and recognize the greatness of His love. Live in faith! Through me, my Son is preparing you for the works which He desires to do through you – works through which He desires to be glorified. Give Him thanks. Especially thank Him for the shepherds - for your intercessors in the reconciliation with the Heavenly Father. I am thanking you, my children. Thank you."

March 18, 2014

Several thousand pilgrims gathered in prayer of the Rosary. The apparition lasted from 1:46pm to 1:51pm.

"Dear children! As a mother, I desire to be of help to you. With my motherly love, I desire to help you to open your heart and to put my Son in the first place in it. Through your love for my Son and through your prayer, I desire for God's light to illuminate you and God's mercy to fill you. In this way, I desire for the darkness, and the shadow of death which wants to encompass and mislead you, to be driven away. I desire for you to feel the joy of the blessing of God's promise. You, children of man, you are God's children - you are my children. Therefore, my children, set out on the ways on which my love leads you, teaches you humility and wisdom, and finds the way to the Heavenly Father. Pray with me for those who do not accept me and do not follow me - those who, because of hardness of their hearts, cannot feel the joy of humility, devotion, peace and love — the joy of my Son. Pray that your shepherds, with their blessed hands, may always give you the joy of God's blessing. Thank you."

March 18, 2015

Several thousand pilgrims gathered in prayer of the Rosary. The apparition lasted from 1:47pm to 1:53pm.

"Dear children! With a full heart I am asking you, I am imploring you children: cleanse your hearts of sin and lift them up to God and to eternal life. I am imploring you: be vigilant and open for truth. Do not permit for all that is of this earth to distance you from the true cognition of the contentment in the communion with my Son. I am leading you on the way of true wisdom, because only with true wisdom can you come to know true peace and the true good. Do not waste time asking for signs of the Heavenly Father, because He has already given you the greatest sign, which is my Son. Therefore, my children, pray so that the Holy Spirit can lead you into truth, can help you to come to know it, and through that knowledge of the truth that you may be one with the Heavenly Father and with my Son. That is the cognition which gives happiness on earth and opens the door of eternal life and infinite love. Thank you."

March 18, 2016

Several thousand pilgrims gathered in prayer of the Rosary. The apparition lasted from 1:50pm to 1:56pm.

"Dear children! With a motherly heart filled with love for you, my children, I desire to teach you complete trust in God the Father. I desire for you to learn by an internal gaze and internal listening to follow God's will. I desire for you to learn to boundlessly trust in His mercy and His love, as I always trusted. Therefore, my children, cleanse your hearts. Free yourselves from everything that binds you to only what is earthly and permit what is of God to form your life by your prayer and sacrifice—so that God's Kingdom may be in your heart; that you may begin to live proceeding from God the Father; that you may always strive to walk with my Son. But for all of this, my children, you must be poor in spirit and filled with love and mercy. You must have pure and simple hearts and always be ready to serve. My children, listen to me, I speak for your salvation. Thank you."

March 18, 2017

Several thousand pilgrims gathered in prayer of the Rosary. The apparition lasted from 1:44pm to 1:48pm.

"Dear children! My motherly desire is for your hearts to be filled with peace, and for your souls to be pure so that in the presence of my Son you could see His face. Because, my children, as a mother I know that you thirst for consolation, hope and protection. You, my children, consciously and unconsciously are seeking my Son. I also, as I passed the time on earth, rejoiced, suffered and patiently endured pains, until my Son, in all His glory, removed them. And that is why I am saying to my Son: help them always. You, my children, with true love, illuminate the darkness of selfishness which all the more envelopes my children. Be generous. May both your hands and heart always be open. Do not be afraid. Abandon yourselves to my Son with trust and hope. As you look towards Him, live life with love. To love means to give oneself, to endure, and never to judge. To love means to live the words of my Son. My children, as a mother I am speaking to you: only true love leads to eternal happiness. Thank you."

Ivanka Ivankovic-Elez

Ivanka Ivankovic-Elez had daily apparitions from June 24, 1981 to May 7, 1985. On that day, Our Lady told her,

"My dear child, today is our last meeting, but do not be sad because I will come to you on every anniversary except this one. My child, do not think that you have done something wrong, and that's why I no longer come. No, this isn't true. The plan which my Son and I have, you accepted with all your heart and completed your part. Be happy because I am your mother, and I love you with all my heart. Ivanka, thank you for having responded to the invitation of my Son and for persevering and for always being close to Him and staying until He had completed that which He asked of you. My child, tell your friends that both I and my Son will always be there for you when you seek or call us. About that which I told you during these years concerning the secrets, it is still not time to tell anyone. Ivanka, the grace which you and the others received, nobody on this earth has received up until now!"

Confiding to her the tenth secret, Our Lady told her that for the rest of her life, she would have one yearly apparition, on June 25th, the anniversary of the apparitions.

June 25, 1995

Ivanka had the six minute apparition at her family home at the end of which she brought this message of Our Lady to those present: "Our Lady blessed every one present at the apparition. She spoke to me about the secrets. She called us to pray for families, because Satan desires to destroy them. In addition, Our Lady called on all people to be messengers of peace."

At the end Ivanka added, "Now I will have to wait a whole year again for another meeting."

June 25, 1996

The apparition took place in her family home and lasted seven minutes. After the apparition Ivanka said that this had been one of the most beautiful apparitions that she had had up to the present. "Our Lady thanks us for our prayer and for our love, and desires that prayer and love become interwoven into every day. In conclusion, She invited us to pray for those who were under diabolic possession."

June 25, 1997

Ivanka had the six minute apparition in her own family home. After the apparition Ivanka said, "Our Lady talked to me about the fifth secret, and spoke the following message,"

"Dear children, pray with the heart to know how to forgive and how to be forgiven. I thank you for your prayers and the love you give to me."

June 25, 1998

Ivanka had the apparition in her home, and it lasted six minutes. After the apparition Ivanka said, "Our Lady was joyful. I asked her to bless everyone, which She did. Our Lady talked to me about all the secrets. She invited us to pray for families at this time, and especially to pray for the sick. She called us to open our hearts and to thank her Son for the grace He has given us. At the end, Our Lady thanked us for our prayers and love."

June 25, 1999

Ivanka had the apparition, which lasted eight minutes, in her own family home. Present for the apparition were only Ivanka's family, her husband and their three children. After the apparition Ivanka said that during the apparition, she prayed for the parish and families, and she recommended all in her prayer. Our Lady gave the following message,

"Dear children, thank my Son for all the graces that He has given you. Pray for peace, pray for peace, pray for peace!"

June 25, 2000

The apparition lasted seven minutes, and Ivanka had it in her family home. Present for the apparition were only Ivanka's family, her husband and their three children. Our Lady gave the following message,

"I introduced myself as 'Queen of Peace'. Again, I call you to peace, fasting, prayer. Renew family prayer and receive my blessing."

Ivanka told us that Our Lady was happy, and that She spoke to her about the sixth secret.

June 25, 2001

Ivanka had the apparition in the presence of her family. She says that Our Lady was joyful, and that She spoke to her about the future of the Church. Our Lady gave the following message,

"Dear angels! Thank you for your prayers, because through them my plan is being realized. This is why, angels, pray, pray, pray, so that my plan may be realized. Receive my motherly blessing!"

June 25, 2002

The apparition lasted six minutes. Ivanka had the apparition at home in the presence of her family, her husband and their three children. Our Lady gave the following message,

"Dear children, do not tire of prayer. Pray for peace, peace, peace."

Our Lady related to Ivanka some new details about Her life. "She gave us her motherly blessing. Our Lady was joyful."

June 25, 2003

The apparition lasted ten minutes. Ivanka had the apparition at home in the presence of her family, her husband and their three children. Our Lady gave the following message,

"Dear children! Do not be afraid; I am always with you. Open your heart for love and peace to enter into it. Pray for peace, peace, peace."

Our Lady was joyful and spoke to Ivanka more extensively about Her life.

June 25, 2004

The apparition lasted nine minutes. Ivanka had the apparition at home in the presence of her family, her husband and their three children. Our Lady gave the following message,

"Dear children! Pray for those families who have not come to know the love of my Son. Receive my motherly blessing."

Our Lady was joyful and spoke to Ivanka more extensively about Her life.

June 25, 2005

The apparition lasted ten minutes. Ivanka had the apparition at home in the presence of her family, her husband and their three children. Our Lady gave the following message,

"Dear children, love each other with the love of my Son. Peace, peace, peace."

Our Lady was joyful and spoke to Ivanka about the 6th secret.

June 25, 2006

The apparition lasted seven minutes. Ivanka had the apparition at home in the presence of her family, her husband and their three children. Our Lady gave the following message,

"Dear children, thank you for having responded to my call. Pray, pray, pray."

Our Lady was joyful, and spoke about the seventh secret.

June 25, 2007

The apparition lasted seventeen minutes. Ivanka had the apparition at home in the presence of her family, her husband and their three children.

After the apparition, the visionary Ivanka said, "Our Lady remained with me for seventeen minutes. She was joyful and spoke to me about Her life. Our Lady said:" *"Dear children, receive my motherly blessing."*

June 25, 2008

The apparition lasted six minutes. Ivanka had the apparition at home in the presence of her family, her husband and their three children. After the apparition, the visionary Ivanka said, "Our Lady spoke to me about the ninth secret. She gave us her motherly blessing."

June 25, 2009

The apparition lasted ten minutes. Ivanka had the apparition at home in the presence of her family, her husband and their three children. After the apparition, the visionary Ivanka said, "Our Lady remained with me for ten minutes and spoke to me of the tenth secret. Our Lady said:"

"Dear children, I call you to be apostles of peace. Peace, peace, peace."

June 25, 2010

The apparition, which lasted six minutes, took place at Ivanka's family home. Only Ivanka's family was present at the apparition. After the apparition, Ivanka said, "Our Lady spoke to me about the fifth secret and, at the end, said:" *"Dear children, receive my motherly blessing."*

June 25, 2011

The apparition, which lasted eight minutes, took place at Ivanka's family home. Only Ivanka's family was present at the apparition. After the apparition, Ivanka said, "Our Lady spoke to me about the first secret and, at the end, said:" *"Dear children, receive my motherly blessing."*

June 25, 2012

The apparition, which lasted 7 minutes, took place at Ivanka's family home. Only Ivanka's family was present at the apparition. After the apparition, Ivanka said, "Our Lady spoke to me about the 5th secret and at the end said:" *"I am giving you my motherly blessing. Pray for peace, peace, peace."*

June 25, 2013

The apparition lasted 2 minutes, and took place at Ivanka's family home. Only Ivanka's family was present at the apparition. After the apparition, Ivanka said, "Our Lady did not give a message. She blessed us with her motherly blessing."

June 25, 2014

The apparition lasted 4 minutes, and took place at Ivanka's family home. Only Ivanka's family was present at the apparition. After the apparition, Ivanka said, "Our Lady gave us her motherly blessing."

June 25, 2015

The apparition lasted 4 minutes, and took place at Ivanka's family home. Only Ivanka's family was present at the apparition. After the apparition, Ivanka said: "Our Lady gave us her motherly blessing and said: *Peace, peace, peace.*"

June 25, 2016

The apparition lasted 4 minutes, took place at Ivanka's family home. Only Ivanka's family was present at the apparition. After the apparition, Ivanka said: Our Lady gave the following message: *"Little children, pray, pray, pray."* Our Lady was joyful and blessed all of us with her motherly blessing.

Jakov Colo

Jakov Colo had daily apparitions from June 25, 1981 to September 12, 1998. On that day, Our Lady told him:

"Dear child! I am your mother, and I love you unconditionally. From today, I will not be appearing to you every day, but only on Christmas, the birthday of my Son. Do not be sad, because as a mother, I will always be with you, and like every true mother, I will never leave you. And you continue further to follow the way of my Son, the way of peace and love, and try to persevere in the mission that I have confided to you. Be an example of that man who has known God and God's love. Let people always see in you an example of how God acts on people and how God acts through them. I bless you with my motherly blessing, and I thank you for having responded to my call."

Entrusting to him the tenth secret, Our Lady told him that for the rest of his life he would have one yearly apparition, on Christmas Day.

December 25, 1998

After the apparition, which began at 11.50am, and lasted twelve minutes, Jakov wrote: "Our Lady was joyful. She greeted me, as always, with *'Praised be Jesus!'* She spoke to me about the secrets and afterwards gave me this message."

"Dear children! Today, on the birthday of my Son, my heart is filled with immeasurable joy, love and peace. As your mother, I desire for each of you to feel that same joy, peace and love in the heart. That is why do not be afraid to open your heart and to completely surrender yourself to Jesus, because only in this way can He enter into your heart and fill it with love, peace, and joy. I bless you with my motherly blessing."

Jakov prayed with his family. He prepared himself for the apparition with confession and Holy Mass. After the apparition, he cried for a while.

December 25, 1999

The apparition began at 3:00pm and lasted for ten minutes. Our Lady came joyfully in a golden dress with the Child Jesus in her arms. She talked about the secrets. She blessed everyone. Our Lady gave the following message.

"Dear children! Today on the birthday of my Son, when my heart is filled with immeasurable joy and love, I invite you to open fully and surrender fully to God. Throw out all the darkness from your heart and let God's light and God's love enter your heart and dwell there forever. Be carriers of God's light and love to all people, so everyone, in you and through you, can feel and experience the authentic light and love that only God is able to give you. I am blessing you with my motherly blessing!"

December 25, 2000

The apparition began at 3:20 pm and lasted ten minutes. Our Lady was joyful with Baby Jesus in Her arms. She blessed everyone and gave a message.

"Dear children! Today when Jesus is born and by His birth brings immeasurable joy, love and peace, I call you, in a special way to say your 'yes' to Jesus. Open your hearts so that Jesus enters into them, comes to dwell in them, and begins to work through you. Only in this way will you be able to comprehend the true beauty of God's love, joy, and peace. Dear children, rejoice in the birth of Jesus and pray for all those hearts that have not opened to Jesus so that Jesus may enter into each of their hearts and may start working through them, so that every person will be an example of a true person through whom God works."

December 25, 2001

The apparition began at 3:30pm and lasted five minutes. Our Lady gave the following message.

"Dear children, today when Jesus is born anew for you, in a special way, I want to call you to conversion. Pray, pray, pray for the conversion of your heart, so that Jesus may be born in you all and may dwell in you and come to reign over your entire being. Thank you for having responded to my call."

December 25, 2002

Our Lady came with the Child Jesus in her arms. The apparition began at 5:20pm and lasted seven minutes. Our Lady gave the following message.

"Dear children! Today on the day of love and peace, with Jesus in my arms, I call you to prayer for peace. Little children, without God and prayer you cannot have peace. Therefore, little children, open your hearts so that the King of Peace may be born in your hearts. Only in this way can you witness and carry God's peace to this peaceless world. I am with you and bless you with my motherly blessing."

December 25, 2003

The apparition began at 3:15pm and lasted eight minutes. Our Lady gave the following message.

"Dear children! Today, when in a special way Jesus desires to give you His peace, I call you to pray for peace in your hearts. Children, without peace in your hearts you cannot feel the love and joy of the birth of Jesus. Therefore, little children, today in a special way, open your hearts and begin to pray. Only through prayer and complete surrender will your heart be filled with the love and peace of Jesus. I bless you with my motherly blessing."

December 25, 2004

The apparition began at 2:30pm and lasted seven minutes. Our Lady gave the following message.

"Dear children! Today, on a day of grace, with little Jesus in my arms, in a special way I call you to open your hearts and to begin to pray. Little children, ask Jesus to be born in each of your hearts and to begin to rule in your lives. Pray to Him for the grace to be able to recognize Him always and in every person. Little children, ask Jesus for love, because only with God's love can you love God and all people. I carry you all in my heart and give you my Motherly blessing."

December 25, 2005

The apparition began at 2:45pm and lasted seven minutes. Our Lady gave the following message.

"Dear children! Today, with Jesus in my arms, in a special way I call you to conversion. Children, through all this time which God permitted me to be with you, I continuously called you to conversion. Many of your hearts remained closed. Little children, Jesus is peace, love and joy; therefore now decide for Jesus. Begin to pray. Pray to Him for the gift of conversion. Little children, only with Jesus can you have peace, joy and a heart filled with love. Little children, I love you. I am your Mother and give you my motherly blessing."

December 25, 2006

The apparition began at 3:23pm and lasted six minutes. Our Lady gave the following message.

"Today is a great day of joy and peace. Rejoice with me. Little children, in a special way, I call you to holiness in your families. I desire, little children, that each of your families be holy and that God's joy and peace, which God sends you today in a special way, may come to rule and dwell in your families. Little children, open your hearts today on this day of grace, decide for God and put Him in first place in your family. I am your Mother. I love you and give you my Motherly Blessing."

December 25, 2007

The apparition began at 2:29pm and lasted six minutes. Our Lady gave the following message.

"Dear children! Today in a special way I call you to become open to God and for each of your hearts today to become a place of Jesus' birth. Little children, through all this time that God permits me to be with you, I desire to lead you to the joy of your life. Little children, the only true joy of your life is God. Therefore, dear children, do not seek joy in things of this earth but open your hearts and accept God. Little children, everything passes; only God remains in your heart. Thank you for having responded to my call."

December 25, 2008

The apparition began at 9:49am and lasted six minutes. Our Lady gave the following message.

"Dear children! Today, in a special way, I call you to pray for peace. Without God you cannot have peace or live in peace. Therefore, little children, today on this day of grace open your hearts to the King of peace, for Him to be born in you, and to grant you His peace, and you be carriers of peace in this peaceless world. Thank you for having responded to my call."

December 25, 2009

The apparition began at 2:35pm and lasted twelve minutes. Our Lady gave the following message.

"Dear children! All of this time in which God in a special way permits me to be with you, I desire to lead you on the way that leads to Jesus and to your salvation. My little children, you can find salvation only in God, and therefore, especially on this day of grace with little Jesus in my arms, I call you to permit Jesus to be born in your hearts. Only with Jesus in your heart can you set out on the way of salvation and eternal life. Thank you for having responded to my call."

December 25, 2010

The apparition began at 2:25pm and lasted seven minutes. Jakov said, "Our Lady spoke to me about the secrets and at the end said, 'Pray, pray, pray.'"

December 25, 2011

The apparition began at 3:30pm and lasted eleven minutes. Our Lady gave the following message.

"Dear children! Today, in a special way, I desire to take you to and give you over to my Son. Little children, open your hearts and permit Jesus to be born in you, because only in this way, little children, will you yourselves be able to experience your new birth and set out with Jesus in your hearts towards the way of salvation. Thank you for having responded to my call."

December 25, 2012

The apparition began at 2:15pm and lasted ten minutes. Our Lady gave the following message.

"Dear children, give the gift of your life to me and completely surrender to me so that I may help you to comprehend my motherly love and the love of my Son for you. My children, I love you immeasurably and today, in a special way, on the day of the birth of my Son, I desire to receive each of you into my heart and to give a gift of your lives to my Son. My children, Jesus loves you and gives you the grace to live in His mercy, but sin has overtaken many of your hearts and you live in darkness. Therefore, my children, do not wait, say 'no' to sin and surrender your hearts to my Son, because only in this way will you be able to live God's mercy and, with Jesus in your hearts, set out on the way of salvation."

December 25 2013

The apparition began at 3:07 pm and lasted 8 minutes. Afterwards Jakov transmitted the following message.

"Little children, today in a special way, Jesus desires to come to dwell in each of your hearts and to share with you your every joy and pain. Therefore, little children, today in a special way, peer into your hearts and ask yourselves if the peace and joy of the birth of Jesus have truly taken hold of your hearts. Little children, do not live in darkness, aspire towards the light and towards God's salvation. Children, decide for Jesus and give Him your life and your hearts, because only in this way will the Most High be able to work in you and through you."

December 25th 2014

The apparition began at 2:40 pm and lasted 8 minutes. Afterwards Jakov transmitted the following message.

"Dear children! Today, on this day of grace, I desire for each of your hearts to become a little stable of Bethlehem in which the Savior of the world was born. I am your mother who loves you immeasurably and is concerned for each of you. Therefore, my children, abandon yourselves to the mother, so that she may place each of your hearts and lives before little Jesus; because only in this way, my children, your hearts will be witnesses of God's daily birth in you. Permit God to illuminate your lives with light and your

hearts with joy, so that you may daily illuminate the way and be an example of true joy to others who live in darkness and are not open to God and His graces. Thank you for having responded to my call."

December 25th 2015
The apparition began at 2:08 pm and lasted 10 minutes. Afterwards Jakov transmitted the following message.

"Dear children! All these years that God permits me to be with you are a sign of the immeasurable love which God has for each one of you and a sign of how much God loves you. Little children, how many graces the Most High has given to you and how many graces he desires to give to you. But, little children, your hearts are closed and live in fear, and do not permit Jesus to have His love and His peace overcome your hearts and to begin to reign in your lives. To live without God means to live in darkness and never to come to know the Father's love and His care for each of you. Therefore, little children, today in a special way pray to Jesus that as of today your life may experience a new birth in God and become a light which will radiate from within you, and thus that you may become witnesses of God's presence in the world to every person who lives in darkness. Little children, I love you and daily intercede before the Most High for you. Thank you for having responded to my call."

December 25th 2016
The apparition began at 2:20 pm and lasted 10 minutes. Afterwards Jakov transmitted the following message.

"Dear children! Today, on this day of grace, in a special way, I am calling you to pray for peace. Children, I came here as the Queen of Peace and how many times have I called you to pray for peace. But, children, your hearts are restless. Sin is preventing you from opening yourselves completely to grace and peace which God desires to give you. To live peace, my children, is to first have peace in your hearts and to be surrendered completely to God and to His will. Do not seek peace and joy in the things of this world, because this is all passing. Long for true mercy and peace which come only from God; and only in this way will your hearts be filled with true joy; and only in this way will you be able to become witnesses of peace in this peaceless world. I am your mother and intercede before my Son for each of you. Thank you for having responded to my call."

Messages to Jelena Vasilj and her Prayer Group

In December 1982, Jelena Vasilj was just ten years old. She came from a local family in Medjugorje that was very devout. The family had always prayed together and lived an active faith life. Jelena began to receive inner locutions from Our Lady at the end of December 1982. While the six visionaries could see Our Lady in three dimensions, and spoke with her as in a normal conversation, Jelena could only hear Our Lady's voice and saw her in a two dimensional interior way. Several months later, in March of 1983, Jelena's friend Marijana Vasilj (they were friends but not related) began also to receive inner locutions.

At Our Lady's request, a prayer group was founded by Jelena in June 1983. According to her testimony, Our Lady speaks to her and teaches her. The prayer group used to meet in the parish hall after the evening Mass under the guidance of Fr. Tomislav Vlasic, and from time to time, other priests were also with the group. During the meetings, which consisted of simple prayer and singing, Our Lady gave messages to the group primarily through Jelena, teaching them how to pray. This prayer group was active until 1987. Those who had joined the group had to make the commitment that during the following four years they would not make any life decisions.

Jelena received the following message,
Our Lady says, *"I want a prayer group here. I will lead the group and will give the group rules of consecration. Everyone else in the world can consecrate themselves according to these rules. Think it over for a month, but tell them about the conditions I am giving."*

"First of all, let them renounce everything and place themselves completely into God's hands. Let each one of them renounce any fear because, if you surrender yourself to God, there is no place for any fear whatsoever. All difficulties that they will meet, will be for their spiritual growth and for the glory of God. I invite the young and single people, because those who are married have their obligations. But anyone who wishes to participate in this program can follow it at least partially. I will lead the group."

In addition to these weekly meetings, Our Lady also requested monthly late night Adoration from the group, which the group did mainly on the night of the first Saturday of the month, ending Adoration with the Sunday morning Mass.

The Beginning

Wednesday, December 29, 1982

Jelena: "May I know the ten secrets?"

"I did not appear to you as to the other six because my plan is different. To them I entrusted messages and secrets. Forgive me if I cannot tell you the secrets which I have entrusted to them; it concerns a grace which is for them, but not for you. I appeared to you for the purpose of helping you to progress in spiritual life, and through being an intermediary I want to lead people to holiness."

Beginning of 1983

Jelena asks the Blessed Virgin about the authenticity of the apparitions of the six visionaries and on the sign which has been promised,

"Pardon me, but you cannot know it; it is a special gift for them. You will have to believe it like all the others. In the meantime, everything that they say corresponds to truth."

Tuesday, March 1, 1983

To Jelena,

"Transcribe all the lessons which I give you for the spiritual life; later you will deliver them to the authorities of the Church."

April 4, 1983 (Easter Monday)

A message addressed by Jelena to Fr. Tomislav, who had written a letter of protest on Good Friday, April 1, regarding problems suffered in the parish.

Fr. Tomislav said: "I was expecting the corrections to be from a canonist, and no one knew anything except the pastor. On Monday, Jelena appeared without knowing anything, and tells me Our Lady said:"

"Do not have recourse to anyone. When you have a problem, you must remain smiling and praying. When God begins a work, no one will stop it."

"Pray, fast, and allow God to act."

To Jelena,

"Do not pity anyone. If the police cause you some anxiety, continue on your way joyful and calm. Pray for them. When God begins His work, no one can stop it."

Fr. Tomislav notes in the "Parish Chronicle" the internal locutions which have been received by Jelena after December 15, 1982. Our Lady's message:

"Hurry to be converted. Do not wait for the great sign. For the unbelievers, it will then be too late to be converted. For you who have faith, this time constitutes a great opportunity for you to be converted and to deepen your faith. Fast on bread and water before every feast, and prepare yourselves through prayer."

"Fast once a week on bread and water outside of Friday in honor of the Holy Spirit."

"Have the largest possible number of persons pray and fast during the novena of the Holy Spirit, so that it may spread over the Church. Fast and pray for the Bishop."

Wednesday, April 20, 1983
To Jelena, the Blessed Virgin, in tears,

"I give all the graces to those who commit grave sins, but they do not convert. Pray! Pray for them! Do not wait for Friday. Pray now. Today your prayers and your penance are necessary to me."

Monday, April 25, 1983
Message received by Jelena:

"Be converted! It will be too late when the sign comes. Beforehand, several warnings will be given to the world. Have people hurry to be converted. I need your prayers and your penance."

"My heart is burning with love for you. It suffices for you to be converted. To ask questions is unimportant. Be converted. Hurry to proclaim it. Tell everyone that it is my wish and that I do not cease repeating it. Be converted; be converted. It is not difficult for me to suffer for you. I beg you, be converted."

"I will pray to my Son to spare you the punishment. Be converted without delay. You do not know the plans of God; you will not be able to know them. You will not know what God will send, or what He will do. I ask you only to be converted. That is what I wish. Be converted! Be ready for everything, but, be converted. That is all I wish to say to you. Renounce everything; all that is part of conversion. Goodbye, and may peace be with you."

Friday, April 29, 1983

Marijana, (aged eleven) sees the Blessed Virgin at the same time as Jelena, but she does not hear her words. Jelena, "Why doesn't Marijana hear?"
"I do not want to separate you."

Wednesday, May 25, 1983

To Jelena,
"Assemble about twenty young people who are ready to follow Jesus without reservation. Bring them together within a month's notice. I will initiate them into the spiritual life. There can likewise be more than twenty. Even some adults and children can participate, all those who will accept the rule."

"I will ask these people to do penance for certain intentions. They will fast and pray for the Bishop. They will give up what they cherish the most, drink, coffee, pleasures, television. It is necessary to have persons who wish to consecrate themselves more specifically to prayer and fasting. I will give them the rules to follow." (See June 16, 1983)

"The persons who will follow these rules will be consecrated whatever their state in life may be."

Saturday, May 28, 1983

To Jelena,
"It is very beautiful to remain on Thursdays for the Adoration of my Son in the Blessed Sacrament of the Altar. It is likewise beautiful to venerate the Cross each Friday. I wish that every Saturday, which is the day that the Church had dedicated to me, you will consecrate to me at least a quarter of an hour. Meditate during this time on my life, my messages, and pray."

310

Friday, June 10, 1983

Jelena, Marijana and Anita, (age eleven), are arguing. The first two make peace, but Anita refuses. The other two enter the church. Anita follows them and suddenly extends to them her hand. An indescribable joy penetrates their hearts.

"I had been waiting for quite a while for your success. Continue in this manner."

Thursday, June 16, 1983

On May 25, 1983, the Blessed Virgin has repeated her desire that a prayer group, totally abandoned to Jesus, be formed. On June 16 she dictated to Jelena the rules for this group:

1. Renounce all passions and inordinate desires. Avoid television, particularly evil programs, excessive sports, the unreasonable enjoyment of food and drink, alcohol, tobacco, etc.

2. Abandon yourselves to God without any restrictions.

3. Definitely eliminate all anguish. Whoever abandons himself to God does not have room in his heart for anguish. Difficulties will persist, but they will serve for spiritual growth and will render glory to God.

4. Love your enemies. Banish from your heart hatred, bitterness, pre-conceived judgments. Pray for your enemies and call the Divine blessing over them.

5. Fast twice a week on bread and water. Reunite the group at least once a week.

6. Devote at least three hours to prayer daily, at least half an hour in the morning and half an hour in the evening. Holy Mass and the prayer of the rosary are included in this time of prayer. Set aside moments of prayer in the course of the day, and each time that circumstances permit it, receive Holy Communion. Pray with great meditation. Do not look at your watch all the time, but allow yourself to be led by the grace of God. Do not concern yourself too much with the things of this world, but entrust all that in prayer to Our Heavenly Father. If one is very preoccupied, he will not be able to pray well because internal serenity is lacking. God will contribute to lead to a successful end the things here below, if one strives to do his utmost in working on his own.

311

Those who attend school or go to work must pray half an hour in the morning and in the evening, and, if possible, participate in the Eucharist. It is necessary to extend the spirit of prayer to daily work, that is to say, to accompany work with prayer.

7. Be prudent because the devil tempts all those who have made a resolution to consecrate themselves to God, most particularly, those people. He will suggest to them that they are praying very much, they are fasting too much, that they must be like other young people and go in search of pleasures. Have them not listen to him, or obey him. It is to the voice of the Blessed Virgin that they should pay attention. When they will be strengthened in their faith, the devil will no longer be able to seduce them.

8. Pray very much for the Bishop and for those who are responsible for the Church. No less than half of their prayers and sacrifices must be devoted to this intention.

To Jelena,
"I have come to tell the world that God is truth; He exists."

"True happiness and the fullness of life are in Him. I have come here as Queen of Peace to tell the world that peace is necessary for the salvation of the world. In God one finds true joy from which true peace is derived."

Spring 1983
To Jelena, concerning Anita, to whom the Blessed Virgin appeared after Good Friday and who only seldom gets together with Jelena and Marijana, because of her many obligations,
"If she cannot come because of her responsibilities, have her pray for a quarter of an hour at least, and I will appear to her and bless her."

Wednesday, June 22, 1983
To Jelena,
"Love your enemies and bless them!"

Tuesday, June 28, 1983
To Jelena,
"Pray for three hours a day. You pray very little. Pray at least a half hour in the morning and in the evening."

Saturday, July 2, 1983
To Jelena,
"Devote five minutes to the Sacred Heart. Each family is an image of it."

Monday, July 4, 1983
To Jelena,
"You have begun to pray three hours a day, but you look at your watch, preoccupied with your work. Be concerned with only the essential. Let yourself be guided by the Holy Spirit in depth; then your work will go well. Do not hurry. Let yourself be guided, and you will see that everything will be accomplished well."

Tuesday, July 26, 1983
To Jelena,
"Be on your guard. This period is dangerous for you. The devil is trying to lead you astray from your way. Those who give themselves to God will be the object of attacks."

Tuesday, August 2, 1983
To Jelena,
"Consecrate yourself to the Immaculate Heart. Abandon yourselves completely. I will protect you. I will pray to the Holy Spirit. Pray to Him also."

Monday, August 15, 1983
To Jelena,
"See how I am happy here! There are many who have come to honor me. In the meanwhile, do not forget that in other places there are still more persons who hurt me and offend me."

"Do not be in anxiety. May peace unite your hearts. Every disorder comes from Satan."

To the young people who are returning to school,
"Be careful not to diminish the spirit of prayer. Satan is enraged against those who fast and those who are converted."

Thursday, September 29, 1983
To Jelena,
"I desire for a great peace and a great love to grow in you. Consequently, pray!"

Thursday, October 20, 1983

To Jelena, for the prayer group,

"I ask you for a commitment of four years. It is not yet the time to choose your vocation. The important thing is, first of all, to enter into prayer. Later you will make the right choice."

Monday, October 24, 1983

To Jelena, for the prayer group,

"If you pray, a source of life will flow from your hearts. If you pray with strength, if you pray with faith, you will receive graces from this source, and your group will be strengthened."

Tuesday, October 25, 1983

To Jelena,

"Pray! Pray! Prayer will give you everything. It is with prayer that you can obtain everything."

Wednesday, October 26, 1983

To Jelena,

"I pour out my blessing over you, and my heart wishes to be with you."

Thursday, October 27, 1983

To Jelena,

"Pray, pray, pray. You do not learn anything from chatter, but only from prayer. If someone asks you about me and about what I say, answer: 'That doesn't explain anything. It is in praying that we will understand better.'"

Friday, October 28, 1983

To Jelena,

"I see that you are tired. I wish to support you in your effort, to take you in my arms so that you may be close to me. All those who wish to ask me questions, I will answer: 'There is only one response, prayer, a strong faith, an intense prayer, and fasting.'"

Saturday, October 29, 1983
To Jelena,

I give you my heart; receive it! I would not want to distress you, or to stop talking to you, but I cannot stay always with you. You have to get used to it. In the meantime, I wish to be constantly with you, from the bottom of my heart. It is necessary to pray very much, not to say: 'If today we have not prayed, it is nothing serious'. You must strive to pray. Prayer is the only road which leads to peace. If you pray and fast, you will obtain everything that you ask for."

Sunday, October 30, 1983
To Jelena,

"Why do you not put your trust in me? I know that you have been praying for a long time, but really, surrender yourself. Abandon your concerns to Jesus. Listen to what He says in the Gospel: 'And who among you, through his anxiety, is able to add a single cubit, to the length of his life?' (Mt. 6:27). Pray also, in the evening when you have finished your day. Sit down in your room, and say to Jesus, 'Thank you.' If in the evening you fall asleep in peace, and in prayer, in the morning you will wake up thinking of Jesus. You will then be able to pray for peace, but if you fall asleep in distraction, the day after will be misty, and you will forget even to pray that day."

Monday, October 31, 1983
To Jelena,

"I know that you prayed today, and that you did all your work while praying. Still, I have a particular intention for which I am asking you to say each day, seven Our Father's, seven Hail Mary's, seven Glory Be's, and the Creed."

Friday, November 4, 1983
To Jelena,

"I wish that you tell them that tomorrow is a day of fasting, in order to sanctify yourselves in the Holy Spirit. And pray! Let this message be conveyed to the group."

Saturday, November 5, 1983
Jelena: "Our Lady looked at us tenderly and said:

'I know, my children, that you have worked and prayed today. But, I beseech you, be generous, persevere, continue to pray.'"

Sunday, November 6, 1983
To Jelena,

"Where are the prayers which you addressed to me? My clothes were sparkling. Behold them soaked with tears. Oh, if you would know how the world today is plunged into sin. It seems to you that the world sins no longer, because here, you live in a peaceful world where there is no confusion or perversity. If you knew how lukewarm they are in their faith, how many do not listen to Jesus. Oh, if you knew how much I suffer, you would sin no more. Oh, how I need your prayers. Pray!"

Monday, November 7, 1983
To Jelena,

"Do not go to confession through habit, to remain the same after it. No, it is not good. Confession should give an impulse to your faith. It should stimulate you and bring you closer to Jesus. If confession does not mean anything for you, really, you will be converted with great difficulty."

Tuesday, November 8, 1983
To Jelena,

"Pray and fast! All that you can do for me is to pray and fast."

Wednesday, November 9, 1983
To Jelena,

"Pray! I have such a great need for your prayers. Give me your hearts."

Thursday, November 10, 1983
To Jelena,

"I ask you to pray. That is all that I expect of you. Do not forget to pray to the Lord, morning and evening. Pray, Pray."

Friday, November 11, 1983
To Jelena,

"Pray! You can do everything, yes, you can do it through prayer. Place an image of the hearts of Jesus and Mary in your homes."

Saturday, November 12, 1983
To Jelena,
"Give me your hearts; open them to me."
"How do we do that?"
"You must redouble your efforts. Day after day, increase your fervor."

Sunday, November 13, 1983
To Jelena,
"Pray, and do it with fervor. Include the whole world in your prayer. Pray, because prayer makes one live."
In response to a question, the Gospa only says,
"Pray and you will understand that someday."

Monday, November 14, 1983
To Jelena,
"Pray, because prayer is life. Through it and in it, you live in prayer."

Tuesday, November 15, 1983
To Jelena,
"Pray and fast!"
For the intention of the group:
"I have often reproached you. Pray with me. Begin right now."

Wednesday, November 16, 1983
To Jelena,
"Pray and fast. Have all the members of your group come on Tuesday as often as possible. Speak to them about fasting. Fast three days a week for the Bishop. If that cannot be done by everyone the same day, have each one do it whenever he is able."

Thursday, November 17, 1983
To Jelena,
"Pray! If I always ask you to pray, do not think that your prayers are not good. But I invite you to prolong your personal prayer, to pray more intensely for the others."

Friday, November 18, 1983

To Jelena,

"At Medjugorje, many have begun well, but they have turned toward material goods, and they forget the only good."

Saturday, November 19, 1983

To Jelena,

"My children, pray only!"

Sunday, November 20, 1983

To Jelena,

"My children, do not believe everything that people tell you. One must not, because of that, weaken in his faith."

Monday, November 21, 1983

To Jelena,

"Tuesday, that is, tomorrow, the whole group will find peace in prayer. All its members will be invigorated in prayer, as it is the wish of Jesus. He entrusts something to each one, and wishes something from each one. It is necessary to make them come back to their promises, which were made at the beginning, and to pray."

Tuesday, November 22, 1983

To Jelena,

"Pray, pray, pray... Pray, my children. Pray, because only prayer can save you."

Wednesday, November 23, 1983

To Jelena,

"Oh, my sweet children, pray! I ask you only to pray. You yourselves can see that only prayer can save."

Thursday, November 24, 1983

To Jelena,

"Pray and fast!"

Friday, November 25, 1983

Jelena: "Our Lady stayed just a short time, and only said: *'Pray and fast.'*"

Sunday, November 27, 1983
To Jelena,
"My children, pray and keep your soul pure. I wish to be constantly with you."

Monday, November 28, 1983
To Jelena,
"Pray, pray! Have the parish pray each day to the hearts of Jesus and Mary during the Novena of the Immaculate Conception."

This same day, prayers were dictated or inspired by Our Lady.

Consecration to the Heart of Jesus

O Jesus, we know that You are sweet (Mt. 11:29),
That you have given Your heart for us.
It was crowned with thorns by our sins.
We know that today You still pray for us
so that we will not be lost.
Jesus, remember us if we fall into sin.
Through Your most Sacred Heart,
make us all love one another.
Cause hatred to disappear among men.
Show us Your love.
All of us love You.
And we desire that You protect us with Your
Heart of the Good Shepherd.
Enter into each heart, Jesus!
Knock on the door of our hearts.
Be patient and tenacious with us.
We are still locked up in ourselves, because we
have not understood Your will.
Knock continuously, O Jesus.
Make our hearts open up to You,
at least in reminding us of the Passion
which you suffered for us. Amen

Consecration to the Immaculate Heart of Mary

O Immaculate Heart of Mary, overflowing
with goodness, show us your love for us.
May the flame of your heart, O Mary,
Descend upon all peoples.
We love you immensely.
Impress in our hearts a true love.
May our hearts yearn for you.
O Mary, sweet and humble of heart,
Remember us when we sin.
You know that all mankind are sinners.
Through your most sacred and maternal heart,
Cure us from every spiritual illness.
Make us capable of looking at the beauty of your maternal heart,
And that, thus, we may be converted
to the flame of your heart. Amen

Tuesday, November 29, 1983
To Jelena,
"Pray!"
For the intention of the group,
"I am your mother full of goodness, and Jesus is your great friend. Do not fear anything in His presence. Give Him your heart, from the bottom of your heart. Tell Him your sufferings; thus you will be invigorated in prayer, with a free heart, in a peace without fear."

Wednesday, November 30, 1983
To Jelena,
"Pray, pray, pray!"

November 1983
Before the Novena to the Immaculate Conception, the Blessed Virgin tells Jelena,
"Before Mass it is necessary to pray to the Holy Spirit."

Jelena, "We followed this message during the Novena, praying before Mass and asking the faithful to respond, 'O come Holy Spirit.' After Communion, we sang the hymn to the Holy Spirit, and then we stopped doing it." In January, 1983, Jelena said that the Blessed Virgin requested that these prayers be resumed. We should not have stopped them. The prayers to the Holy Spirit should always accompany the Mass.

Friday, December 2, 1983
To Jelena,
"Thank you. Thanks to everyone!"

That evening, it was particularly cold,
"You are very good to come to Mass without looking for an excuse. Show me that you have a generous heart."

Sunday, December 4, 1983
To Jelena,
"Pray, pray, pray only. Prayer should be for you not only a habit, but also a source of goodness. You should live by prayer."

Tuesday, December 6, 1983
To Jelena,
"Pray, pray! If you pray, I will keep you, and I will be with you."

Wednesday, December 7, 1983
The Vigil of the Immaculate Conception, to Jelena,
"Tomorrow will really be a blessed day for you, if every moment is consecrated to my Immaculate Heart. Abandon yourselves to me. Strive to make your joy grow, to live in faith, to change your hearts."

Thursday, December 8, 1983
To Jelena,
"Thank you, my children, for having come so often. Thank you. Continue your efforts and be persevering and tenacious. Pray without ceasing."

Sunday, December 11, 1983
To Jelena,

"Pray and fast! I wish that prayer be renewed in your heart every day. Pray more, yes, more each day."

Monday, December 12, 1983
To Jelena,

"Pray, pray; thus I will protect you. Pray and abandon your hearts to me, because I wish to be with you."

Tuesday, December 13, 1983
To Jelena,

"Pray and fast! I do not wish to say anything else to you."

Thursday, December 15, 1983
To Jelena on the subject of catastrophic predictions,

"That comes from false prophets. They say: 'Such a day, on such a date, there will be a catastrophe.' I have always said that evil will come if the world does not convert itself. Call the world to conversion. Everything depends on your conversion."

Saturday, December 17, 1983
To Jelena,

"Pray and fast!"

Sunday, December 18, 1983
To Jelena,

"In this Novena for Christmas, pray as much as you can. I ask you."

Monday, December 19, 1983
To Jelena,

"Pray!"

Tuesday, December 20, 1983
To Jelena,

"Pray!"

For the intention of the group,
"Fast on Wednesday, Thursday, and Friday."

Wednesday, December 21, 1983
To Jelena,
"My children, I say to you again, pray and fast."

Thursday, December 22, 1983
To Jelena,
"Pray! What is most important for your body is prayer."

Friday, December 23, 1983
To Jelena,
"Pray, pray, especially tomorrow. I desire your prayers."

Saturday, December 24, 1983
To Jelena,
"Pray, pray, my children. I wish that this night be spent in prayer."

Sunday, December 25, 1983
To Jelena,
"My children, pray! I cannot tell you anything else than pray. Know that in your life, there is nothing more important than prayer."

Monday, December 26, 1983
To Jelena,
"My children, pray, pray more. It is not necessary to say that 'Our Lady only repeats pray.' I cannot tell you anything else than to pray. You would need to live this Christmas in prayer. You have rejoiced very much this Christmas, but your hearts have not attained and lived what you have desired. No one withdrew to his room to thank Jesus."

Tuesday, December 27, 1983
To Jelena,
"My children, pray, pray, pray. Remember that the most important thing in our lives is prayer."

Thursday, December 29, 1983
To Jelena,
"I wish that one love, one peace, flourish in you. Pray then."

Friday, December 30, 1983
To Jelena,
"My children, pray and fast. I wish to strengthen you, but prayer alone is your strength."

Saturday, December 31, 1983
To Jelena,
"For you, I only wish that this New Year will really be a holy one. On this day go then to confession, and purify yourself in this New Year."

Our Lady asks the group to continue to pray for the Bishop.

Wednesday, January 18, 1984
To Jelena,
"Pray and fast!"

For the intention of the group,
"Have everyone get up early - some to go to school, others to go to work, still others to help the poor like themselves, also those who need help."

Tuesday, January 31, 1984
To Jelena,
"Pray! Do not think of anything. Pray! Do not think of anything else except those for whom you pray. Then prayer will be better, and you will be faithful to it."

To the group,
"Continue to help the poor, the sick, and to pray for the dead. You should not feel any fear. Let all free themselves completely, and let them abandon their hearts to me so that I can be with them. Have them listen to me and discover me in the poor and in every person."

Friday, February 3, 1984

To Jelena,

"It is up to you to pray, and I will take care of the rest. You cannot even imagine how powerful God is. That is why you pray. Pray because he wants to be with you and wants to cleanse you from all sin."

Sunday, February 5, 1984

And especially for the prayer group,

"Some of them still have a week of rest. They do not fast... others have come here and fast on Wednesday, Thursday, and Friday; others help the poor and the sick; others love everybody and want to discover Jesus in each one. Some are not convinced; others are. They are mine. See how they honor me. Lead them to me so that I may bless them."

Wednesday, February 8, 1984

To Jelena,

"From you I expect only prayer. Thus, pray."

Monday, February 13, 1984

To Jelena,

"Fast and pray! Give me your hearts. I desire to change them completely. I desire for them to be pure."

Tuesday, February 28, 1984

For the intention of the group,

"Have each one decide alone. In the meantime, it would be good that this week they fast on Thursday. Have them read the Bible and meditate on it."

Thursday, March 1, 1984

Message to Marijana:

"Pray and fast. When I tell you to pray, do not think that you have to pray more, but pray. Let prayer and faith awaken in your hearts."

To Jelena,

"Each Thursday, read again the passage of Matthew 6, 24-34, before the most Blessed Sacrament, or if it is not possible to come to church, do it with your family."

Monday, March 5, 1984

To Jelena,

"Pray and fast! Ask the Holy Spirit to renew your souls, to renew the entire world."

Saturday, March 17, 1984

To Jelena, during the Novena in preparation for the Annunciation,

"Pray and fast so that during this Novena God will fill you with His power."

Wednesday, March 21, 1984

To Jelena,

"Today I rejoice with all my angels. The first part of my program has been achieved."

Then, while crying,

"There are so many men who live in sin. Here there are likewise among you some people who have offended my heart. Pray and fast for them."

Thursday, March 22, 1984

To Jelena,

"Yesterday evening I said that the first wish of my plan was realized."

Tuesday, March 27, 1984

To Jelena,

"In the group, some have given themselves up to God so that He may guide them. Let the will of God be realized in you."

Friday, March 30, 1984

To Jelena,

"My children, I wish that the Holy Mass be for you the gift of the day. Attend it; wish for it to begin. Jesus gives Himself to you during the Mass. Thus, look forward to that moment when you are cleansed. Pray very much so that the Holy Spirit will renew your parish. If people attend Mass with luke-warmness, they will return to their homes cold and with an empty heart."

Tuesday, April 3, 1984

To Jelena,

"I ask for you to pray for the conversion of all men. For that I need your prayers."

326

Saturday, April 14, 1984
To Jelena,

"How can you not be happy? Jesus gives Himself to you. I wish to inundate souls. If I am sad this evening, the reason is that many have not prepared themselves for Easter. They do not permit Jesus on that day to unite Himself to their souls."

Holy Week April 15-22, 1984
To Jelena,

"Raise your hands and open your hearts. Now, at the time of the Resurrection, Jesus wishes to give you a special gift. This gift of my Son is my gift. Here it is. You will be subjected to trials, and you will endure them with great ease. We will be ready to show you how to escape from them if you accept us. Do not say that the Holy Year has ended and that there is no need to pray. On the contrary, double your prayers, because the Holy Year is just another step ahead."

At this time, the risen Jesus appeared. Rays of light came forth from His wounds. He said,

"Receive my graces and tell the whole world that there is no happiness except through Me."

Holy Thursday, April 19, 1984
To Jelena,

"I'm going to reveal a spiritual secret to you: if you want to be stronger than evil, make yourself a plan of personal prayer. Take a certain time in the morning, read a text from Holy Scripture, anchor the Divine Word in your heart, and strive to live it during the day, particularly during the moment of trials. In this way, you will be stronger than evil."

That same day, Our Lady dictated the following prayer to Jelena,

How to Give Oneself to Mary,
Mother of Goodness, of Love, and of Mercy

O my Mother!
Mother of goodness, love and mercy!
I love you immensely, and I offer myself to you.
Through your goodness, your love,
And your mercy, save me!
I wish to be yours.
I love you immensely,
And I wish that you protect me.
In my heart, O Mother of goodness,
Give me your goodness,
So that I go to Heaven.
I ask you for your immense love
That you may give me the grace
That I will be able to love each one
Just like you loved Jesus Christ.
I ask you in grace
That I be able to be merciful* to you.
I offer myself completely to you,
And I wish that you will be with me at each step,
Because you are full of grace.
I wish never to forget your grace,
And if I should lose it,
I will ask to make me find it again. Amen.

* - According to Fr. Slavko, this statement means:
'That I know how to love your will when it differs from mine.'

To Tomislav Vlasic's question, asked by Jelena:
"How could Jesus pray all night? With what method?"
"He had a great longing for God and for the salvation of souls."

"If you want to be stronger against evil, have an active conscience. For that, pray very much in the morning and read a passage from the Gospel. Plant the Divine Word in your heart and live it during the day, in this special way, in trials and in the evening; you will be very strong."

Good Friday, April 20, 1984

To Jelena,

"You should be filled with joy. Today Jesus died for your salvation. He descends into Hell and opens the gates of paradise. Let joy reign in your hearts!
When you pray, seek the advantage of prayer. Prayer is a conversation with God. To pray means to listen to the Lord. Prayer is for me a service, because after it all things become clear. Prayer leads to knowing happiness."

Holy Saturday, April 21, 1984

To Jelena,

"Raise your hands; yearn for Jesus because in His Resurrection, He wants to fill you with graces. Be enthusiastic about the Resurrection. All of us in Heaven are happy, but we seek the joy of your hearts. My Son's gift and mine, at this moment, is this: you will be comforted in your trials. They will be easier for you because we will be close to you. If you listen to us, we will show you how to overcome them."

"Pray very much tomorrow. May Jesus truly rise in your families, that peace be established there where there are wars. I wish that someone is born again in your hearts. My children, I thank you. Continue to bring about the Resurrection of Jesus in all men. The Holy Year has ended, but it represents only a step in our life. Continue to pray."

Tuesday, April 24, 1984

To Jelena,

"Many times, confronting justice and confronting your sins, many times I returned from your home in tears. I could not say a single word. I am your Mother, and I do not want to oppose you. But on you will depend what I wish to do in you. We must rejoice in Jesus to make Him happy."

Saturday, May 19, 1984

To Jelena,

"Dear children, at this time it is especially necessary for you to consecrate yourselves to me and to my heart. Love, pray, and fast."

Monday, May 21, 1984
To Jelena,

"O dear children, how I wish that you would turn to me. Imagine, my little children, that it is the end of the school year, and you have reached halfway. That is why now you must become a little more serious."

Wednesday, May 23, 1984
To Jelena,

"I wish that the parish prepare itself through a novena to receive the sacrament of Confirmation on the day of the feast of the Ascension."
(Which will take place May 31)

Friday, May 25, 1984
To Jelena,

"I truly wish that you would be pure on the day of Pentecost. Pray, pray that your spirit be changed on that day."

Saturday, May 26, 1984
To Jelena,

"Dear children, thank you for every prayer. Try to pray continuously, and do not forget that I love you and wish that all of you would love one another."

To Jelena, who is requested to ask questions of Our Lady,

"For all of these questions, there is an answer: Pray to the Holy Spirit so that He may enlighten you, and you will come to know all that you wish."

Monday, May 28, 1984
To Jelena,

"Love is a gift from God. Pray then, that God may give you the gift to love."

Wednesday, May 30, 1984
To Jelena,

"The priests should visit families, more particularly those who do not practice anymore and who have forgotten God. Priests should carry the Gospel of Jesus to the people and teach them the way of prayer. And the priests themselves should pray more and even fast. They should give to the poor what they don't need."

330

May 1984

To Jelena, after inquiring about August 5, 1984, if they would be celebrating her two thousandth birthday,

"Throughout the centuries, I have given myself completely to you. Is it too much to give me three days? Do not work on those days. Take your rosaries and pray. Fasting has been forgotten during the last quarter of the century within the Catholic Church."

Jelena, "I know that all families can pray four hours a day. But, if I tell that to people, they will back out."
"Don't you understand that it is only one-sixth of the day?"

Friday, June 1, 1984

To Jelena,
"May the love of God be always in you, because without it, you cannot be fully converted. Let the rosary in your hands make you think of Jesus."
"Dear children, strive to be absorbed in Mass, just as you should."

Saturday, June 2, 1984

To Jelena,
"Thank you for every prayer. Continue to pray, but pray with the heart. Dear children, again it is necessary for you to pray to the Holy Spirit, and it would be good for you to pray seven Our Father's in the church as one does for Pentecost."

During the novena, in preparation for Pentecost, the priest who leads the prayer makes a brief introduction before each Our Father to ask for the seven gifts of the Holy Spirit.

Friday, June 8, 1984

To Jelena,
"Dear children, you need love. I have said it to you many times, and I remind you. Continue only to pray and be happy because I am with you."

Monday, June 11, 1984

To Jelena,
"I wish that you continue to pray and to fast."

To the group,
"I wish that you would become like a flower in the spring. The love which I give you is great, but sometimes you reject it, and thus, it becomes less. Always accept immediately the gifts which I give you, so that you may profit from them."

Middle of June, 1984
To Jelena,
"Prepare yourselves through prayer for the third anniversary of the beginning of the apparitions. June 25 should be celebrated as the Feast of Mary, 'Queen of Peace'."

Thursday, June 21, 1984
To Jelena,
"If you knew how much I love you, you would cry with joy. When anyone is before you and asks you something, you will give it to him. I am before so many hearts, but they remain closed. Pray so that the world receives my love."

"Each member of the group is like a flower; and if someone tries to crush you, you will grow and will try to grow even more. If someone crushes you a little, you will recover. And if someone pulls a petal, continue to grow as though you were complete."

To Marijana,
"My only wish is that you become as joyful and enthusiastic as you were during the first days of my apparitions."

Saturday, June 23, 1984
After Easter, Our Lady does not speak to Jelena or Marijana every day, but on Tuesday, Wednesday, Saturday and Sunday.

Beginning of August 1984
To Jelena,
"This message is dedicated to the Pope and to all Christians. Prepare the second millennium of my birth, which will take place August 5, 1984. Throughout the centuries, I consecrated my entire life to you. Is it too much for you to consecrate three days for me? Do not work on that day, but take up the rosary and pray."

Monday, September 10, 1984

To Jelena,

"Dear children, you must understand that one has to pray. Prayer is no joke; prayer is a conversation with God. In every prayer you must listen to the voice of God. Without prayer one cannot live. Prayer is life."

Friday, October 5, 1984

To Jelena, *"I love you. Love me; love one another."*

Saturday, November 17, 1984

To Jelena,

"Pray. Do not ask yourself about the reason why I constantly invite you to prayer. Intensify your personal prayer so that it will become a channel for others."

Thursday, December 20, 1984

To Jelena,

"Today I am asking you to do something concrete for Jesus Christ. On the day of joy, I would like every family of the parish to bring a flower as a sign of self-offering to Jesus. I would like every member of the family to have a flower next to the crib so that Jesus can come and see your offering of self to Him."

Friday, December 29, 1984

To Jelena,

"I want you to be a flower which will blossom for Jesus on Christmas, a flower that will not stop blooming when Christmas is over. I want your hearts to be shepherds to Jesus."

Saturday, December 29, 1984

To Jelena, on the anniversary day of her first apparition, "Today is the feast of the Mother of goodness, of mercy, and of love. Then she gave us her blessing saying, *'Up until now I have not given it to you.'"*

"And the group felt strongly changed because of it. She motivated them to receive this blessing,"
"Receive it; do not neglect it as before. I can give you my blessing, but I cannot give it to you if you do not want it."

To Jelena,

"I wish that a great love, a great peace would flourish in you. Thus, pray."

Wednesday, February 20, 1985 (Ash Wednesday)

To Jelena,

"I give you advice; I would like for you to try to conquer some fault each day. If your fault is to get angry at everything, try each day to get angry less. If your fault is not to be able to study, try to study. If your fault is not to be able to obey, or if you cannot stand those who do not please you, try on a given day to speak with them. If your fault is not to be able to stand a proud person, you should try to approach that person. If you desire that person to be humble, be humble yourselves. Show that humility is worth more than pride."

"Thus, each day try to go beyond and to reject every vice from your heart. Find out which are the vices that you most need to reject. During this Lent, you should try and truly desire to spend it in love. Strive as much as possible."

Monday, February 25, 1985

To Jelena,

"Know that I love you. Know that you are mine. I do not wish to do anything more for anyone that I do not wish to do for you. Come, all of you, to me. Remain with me, and I will be your Mother always. Come, because I wish to have all of you."

Lent 1985 (February 20-April 6)

To Jelena,

"Fast on bread and water during the first week of the Passion and on Holy Wednesday, Holy Thursday, and Good Friday."

Monday, March 25, 1985 (Feast of the Annunciation)

Jelena: "Why are you so beautiful?"

"I am beautiful because I love. If you want to be beautiful, love. There is no one in the world who does not desire beauty."

334

Thursday, March 28, 1985
To Jelena,

"You all know the flowers. A flower must blossom, and each part of the flower is very important. But there is a moment when the flower must wilt so that the seed can ripen, and after, when the seed is ripe, other flowers will come."

Jelena did not know how to explain this parable. But Fr. Tomislav Vlasic explained, "One finds in it the whole liturgy of this evening (Saturday, Vigil of Palm Sunday); one must die in order to be able to rise again. We say sometimes that it is sad that a flower must wilt. But, if it does not wilt, it is not able to ripen the seed from where the other flowers come. If it does not die, life cannot multiply itself."

Friday, May 3, 1985
To Jelena,

"Sometimes prayers said in a loud voice keep Jesus at a distance, because when men want to conquer with their own power, there is no place for God. Prayers said in a loud voice are good when they come from the heart."

Sunday, May 19, 1985
To Jelena,

"Dear children, at this time I ask you particularly to consecrate yourselves to me and to my Immaculate Heart. Love, pray, and fast."

Saturday, June 1, 1985
To Jelena,

"Always have the love of God in you, because without this love, you are not able to convert yourselves completely. Let the rosary be in your hands in memory of Jesus. Dear children, strive to deepen your knowledge of the Mass as you should."

Tuesday, June 25, 1985
To Jelena,

"A heart which belongs to the Lord is splendid, even if it is flooded with difficulties and trials. But if the heart is engaged in difficulties, strays away from God, it loses its splendor."

June 1985
To Jelena,

"Dear children, if there is someone who asks you for something, give it to him. I, too, ask before many hearts, and they do not open up. Pray so that the world may receive my love."

Saturday, December 7, 1985
To Jelena,

"I have only one wish for tomorrow's feast. I ask of you to find at least a quarter of an hour for you to come before me and entrust your problems to me. No one will understand you as I do."

Tuesday, December 31, 1985
To Jelena, during the eve of December 31,

"Next year is the year of peace, not because men have named it so, but because God has programmed it. You will not have peace through the presidents, but through prayer."

Through one of the little members of the group, during this same vigil, Jesus said,

"When you hear the clocks at midnight, you will fall on your knees, and bow your head to the ground so that the King of Peace will come. This year I will offer my peace to the world. But afterwards, I will ask you where you were when I offered you my peace."

Tuesday, January 21, 1986
It was the second day of retreat for a prayer group, probably that of Jelena.

"This evening, rest."

Wednesday, January 22, 1986
To the same group,

"I know that you are tired, but I cannot tell you to rest. Today I tell you to pray, and do not go to bed before having prayed at least a quarter of an hour for the group. Tomorrow will be a better day."

Saturday, February 22, 1986
At the end of the meeting of the prayer group, before the blessing,
"Dear children, you will be able to receive Divine Love only in proportion to your understanding that on the Cross, God offers you His immense love."

Monday, March 24, 1986
To the prayer group,
"Dear children, receive all that the Lord offers you. Do not have your hands paralyzed, and do not repeat: 'Jesus, give me.' But open your hands, and take everything that the Lord offers you."

Tuesday, June 24, 1986
To the prayer group,
"I beseech you, withdraw in silence. Your obligation is not so much to do, but to adore God, to stay with Him."

Messages to Jelena No Exact Dates

JOURNAL OF JELENA

Questioned on the similarity between the signs announced in Medjugorje, and the third secret of Fatima, Jelena responds, "About these things the Gospa told us,

Do not fear anything. You must forget what is behind you in your life. I only want that from now on, you be new people. Do not fear anything when I am near you. I love you."

To Jelena,

"The subject concerning the certainties of catastrophes comes from false prophets. They say on such a day, at such an hour, there will be a catastrophe. I have always said, 'Punishment will come about if the world is not converted.' Call all mankind to conversion. Everything depends on your conversion."

To Jelena,

"When others cause you some difficulty, do not defend yourself; rather, pray."

To Jelena,

"I desire that you be a flower, which blossoms for Jesus at Christmas, a flower which does not cease to bloom when Christmas has passed. I wish that you have a shepherd's heart for Jesus."

"Dear children, when someone comes to you and asks you a favor, answer by giving. I find myself before so many hearts which do not open themselves to me. Pray, so that the world willingly wants to accept my love."

To Jelena,

"Christians make a mistake in considering the future because they think of wars and of evil. For a Christian, there is only one attitude toward the future. It is the hope of salvation."

"Your responsibility is to accept divine peace, to live, and to spread it not through words, but through your life."

To Jelena,
"*The only attitude of the Christian regarding the future is the hope of salvation. Those who think only of wars, evils, punishment, do not do well.*"

"*If you think of evil, punishment, wars, you are on the road to meeting them. Your responsibility is to accept divine peace, live it and spread it*"

"*If you have not listened to my messages, the day of joy will become for me a day of sadness.*"

To Jelena, in 1983,
"*Take me seriously. When God comes among men, He does not come to joke but to say serious things.*"

"*It is better to stay in church and pray with faith than to gather together with onlookers near the visionaries during an apparition.*"

Message to the prayer group which had received many messages during Lent and was surprised not to receive any more after Easter,
"*Thank you to all those who pray and feel my presence. I regret that some individuals say the Gospa is no longer among us. Pray, and you will feel that I am present.*"

In a meeting of her prayer group, Jelena saw the desert, and in the desert, a tree, and under the tree, where the sun was shining. In this sun she recognized Jesus Christ. Our Lady told her, among other things,
"*To this group many graces have been given, but you must not reject them.*"

To Jelena's group toward the beginning of July 1985,
"*I cannot speak to you. Your hearts are closed.*"

"*You have not done what I told you; I cannot speak to you. I cannot give you graces as long as you remain closed.*"

To Jelena for her group,
"*Each of you has a special gift which is your own, and which you alone can understand it interiorly.*"

To Jelena's prayer group,

"It seems when you carry my messages, be on your guard that they are not lost. Carry my messages with humility, in such a way that on seeing happiness in you, persons will desire to be like you. Do not carry my messages to simply throw them to others."

In the middle of June, 1985, Jelena saw a splendid pearl, which divided itself. Each part glittered, and then it faded. Jelena heard this explanation,

"Jelena, man's heart is like this splendid pearl. When he belongs completely to the Lord, he shines even in the darkness. But when he is divided, a little to Satan, a little to sin, a little to everything, he fades and is no longer worth anything."

To Jelena, during the week of July 28 to August 4,

"During these days I wish that you consider this idea: After so long and so much time, I have not met Jesus, my friend. After so long and so much time, I have not encountered my Mother Mary. In these days, I want to encounter them.

Do not be afraid of Satan. That isn't worth the trouble, because with a humble prayer and an ardent love one can disarm him."

Prayer given to Jelena for her group,

"My soul is full of love like the sea. My heart is full of peace like the river. I am not a saint, but I am invited to be one."

To Jelena, three evenings in succession, between October 10 to 15,

"If you wanted to accept my love, you would never sin."

On the following evening (the fourth day), Jelena asks, "Why do you always repeat the same message?"

"But I don't have anything else to say to you."

And she cries.

"There are many who finish their prayers, even without entering into them."

A question from the pilgrims of Milan to Jelena,

"We have come to you, Dear Mother. When will you come to Milan?"

Our Lady's answer through Jelena, *"When you open your hearts to me."*

"If you want to be stronger than evil and grow in goodness, then develop an active conscience."

To a prayer group, after an hour of prayer, in which their prayer of petition had prevailed,
"Have you forgotten that you are in my hands?"

To Jelena, for her prayer group, after prayer and fasting,
"I have listened to your prayer, and yet you will not receive what you have wished. You will receive other things because it is not up to you to glorify yourself but to me to glorify myself in you."
"Do not be afraid. Confide yourself to the Father. Pray until you are sure that He guides everything. In difficulties, when you carry the cross, sing; be full of joy."

To Jelena, for her group,
"I wish only that you would be happy, that you would be filled with joy, that you be filled with peace and announce this joy."

To Jelena,
"When people ask you to speak about the apparitions, say: 'Let us pray together to understand the apparitions of the Gospa'."

To the group on March 25, on the Feast of the Annunciation,
"Today before God I say my 'Fiat' for all of you. I repeat it: I say my 'Fiat' for all of you. Dear Children, pray so that into the whole world may come the Kingdom of Love. How mankind would be happy if love reigned!"

Some in the prayer group found the advice from Our Lady too rigid.
"Why shut down the television? Why not even read the newspaper?"
"If you look at the programs, if you look at the newspapers, your heads are filled with news; then there is no longer any place for me in your hearts."

"Pray. Fast. Let God act! Pray for the gift of love, for the gift of faith, for the gift of prayer, for the gift of fasting."

341

To Jelena, for her group,
"I beg you, destroy your house made of cardboard, which you have built on desires. Thus I will be able to act for you."

To Jelena, during the autumn of 1983,
"Dear Children, one lives not only from work; one lives also from prayer."

To the prayer group during the week preceding May 3,
"I give you the best that I can give anyone. I give myself and my Son."

Toward May 12 (at the beginning of the Novena of Pentecost) to the prayer group,
"You will be happy if you do not judge yourselves according to your faults, but if you understand that in your faults even graces are offered to you."

"Love. If you do not love, you are not able to transmit the testimony. You are not able to witness, either for me, or for Jesus."

"I wish for all of you to be the reflection of Jesus. He will thus illuminate this unfaithful world, which moves in darkness."

"Pray before the Cross. Special graces come from the Cross. Consecrate yourselves to the Cross. Do not blaspheme either Jesus or the Cross."

"You will have as many graces as you want. That depends on you. You will have love when you want it, as long as you want it. That depends on you."

To the prayer group, before giving her blessing, at the end of an evaluation of the group,
"I thank you for that. You have done well, but do not forget that God's will is decisive."

"I wish only that for you the rosary become your life."

"Read each Thursday the Gospel of Matthew, where it is said, 'No one can serve two masters… You cannot serve God and money.'"

To the prayer group,
"If you would abandon yourselves to me, you will not even feel the passage from this life to the next life. You will begin to live the life of Heaven from this earth."

To Jelena, the beginning of September 1986,
"Today it is not words or deeds which are important. The important thing is only to pray, to remain in God."

Message from Jesus through Jelena,
"I am joyful, but my joy is not complete until you are filled with joy. You are not yet filled with joy because you are not yet at the stage of understanding my immense love."

Special Prayers Given by Our Lady to Jelena Vasilj

Consecration to the Heart of Jesus
(Given by Our Lady to Jelena Vasilj, 11/28/1983)

O Jesus, we know that You are sweet (Mt. 11:29),
That you have given Your heart for us.
It was crowned with thorns by our sins.
We know that today You still pray for us
so that we will not be lost.
Jesus, remember us if we fall into sin.
Through Your most Sacred Heart,
make us all love one another.
Cause hatred to disappear among men.
Show us Your love.
All of us love You.
And we desire that you protect us with Your
Heart of the Good Shepherd.
Enter into each heart, Jesus!
Knock on the door of our hearts.
Be patient and tenacious with us.
We are still locked up in ourselves, because we
have not understood Your will.
Knock continuously, O Jesus.
Make our hearts open up to you,
at least in reminding us of the Passion
which you suffered for us. Amen

Consecration to the Immaculate Heart of Mary
(Given by Our Lady to Jelena Vasilj, 11/28/1983)

O Immaculate Heart of Mary, overflowing
with goodness, show us your love.
May the flame of your heart, O Mary,
Descend upon all peoples.
We love you immensely.
Impress in our hearts a true love.
May our hearts yearn for you.
O Mary, sweet and humble of heart,
Remember us when we sin.
You know that all mankind are sinners.
Through your most sacred and maternal heart,
Cure us from every spiritual illness.
Make us capable of looking at the beauty of your maternal heart,
And that, thus, we may be converted
to the flame of your heart. Amen

How to Give Oneself to Mary
Mother of Goodness, of Love and of Mercy
(Given by Our Lady to Jelena Vasilj, 4/19/1984)

O my Mother!
Mother of goodness, love, and mercy!
I love you immensely, and I offer myself to you.
Through your goodness, your love,
And your mercy, save me!
I wish to be yours.
I love you immensely,
And I wish that you protect me.
In my heart, O Mother of goodness,
Give me your goodness,
So that I go to Heaven.
I ask you for your immense love
That you may give me the grace
That I will be able to love each one
Just like you loved Jesus Christ.
I ask you in grace
That I be able to be merciful* to you.
I offer myself completely to you,
And I wish that you will be with me at each step,
Because you are full of grace.
I wish never to forget your grace,
And if I should lose it,
I will ask to make me find it again. Amen.

* - According to Fr. Slavko, this statement means:
    'That I know how to love your will when it differs from mine.'

Petition to God
(Given by Our Lady to Jelena Vasilj, 6/22/1985)

Recite three Glory Be's.

O God, our heart is in deep obscurity,
in spite of our union with Your Heart.
Our heart is struggling between You and Satan;
do not permit it to be in this manner!

Every time that the heart is divided
between good and evil,
let it be enlightened by Your light
and let it be unified.

Never permit
for there to be able to exist in us two loves,
for there can never co-exist in us two faiths,
nor can there ever co-exist in us
lying and sincerity,
love and hatred,
honesty and dishonesty,
humility and pride.

Help us on the contrary,
so that our hearts may be elevated toward You
just like that of a child.
May our hearts be ravished with peace
and continue to always have the nostalgia for it.

May Your Holy will and Your love
find a permanent place in us, that at least
sometimes we would really wish to be Your
children and when, O Lord,
we will desire to be Your children,
remember our past desires
and help us to receive You again.

We open our hearts to you
so that Your holy love will remain in us.
We open our souls to you,
so that they may be touched by Your holy mercy,
which will help us to see clearly all our sins
and will make us realize that
that which makes us impure is sin.

God, we want to be Your children,
humble and devout,
to the point of becoming your cherished and
sincere children,
such as only the Father
would be able to desire that we be.
Help us, Jesus, our brother,
to obtain the goodness of the Father in our regard,
and to be good to Him.

Help us, Jesus,
to understand well what God gives us,
although sometimes we fail to perform a good act,
as though it were for us an evil.

Prayer for a Sick Person
(Given by Our Lady to Jelena Vasilj, 6/22/1985)

Recite three Glory Be's.

O, my God,
behold this sick person before You.
He has come to ask You
what he wishes
and what he considers as the most important thing
for himself.
You, O my God,
make these words enter into his heart:
What is important is the health of his soul.

Lord, may Your will in everything
take place in his regard, if You want for him to
be cured.
Let health be given to him;
but if Your will is something else,
let him continue to bear his cross.

I also pray to You for us,
who intercede for him;
purify our hearts
to make us worthy to convey
Your holy Mercy.

Protect him and relieve his pain,
that Your holy will be done in him,
that Your holy name be revealed through him;
help him to bear his cross with courage.

The Jesus Rosary
(Given by Our Lady to Jelena)

This special rosary has a crucifix, and one bead on the tail, and continues with a circular formation of seven sets of beads, each containing five beads.

Pray the Creed.

1. Mystery: Contemplate the birth of Jesus.
Intention: Pray for peace.
Five Our Father's
Prayer: "O Jesus, be strength and protection for us."

2. Mystery: Contemplate that Jesus helped and gave all to the poor.
Intention: Let us pray for the Holy Father and for the Bishops.
Five Our Father's
Prayer: "O Jesus, be strength and protection for us."

3. Mystery: Contemplate that Jesus trusted in his Father completely and carried out His will.
Intention: Pray for priests and for all those who serve God in a particular way.
Five Our Father's
Prayer: 'O Jesus, be strength and protection for us.'

4. Mystery: Contemplate that Jesus knew he had to give up His life for us, and that He did so without regrets because He loved us.
Intention: Pray for families.
Five Our Father's
Prayer: "O Jesus, be strength and protection for us."

5. Mystery: Contemplate that Jesus made His life into a sacrifice for us.
Intention: Pray so that we, too, may be capable of offering our life for our neighbor.
Five Our Father's
Prayer: "O Jesus, be strength and protection for us."

6. Mystery: Contemplate the victory of Jesus over Satan. He is risen.
Intention: Let us pray that all sins may be eliminated so that Jesus may relive in our hearts.
Five Our Father's
Prayer: "O Jesus, be strength and protection for us."

7. Mystery: Contemplate the Ascension of Jesus into Heaven.
Intention: Let us pray that the will of God may triumph, so that His will may be done
Five Our Father's
Prayer: "O Jesus, be strength and protection for us."

After this, contemplate how Jesus sent us the Holy Spirit.
Intention: Pray so that the Holy Spirit may descend upon us.
Seven Glory Be's

Notations

October 1, 1981 - "Are all religions the same?" Page 59.

The answer is a clarified response following a discussion between Vicka and Fr. René Laurentin.

October 12, 1981 - *"I went to Heaven before death."* Page 60.

This would indicate that Our Lady's soul was assumed while She was still alive. Anne Catherine Emmerich did believe that a tomb had been erected somewhere in the environs of Ephesus, but no tomb has ever been found. She was more hopeful than infallible, it seems, when she stated that she believed the tomb still existed and would be found some day. Even if a tomb were discovered, it does not contradict Mary's statement in the message. The tomb could well have been prepared ahead of time by devotees wanting to make sure that Our Lady's body would have an appropriate resting place when She departed from this earth. Even if a tomb existed, Mary could have been placed in that tomb after "falling asleep in the Lord," without having officially died as we understand death. Perhaps some state of apparent death or altered state of consciousness may even have been interpreted as her bodily death. At any rate, Mary would not have died a physical death as a result of sin, whether original or personal. She was immaculately conceived and never sinned either mortally or venially during her life. Her statement to the Medjugorje seers about being assumed before death is best interpreted then as denoting an action of God, in which God raised Mary's body and soul to heaven without the usual formalities that surround normal physical death, including burial rites and entombment.

August 31, 1982 - *"I do not dispense all graces."* Page 82.

The Dogma of Mary Mediatrix of All Graces has not yet been defined by the Church; it is still being discussed by theologians and Mariologists. However, there is no contradiction between what Our Lady has said and what might be expressed in the possible forthcoming dogma. There is a belief that Mary dispenses ALL graces. Does this mean that Jesus channels ALL graces through Mary, or could it be construed, to correspond to Our Lady's words, that she dispenses ALL graces that She herself has requested from Jesus?

August 25, 1994 – *"Today I am united with you in prayer in a special way, praying for the gift of the presence of my most beloved son* in your home country."* Page 161.
* Our Lady is referring to Pope John Paul II.

Other Books: If you enjoyed this book,
you might also enjoy our companion book:

Prayers from the Heart – A Medjugorje Prayer Book
6"x9" Softcover – 203 Pages $16.00 B&W, $29.00 Color

Each year, over a million pilgrims from around the world travel to Medjugorje, a tiny village in Bosnia and Herzegovina, to pray at the site where Mary, the Mother of Jesus, has been appearing since 1981.

The hills of Medjugorje resound with the reverent and peaceful prayers of pilgrims every day. This book is a collection of many of the most popular prayers from Medjugorje; prayers that Our Lady has given and requested us to pray, as well as popular devotions and novenas from our Catholic faith that truly lend themselves to being prayed from the heart.

The Mysteries of the Rosary, as well as the Stations of the Cross, include pictures of the bronze reliefs sculpted by the Italian artist Carmelo Puzzolo, which are found on Apparition Hill and Cross Mountain in Medjugorje. The mosaics of the Luminous Mysteries are located behind the church of St. James in Medjugorje.

http://www.medjugorje.org/ccart

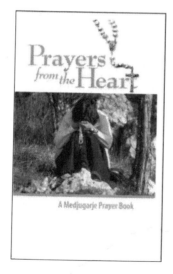

Made in the USA
Middletown, DE
30 May 2017